CHOSEN

A chosen generation for a chosen new Messianic Era

ALI MAHJOUB

Chosen
by Ali Mahjoub

Printed in the United States of America

ISBN: 978-0-692-17516-3

Edited by Elizabeth Cooper
Designed by Suzanne Parada

Dedication

To God Almighty, the most loving, merciful and compassionate God, I give thanks for his never-ending inspiration, encouragement and protection throughout my life and while writing this book. My warmest thanks and appreciation to the late Rev. Sun Myung Moon and Han Hak Ja, God's present day messengers and mankind's True Parents for revealing his plan and hope for the world. Individually and together, they endured immeasurable suffering and a humiliating course in conveying God's truth.

My warmest and heartfelt appreciation to my closest and loving members of my family: my wonderful wife, Cynthia, and, particularly, my daughter, Alisa, to remind her of her heritage and how important she is as blessed child. I also extend my warmest love and appreciation to my family members in Tunisia, especially to my brother, Khaled, and my older sister, Aisha, who have been so kind and gracious to me. Also, I would extend my love and appreciation to my two guardian angels in the spiritual world, my brother Mohammed, and my Uncle Taib, with whom I communicate in my dreams. Finally, I would like to extend my love and appreciation to two very special people, Jacinta Kreft and John Weiman, (Unification Church missionaries) who witnessed and took good care of me during my early months in the Unification Church Movement.

Table of Contents

"I am no prophet, nor a prophet's son; but I am a herdsman, and a dresser of sycamore trees, and the Lord took me from following the flock, and the Lord said to me, 'Go prophesy to my people of Israel.'"

(Amos 7:14-15)

Acknowledgments

As I start to take on the awesome task of writing this extraordinary book, I wish to convey my deepest and heartfelt gratitude and thanks to the men and women of God, from the past and present, who put their lives on the line to bring God's truth to mankind. Without their work and sacrifices, the world would have been kept in darkness and hopelessness. People like the great man of God and martyr William Tyndale, whose remarkable story is noted in the preface of the Revised Standard Version of the Bible. Labeled as a heretic for translating the Bible into English from the original Hebrew and Greek, Tyndale was burned at the stake in 1536. Until then, the Bible was read and interpreted by only priests and the privileged few.

My special thanks to the contemporary men and women of God for their great work for which I am so grateful. Without their help, my book would not have been completed.

I also want to give my special thanks to the Rev. Sun Myung Moon and HSA Publications for its many inspiring publications and, in particular, the Divine Principle.

My thanks to great people, such as Michael Breen, author of *Sun Myung Moon: The Early Years 1920-53*; Kevin McCarthy, author of *The Master Plan: God's Hope to Heal Humanity*; the great woman of God and martyr, Benazir Bhutto, author of *Reconciliation: Islam, Democracy and the West*; the Rev. Billy Graham, evangelist and author of *Just As I Am: The Autobiography of Billy Graham*; Mark Gibbs, author of *The Virgin & the Priest: The Lost Secrets of the Messianic Code*; John Hogue, author of *Nostradamus and The Millennium*, and *Nostradamus: The New Millennium*; Arthur Ford, author of *Unknown But Known: My Adventure into the Meditative Dimension*; and, Mo Koo Sung, author of *Who Is He?* And, last, but not least, my thanks to Elizabeth Cooper for her enduring patience in editing and clearing my often complicated writing on new thought-provoking concepts on God's new revelations spoken by the Rev. Sun Myung Moon.

Part One

Chosen

Introduction

A chosen generation for a chosen new messianic era

We are living in a time of rapid change that is nothing like the past. A little less than a century ago, we had no commercial airlines, no Internet, no Facebook or Google and no cell phones. The world at that time could be equated to the world of the Middle Ages. People were traveling on horseback, and messages and news took weeks to reach their destinations. I remember the village I grew up in the 1960s. Like other areas of the world, we didn't have electricity, television or social media.

We are truly living in a miraculous time no history in the past could be compared to our time.

Undoubtedly, our world has entered an exceptional period in human history, one that can be described in religious terms as "The Messianic Era." Signs of the imminent return of Christ have been amassing since the turn of the 20th century. After World War I and II, we entered a new and unprecedented messianic era. There have been more prophecies fulfilled in the 20th century than during any other time in Christian history. One of the greatest biblical prophecies was made by Jesus in Matt. 24:32-34. It was fulfilled in 1948 when the Jewish people returned to their Holy Land.

As neuropsychiatrist Shafica Karagula was quoted in the book, "Worker in the Light":

> "The twentieth century has been designated as the 'Age of Breakthroughs.' We have broken through the tight structure of the atom, we have broken the sound barrier, we have broken the earth's gravitational pull and man has walked on the moon" (Noory and Byrnes, 2006).

We have moved through the 20th century so completely enamored by man's scientific discoveries that we have paid little attention to our perspective on the avalanche of religious and spiritual phenomena, such as ESP, dreams and other psychic phenomena that are occurring in tandem.

Advanced technological achievements have impowered

archaeologists in unearthing shocking new discoveries of ancient civilizations, some of which connected the present to thousands of years in the past. The Dead Sea Scrolls, found in the West Bank between 1946 and 1956, were written by a devout Jewish sect, the Essenes, who lived during Jesus' lifetime and who greatly influenced Him and early Christian beliefs. In addition to the Dead Sea Scrolls, there was the discovery of the Naj Hammadi Scrolls, found in 1947 in Egypt, as well as other ancient manuscripts. These documents revealed new thought-provoking concepts that panicked many Christian theologians.

I must caution you: some of what you will discover in the chapters ahead might offend the ecclesiastical sensitivities so prevalent in our modern age. A perfect example of this is the Pharisees of the New Testament days and how they completely missed the coming of the Messiah for whom they had so urgently longed. And, remember, they were the Bible *experts* of their day. They were the commentators, professors, preachers and academic scholars of religious thought. They were the guardians of theological "truth," very much like Christian educators and theologians of today.

The fact the much-prepared and chosen people couldn't recognize Jesus as the Messiah makes one wonder and ask why? For sure, it wasn't because of their lack of faith; they had too much of that. So, how could the Pharisees have so badly messed up and not recognizing Jesus as the Messiah? Their mistaken biblical interpretation, their dogma, their prejudices and their traditional teaching about the Messiah—all of it—served as stumbling blocks in disbelieving in Jesus as He stood right before them. Could it be that the real reason lies in their mistaken interpretation of prophecies concerning the nature of how the Messiah would appear? The Pharisees were gazing at the sky expecting the Messiah to magically appear from the sky. Why? Because their scripture says so. Take a close look at the book of Malachi, the last chapter of the Old Testament. Mal. 4:5-6, indicated that, as a sign, God will send them back the prophet Elijah before the coming of the Messiah.

> "Behold, I will send you Eli'jah the prophet before the great and terrible day of the Lord comes. And he will turn

the hearts of fathers to their children and the hearts of children to their fathers, lest I come and smite the land with a curse."

This prophecy was the surest sign God gave to the Israelites. I will speak on this subject at length in the coming chapters.

Unfortunately, as Jesus warned, this very mistake can possibly be repeated by the Christians, who are eagerly awaiting the second coming of Christ and are armed with same failed concepts, such as the mistaken biblical interpretation about his literal return on the clouds.

This book, although it is about the power of dreams and divine acts of coincidences, is about my story about how dreams played major roles in leading me to join the controversial Unification Movement of the Rev. Sun Myung Moon. Moon and his Unification Movement had gone through untold persecution and false accusations by Christians and communists alike. He was jailed six times for his faith and tortured almost to death by North Koreans and sent to the Heungnam Prison, known as the world's severest prison, to die. In America, he was greatly welcomed at first. but, that didn't last. False accusations by Christians and bad rumors followed him from Korea. They were spread by the media like wildfire, and the tide was turned against him. For almost all the five decades since coming to America in 1968, the mainstream media made a mockery of Moon's name and his movement. As he noted in his book, *As a Peace-Loving Global Citizen*: "Words like heretic and pseudo were placed in front of my name so often that they seemed to become part of my name" (Moon, 2010). In the 1980s, there wasn't a day when Moon's name wasn't mentioned. He was accused of using kids to amass a lot of money and was called a "prophet for profit." His followers were treated badly and persecuted everywhere they went.

In this book, you will learn the truth about the movement by reading how I was introduced to it. I wasn't young when I was introduced to the movement. I was a successful middle-aged man, had traveled to more than 20 countries and had lived in six different countries. I was politically, religiously, and spiritually well-attuned to be fooled into joining a controversial religious movement. But, what lead me to the Unification Movement is a powerful force to be reckoned with. It is the force and power of dreams and divine acts of coincidences that drove me toward it.

What you are about to read is my personal life story. It is a real-life journey, rich in fascinating dreams and spiritual experiences. Although many of these dreams pertained to my own spiritual growth, a few prophetic dreams revealed clairvoyance on a worldly scale.

Everyone dreams. But, not all dreams are what they appear to be. Some dreams are far from regular; they are sacred and prophetic dreams that carry messages from God.

As you will soon learn in the coming chapters, it is these sorts of prophetic, life-changing dreams that I am compelled to write about. These dreams alone can tell you why I joined the Unification Movement. After all, the Bible tells us that in Last Days, and I believe our time can possibly be the Last Days, God said "I will pour out my spirit upon all flesh, … and your young men shall see visions and your old men shall dream dreams" (Acts 2:17).

We marvel at stories told in dreams in the Bible. Jacob dreamed he saw a ladder set up on Earth that could reach to heaven (Gen. 28:10-17). Joseph dreamed about the Sun, Moon and 11 stars bowing down to him (Gen. 37:9). People of the scriptures, whether they are Jewish, Christian or Muslim, believed in these Bible stories but never considered that God can still communicate with us modern-day people through dreams just as He did then.

This book is not about ordinary dreams and visions nor is it about ordinary encounters with coincidence. Although this book includes all the above, the purpose behind my writing this book is about the extraordinary, beyond the menial and everyday things. It is about the New Era we are living in and the special prophetic dreams, visions, and phenomena of unexplained coincidences we encounter in our life.

I know. It's hard to speak about prophetic dreams these days, especially ones that are related to religious subjects, such the Last Days and the Second Coming of Christ. This is a time where people, particularly the younger generations, most of whom were influenced by secular cultures, despise religion and are fearful of what they consider "organized" religions.

Added to the confusion are the atrocities that were done in the name of God by certain overzealous religious leaders. Jim Jones, the founder of the People's Temple and Jonestown, was responsible for the mass suicide of more than 900 of his followers in November 1978. David Koresh believed himself to be the Messiah and died, along with 75 of his followers, in a fire at their Waco, Texas, compound, ending a 51-day standoff with the FBI on April 19, 1993. ISIS (Islamic State in Iraq and Syria) is a powerful terrorist militant group that has seized control of large areas of the Middle East and is infamous for its brutal violence and gruesome killings. It was these fanatical groups that caused a great mess of religion in general and made people less trusting of anything to do with religion.

Life is a precious journey given to us by God. In life, every human being, without exception, from childhood to adulthood, encounters a collection of profound events and unexplained phenomena. These phenomena resonate in his or her conscious mind, whether they are fairy tales, personal experiences, mysterious occurrences, dreams or "coincidences." The subconscious files them away like "seeds" that lay dormant for years, only to resurface at the appropriate hour to serve as a source of inspiration, guidance, and support when people are making critical life decisions.

Without my collection of spiritual "seeds" and God's constant help and support, I do not think I could have written this book. Throughout my spiritual journey, I have learned that God does not work randomly. He is organized and systematically gives strategic guidance—selecting and preparing His people through a variety of spiritual means, such as prophetic dreams and divine acts of coincidences. He synchronizes time, places and events. God also works with people "just as they are," whatever their passions may be. Whether it is spirituality, religious truth, politics or love, these passions are like an irresistible lure God uses to guide us down a predestined path. I urge people to look deeply inward and realize their calling. I sincerely hope you will enjoy reading this book and find your calling.

CHAPTER 1

Prophetic Dreams

> "Since time immemorial, our dreams have been a source of awe and wonder. At various points in history, they have been seen as messages from the gods, and supernatural experiences involving visions of the future, as well as indications of the state of our physical and mental health. Dreams have been used to shed light on the past, and even predict the future. This has not only been true for individuals, but also for whole nations. Some dreams have even changed the course of history" (O'Connell, Airey and Craze, 2012).

The Power of Dreams and Visions

We are not alone!

We are not alone as many people think. We are constantly watched over, guided and protected by forces greater than us. Some are from the angelic world and others are our departed loved ones who communicate with us through dreams, mysterious coincidences and other psychic elements. Life in the spiritual world is just as real as life on Earth. Unfortunately, the spiritual senses of human beings have been severely damaged because of the fall. The following dream stories illustrate how dreams reveal to us important messages from the other side and influence our decisions in critical times.

Every night, we dream. What we dream about can be hard to remember. Or, when we do remember, they may be difficult to comprehend. During sleep, the brain is active, and our dreams are perceived through the deeper layers of the subconscious mind. The subconscious does not communicate in words or through reason but through visual images to stimulate intuition and feelings. When we wake up, we are left with a residual "sense of" something that stays with us throughout the day. It imprints in our memory like a footprint in the sand.

Dreams are facets of intuition. However, most of the time, we dismiss them because we've been told since childhood that dreams are only fabrications of our imagination. But, our imagination is intuitive as well. I will never forget the shock I had when a magazine looking for stories on dreams and spiritual experiences replied to my story on dreams. The magazine editor once said to me: "I don't think our magazine would include prophetic dreams because I have found dreams are so intensely personal. Although what you experienced has great meaning for you, for someone reading it, it may just seem like a lot of strange images with an explanation tailored to fit."

OK. It sounded like an acceptable response, but, in truth, it wasn't. If you accepted this editor's view on prophetic dreams, you might as well forget biblical dreams all together!

Dream analysis, also referred to as dream interpretation, hinges on the idea you can attach meaning to your dreams. This process has been used in a wide variety of settings, including ancient civilizations and religions—Christianity being one of them. You can go to a bookstore and pick up a book that will help you interpret your own dreams. In modern times, we find volumes upon volumes of books written about dreams. Famous artists, inventors, writers, and scientists have resolved problems in their dreams. Dreams have played an important role in religion and have often guided actions during critical times in a religion's development. The Bible alone contains 576 references to dreams.

Dreams come in many types. Some dreams warn us of danger. Some reveal solutions and some heal. Others reveal prophecies on a worldly scale. We can see this sort of worldly scale revelation mostly in religious dreams. There are four basic types of dreams: precognitive, clairvoyant, apparitions and telepathic.

Precognitive dreams: Precognitive dreams are the most powerful. It is estimated 40 percent of reported psychic experiences concern knowing the future in some way. Dreams are the most common way for premonitions to appear. In a precognitive dream, a dreamer receives information about the future that subsequently turns out to be true by current events. This information could not have been obtained or inferred any other way.

Clairvoyant dreams: These are dreams about an event that is occurring at the same time as the event. There is absolutely nothing you can do about changing or preventing anything you see in a clairvoyant dream, although the information can be used to help people.

Dreams of apparitions: These dreams involve the deceased. I believe we are visited by our departed loved ones and distant ancestors. But, it doesn't matter if you know the person. The person appears in a dream to convey a personal message. However, this message is not necessarily for the dreamer. At times, the message is to be passed onto the loved ones of the deceased.

Telepathic dreams: Communication is made directly from one energy source to another without any mechanical assistance of any kind. These dreams tend to show us people and events not in our immediate environment. Such dreams sometimes occur when someone is either in danger or in an unusual predicament.

Let us now take a closer look at how these four types of dreams have played major roles in changing world history and our lives. Let us begin with dreams in religion.

In scripture, a dream is not only called a "dream," but also "a vision of the night" (Job 33:14-18):

> "For God may speak in one way, and in two, though man does not perceive it. In a dream, in a vision of the night, when deep sleep falls upon men, while they slumber on their beds, then He opens the ears of men, and terrifies them with warnings."

The Old Testament has a collection of profound dreams in which God's vision and voice were seen and heard by his messengers. Jacob heard God's voice in a dream about the Promised Land (Gen. 28:10-22). Joseph, the youngest son of Jacob, saw his future in a dream with a falling sun, moon and seven stars. When he told his father about it, he was rebuked. Joseph's father replied:

> "What is this dream that you have dreamed? Shall I and your mother and your brothers indeed come to bow down ourselves to the ground before you? (Gen. 37:10).

Years later, Joseph was made the pharaoh's second-in-command after he successfully interpreted his complicated dream. When Joseph's father and brothers sought help from the pharaoh, they didn't realize the man they were bowing down to was Joseph (Gen. 41:14-25).

In the New Testament, we find the dream that led the Magi, or Wise Men, to the stable to protect the baby Jesus: "And being warned in a dream not to return to Herod, they departed to their own country by another way" (Matt. 2:12). Before Jesus was born, Joseph, Mary's fiancé, had planned "to divorce her quietly" (Matt. 1:19). That evening, however, an angel appeared to Joseph in a dream and said:

> "Joseph, son of David, do not fear to take Mary your wife, for that which is conceived in her is of the Holy Spirit; she will bear a son, and you shall call his name Jesus, for he will save his people from their sins" (Matt. 1:20-21).

During Jesus' trial, Pontius Pilate received a note from his wife that said: "Have nothing to do with that righteous man, for I have suffered much over him today in a dream" (Matt. 27:19).

Dreams also played an important part in the early formation of Islam. In the *Night Journey*, a Sura, or chapter in the Qur'an, the prophet Mohammed dreamed of traveling with the Archangel Gabriel on the back of a magical flying horse—half-human, half-beast—to the Temple Mount in Jerusalem. There, he met with Abraham, Moses, and Jesus, and was later escorted by Gabriel to the seventh level of heaven to meet with God.

The most stunning prophecies ever told that were fulfilled in real life are the prophecies told in the Old Testament of the Bible about the birth and fate of Jesus Christ. These were made by prophets who lived 400 to 800 years before Jesus' birth. These prophecies are taken by Christians as prophetic, and name Jesus Christ as the Messiah. Among them are:

> "But, you, O Bethlehem Eph'rathah, who are little to be among the clans of Judah, from you shall come forth for me one is to be ruler in Israel, whose origin is from of old, from ancient days" (Mic. 5:2).

> "Say to those who are of a fearful heart, 'Be strong, fear not! Behold, your God will come with vengeance, with the recompense of God. He will come and save you.' Then the eyes of the blind shall be opened, and the ears of the deaf unstopped; then shall the lame man leap like a hart, and the tongue of the dumb sing for joy. For waters shall break forth in the wilderness, and streams in the desert" (Isa. 35:4-6).

> "Rejoice greatly, O daughter of Zion! Shout aloud, O daughter of Jerusalem! Lo, your king comes to you; triumphant and victorious is he, humble and riding on an ass, on a colt the foal of an ass" (Zech. 9:9).

> "He was despised and rejected by men; a man of sorrows, and acquainted with grief, and as one from whom men hide their faces he was despised, and we esteemed him not. Surely, he has borne our griefs and carried our sorrows; yet we esteemed him stricken, smitten by God, and afflicted. But, he was wounded for our transgressions.He was bruised for our iniquities; upon him was the chastisement that made us whole, and with his stripes we are healed" (Isa. 53:3-5).

> "Yea, dogs are round about me; a company of evildoers encircle me; they have pierced my hands and feet—I can count all my bones—they stare and gloat over me; they divide my garments among them, and for my raiment they cast lots" (Psalm 22:16-18).

These biblical verses are held by Christians to accurately predict key events in Jesus' life: His birth at Bethlehem; His miraculous cures; His entry into Jerusalem on an ass; His betrayal for 30 pieces of silver; His arrest and beating, and His crucifixion.

In modern times, we also find volumes of books written about dreams. Famous artists, inventors, writers and scientists have resolved many of their problems through dreams. In 1965, Paul McCartney found the melody for "Yesterday" in a dream. Madam C.J. Walker, the first African-American female entrepreneur, had a dream about beauty and hair products for black women. She is cited by the "Guinness Book of Records" as the first self-made, female millionaire in U.S. history. President Abraham Lincoln had a dream about his assassination.

Although I am fascinated by the wealth of help and information an individual can reap from dreams, to be quite honest, that is not the main reason I began this chapter on "Prophetic Dreams." What ignited my passion to write this chapter was the seemingly unending chain of dreams and uncanny coincidences that have forever altered the course of my life. In this book, I included 12 of these powerful dreams that dramatically changed my views on God, religion, and life. As you will see throughout my story, dreams and coincidences intertwined with my life's events and played large parts in the development of my spiritual journey.

Let us now move on to present-day dreams and how they affect our lives in many ways. Before I begin with my own story and how I got here—talking about dreams and visions, I would like to give you a few examples of dreams and what I call divine acts of coincidence that I found while researching stories on dreams, prophecies, fate, destiny and coincidences. All these spiritual phenomena are all connected and work together for the same purpose, just like in an orchestra.

Dreams and Voices Within

Something out there is watching over us.

The act of listening to your inner voice is not something you need to turn on. It is always on. But, you need to learn to recognize the instinctive signal from which you get the information. It is faint, so we must learn how to amplify it and differentiate it from the rest of the data we process every day. The voice usually carries urgent warnings. What follows is an example of a clairvoyant dream. It is one I had about an accident that really happened.

January 1984 was a very difficult and extremely busy month for me. While I was traveling on a witnessing mission with IOWC (International One World Crusade), there were many things happening in our movement. We were in Los Angeles at the time. The spirit world was very active, and I received a frightening dream about an upcoming accident that happened exactly the way I saw it in the dream. It follows.

Dec. 10, 1983. In this dream, our five-member team was sitting in our van ready to leave for our next destination, when, suddenly, a big machine, such as a forklift, attached itself to our van and began to lift it upward. I could hear it clang as it grabbed our van, and I heard a rattling noise. After a while, the machine seemed to reach its destination. It placed the van on top of a high mountain peak. While this was going on, Annie, one of our sisters, was screaming and saying, "No! No! I don't want to go! I want to get off here." The machine pushed us off the mountain! In the dream, the driver was a Japanese lady whose name was Hiromi. She was one of the Japanese team leaders. I was in the front passenger seat, telling her to drive on the smooth icy surface and avoid any big gaps. I guided her until we got to the bottom of the mountain and headed straight into a big lake that was nestled between three mountains. As we got close to the lake, a line of rocks appeared. They formed a straight line that went down into the lake. I told Hiromi to drive straight for the rocks, hoping we could use them to reduce speed and avoid a crash. She followed all my instructions and drove through the rocks, and we were safe!

The Accident

About two weeks after I had this dream, our group was divided into three teams. It was Jan. 1, 1984, New Year's Day. We had just celebrated a church holiday called "God's Day," one of the Unification Church's important holidays. We loaded our materials into three vans and were getting to leave. Suddenly, Annie, the girl who wanted to get out of the van in my dream, had changed her mind and decided to stay for the seven-day week-long workshop. She persuaded her guest to stay as well. We unloaded her suitcases off the van and headed to our next destination, Portland, Oregon.

Our team commander left for an emergency leaders' meeting in New York with the Rev. Moon. Moon had just returned to the

United States after a long speaking tour in South Korea when he heard about his son, Heung Jin, dying in a car accident.

Heung Jin, the second son of Rev. Moon, was driving on an icy U.S. Route 9 in Hyde Park, New York, on Dec. 23, 1984, when a tractor-trailer collided with his car. The passengers were unharmed, but Heung Jin lost his life.

I was left in charge of the teams. In my van, there were four others: Hiromi, Takumi, Dennis, a spiritually open guy, and Maloney, a tall, thin African-American girl. I was in high spirits after breaking my fast. I had offered to partake in a three-day fast before the New Year as part of my resolution. We were all excited about the trip, and when it was time for us to leave, brothers and sisters came out to say goodbye. Later, in the evening, we stopped in a motel parking lot and slept in our vans to save money. Everything was fine until the next day when we changed drivers. I began to sense signs of danger! There were other strange things going on. Maloney was complaining about the lack of sleep she was getting and about eating tuna sandwiches for breakfast, lunch, and dinner (the cheapest and most convenient way for missionaries to save money). I was fighting with the Japanese members who wouldn't let me eat what I wanted after I finished my fast. For the sake of my health, they wanted to restrict me to soft food and yogurt, but I REALLY wanted a juicy hamburger. Dennis was mumbling to himself and reading the Tibetan Book of the Dead! The whole atmosphere was weird and spooky!

After driving for a few hours, we stopped at a gas station for some gas. I was overwhelmed with the voices inside my head that were begging me to change vans. I wouldn't, however, because I was in charge of overseeing that van, and I couldn't place another person in harm. We drove for another three or four hours. Again, we stopped to use the bathroom and get some gas. The voices were again begging me to change vans. This time, however, the voices were so strong, they really worried me. I went to the other vans to see whether I could find an empty seat. I struggled with the idea of asking someone else to take my seat, but my conscience wouldn't allow it. So, despite all the warnings, I went back to my seat.

We continued on our journey. I changed seats with the Japanese sister, so she could sit next to the driver and talk to her in Japanese. I moved to the middle seat behind the driver, keeping watch on the road. Dennis, who was in the seat behind me, was still reading his book and telling us creepy stories he had just read about dead people. As time passed, it became darker and rainier. After a while, things got quiet, and I found myself fighting to stay awake. Soon, I was asleep.

Not long after I fell asleep, however, the accident happened. The interesting thing about it was, while I was in a deep sleep, I was also sensing what was happening and following the accident as it happened. I felt my body flying around inside the van like a piece of cloth as the van tumbled and rolled off the road. In my mind, I said to myself: "If I make this last tumble, I am going to be fine." And, sure enough, it was the last rollover! I don't know how long we were there before help came. But, but I do know most of us woke up when the ambulance and police arrived. Help seemed to have come very quickly. It was as if they were waiting for the accident to happen. The van was sitting on its side. I don't recall how we got out.

I can recall vividly the love I experienced at that time. It was as if God himself was reaching out to me through every person who helped—the police, paramedics and the ordinary people. Instead of worrying about my state of health, I was deeply moved and grateful for this wonderful and blessed country: America! It was an amazing experience that I will never forget.

After the ambulances took us to the nearest hospital and we were checked for internal injuries, we were released. We resumed our journey to Portland. This time, we traveled in two vans. Coming from a frightening ordeal, no one was complaining. We were just grateful to be alive. It is interesting to note that had Annie, the sister who didn't want to go with us in the dream, come with us, she would have died or been severely injured. This is another clairvoyant dream. There was no way to avoid such a dream.

A Mother Who Saved Her Son

Psychiatrist Carl Jung relates the following story in one of his books:

During World War II, American soldiers were stationed on one of the Pacific Islands preparing for an offensive attack against Japan.

Late one night, one soldier, whose name was Johnny, was resting inside his tent. Inexplicably, he heard his mother's familiar and beloved voice calling him urgently: "Johnny! Johnny!"

Johnny chuckled. His mother was thousands of miles away in the United States. It obviously had to be a bored soldier playing a trick on him by imitating his mother's voice. But, who that soldier could be and how he had been so accurate with his mother's voice, he didn't know. No one had ever met his mother before, so, how could someone mimic her voice so convincingly? Curious and perplexed, Johnny rose from his cot and went out into the darkness to find the man who had pulled the prank.

Johnny expected to find the prankster somewhere nearby, laughing uproariously. But, to his amazement, there was no one in the immediate vicinity.

Johnny was tenacious and didn't easily give up. He also didn't like being duped. So, he wandered far away from his tent, determined to track down the perpetrator of the practical joke. But, everyone seemed to be sleeping soundly. No one was up.

After his investigation proved fruitless, Johnny finally gave up the hunt and returned to his tent. But, the area where the tent had stood only minutes before was now was a giant smoking crater.

During Johnny's absence, Japanese mortar shells had landed directly onto where his tent had been. All the soldiers who were inside the tent were killed instantly. Johnny's life had been saved by the mysterious prankster.

Several months later, Johnny returned safely to the United States and the warm embrace of his mother. As he told the tale of his narrow escape from death, she shared with him a story of her own.

On that fateful night, when Johnny said he heard his mother calling, his mother, who was asleep in Oklahoma, had had a powerful dream at the exact time. In the dream, her son's tent was being bombarded by mortar shells. The dream seemed so real she screamed out in her sleep: "Johnny! Johnny!" Her shrieks did not abate until her husband roused her from her nightmare.

Her husband tried to calm her—saying repeatedly, "It's a dream, only a dream." Finally, she stopped screaming.

Mysteriously, her voice had traveled directly into her son's ears thousands of miles away and saved his life (Rushnell 2006).

CHAPTER 2

Coincidence

Coincidence is God's way of remaining anonymous.
Albert Einstein

How can coincidences be explained? The standard answers are God/Universe and random chance. The trouble with these answers is they exclude you and me. We have something to do with creating coincidences. First, a conscious mind needs to notice them. How else do we participate in coincidence formation? We sometimes use coincidences to help solve our own psychological problems, as some psychoanalysts suggest. How do we explain the uncommon experience of feeling the pain of a loved one who is far away? Or knowing something specific will happen or is happening some distance away? A coincidence is a remarkable concurrence of events or circumstances without any apparent connection.

Every time you experience a coincidence or answered prayer, it's a direct and personal message of reassurance from God to you.

The following story is about the famous American evangelical preacher, the Rev. Billy Graham.

Billy Graham

When passion intersects with coincidence, things happen.

The following story can be found in Squire Rushnell's book, "When God Winks at You" (2006).

Billy Graham was only 5 when he became excited by the preacher's words. From where he was sitting, next to his father, he could see other people were feeling it, too. The passionate word of evangelist Billy Sunday filled the huge tent, and everybody was moved. As he grew up, Graham thought a lot about the power of words to arouse emotion.

When Graham was 16, the oratorical skills of evangelist Dr. Mordecai Fowler Ham grabbed his mind and gripped his heart. He was further fascinated by the ability of some people to captivate others with their words. Four years later, as a student at the Florida Bible Institute in Tampa, Graham pursued his own emerging talents to preach—wherever possible. "I would paddle a canoe out to a little island where I could address all creatures great and small … from alligators to birds," he wrote in his autobiography, *Just As I Am* (Graham, 2007). And, he was once seen sermonizing to a 4-year-old boy who was sitting on top of a chest of drawers in the men's dormitory.

But, the wish Graham held the highest was the chance to preach at the West Tampa Gospel Mission in the city's Hispanic district. He ruminated as to how he could possibly get an invitation to speak there. One day, as he passed the mission, he decided to pray about it. He knelt on the lawn and prayed.

Moments later, Graham stood up and was startled to see the kindly old man who ran the mission, whom everyone knew simply as Mr. Corwin, approaching him.

"Billy," said Mr. Corwin, "our scheduled speaker for tomorrow had to cancel. Could you fill in for him?"

Absolutely astonished by such an immediate answer to his prayer, Graham could only nod. He could never have measured how pivotal that godwink was to become.

Graham's delivery was so impressive Mr. Corwin invited him to speak again, and again, and again. And, with that endorsement came the confidence to take his preaching into the streets of Tampa. Every weekend, six or seven times a day, Graham would strengthen the power of his communication by preaching to whoever would gather. With every sermon, Graham honed his unique style.

After college, Graham took his mission on the road. He would travel from town to town, preaching from temporary stages in tents to churches that offered pulpits. As he built his reputation in one community at a time, national prominence seemed to be sitting off somewhere in the distance.

One can never underestimate the power of godwinks, or the force of a simple little grandmother. No one knew her name, but she attended one of Graham's revivals in a small American town. She was mesmerized by his unique abilities to articulate the English language. She thought everyone should know about him and decided to do something about it.

Picking up the phone, she called information and asked for the number for the home of William Randolph Hearst, the newspaper magnate. What are the chances Hearst would answer the phone? He did. And, in a clear and persuasive voice, she told the world's most powerful publisher exactly how she felt about a young preacher named Billy Graham.

Hearst hung up the phone and directed his secretary to send a telegram to every one of his editors. It simply said, "Puff Graham."

Within days, newspaper readers across the United States were reading stories about a dashing young preacher who was engaging audiences with his words. Within weeks, Billy Graham was a household name.

Two small godwinks, each beyond most people's comprehension, had propelled the career of Billy Graham: A prayer instantaneously answered on a campus in Tampa and the absurdly optimistic initiative of one lonely woman who decided to call one of the most powerful men of the day.

From there on, Graham had the unparalleled stature of being the spiritual adviser to every president from Harry S. Truman to Barack Obama.

But, the famous preacher would not have reached his destiny had he not gotten onto his universal highway and headed in the direction he believed his destiny to be. Once he did, God put things in motion.

Graham did not sit by the side of the road with his belongings and wait for his destiny to come to him. Nor should you. He listened to the small voice within and made the choice to strike out, girded by faith, in the direction he believed his destiny was (Rushnell, 2006).

The man of humble beginnings who grew up to become "America's pastor" passed away peacefully Feb. 21, 2018, at his North Carolina home. His body lied in state at the U.S. Capitol, an honor given to only three other private citizens. This is a testament to how much he meant to the country.

Awakening Coincidence

When God calls you to preach, you preach. You hear?

Deep in my heart, I knew there was always something incredibly meaningful about the coincidences we experience in our lives. While researching coincidence, I found a great book called *Small Miracles of the Holocaust: Extraordinary Coincidences of Faith, Hope and Survival* (2008), written by two devoutly Jewish ladies, Yitta Halberstam and Judith Leventhal. These best-selling authors have both experienced an inordinate number of coincidences firsthand.

Halberstam, a writer and lecturer on spirituality, has had her work appear in many magazines, including *Parade, New York, Money,* and *Working Woman.* Leventhal is a Gestalt therapist. They both live in Brooklyn, New York.

Small Miracles of Love and Friendship: Remarkable Coincidences of Warmth and Devotion (1997) is a collection of short stories that are moving, heartwarming and inspirational. These remarkable coincidences—often containing profound teachings, important moral lessons and even divine messages—draw us out of the ordinary. If you can open yourself to receiving and understanding the meaning of these gifts, you will experience the possibilities, blessings, and sense of harmony within the universe they offer.

According to these gifted authors, coincidence is "all part of creation and God's plan and our response. We just have to be open to seeing it" (Halberstam and Leventhal, 1997).

A coincidence is like a dream and intuition. It is a feeling that lets us know something important is coming. Have you ever experienced a moment when a seemingly random event also seemed strangely meaningful or even miraculous? Have you ever anticipated a phone call? What about thinking about someone you haven't heard from or seen in years and, suddenly, he or she shows up at our door? What you experienced may be more significant than you thought. It may be nothing less than a small miracle—possibly the work of angels or a message from a higher power.

As I read the stories in Halberstam and Leventhal's book, I was reminded of a powerful spiritual experience I had.

In the early years of my new faith, while I was doing missionary work in Minneapolis with the ICC (Inter-Denominational

Conference for Clergy) conference, I visited churches and invited ministers to attend the conference. Early one Sunday morning, I visited a dear friend, the Rev. Delpino, who I had seen in the past. As I merged onto Interstate 94 and drove for about a mile, God's words suddenly enveloped me. I was alone in my car, but I was preaching God's words so loudly that tears poured down my cheeks.

A moment later, I heard a whisper within me telling me I should write these words down. Realizing their importance, I reached for a pen and opened my notebook, which I always carried with me, and began to write. My car was swerving from left and right, and the other drivers were honking their horns as they swerved to avoid me. By the time I came to the exit, I had written most of the message. I got off the interstate and finally arrived at my friend's house. Our meeting was a joyful one; it was filled with God's love and inspiration.

At the end of our discussion, as we said our goodbyes, my friend leaned forward, looked me in the eye and shook me with astonishment. He said: "Look here, young man! When God calls you to preach, you preach. You hear?"

I responded: "Yes, of course, I will." I returned home just in time for Sunday service at my church. I didn't know God had a surprise waiting for me.

As soon as I stepped out of my car, two sisters ran to me. It was clear they were troubled by something. They told me our minister had left for an emergency meeting in New York, and he had left a message I was to substitute for the services today. At first, I was panic-stricken. Then, I managed to pull myself together. I realized the spiritual message I received was meant for this service. I went to my room, prayed for help and arranged my message in the form of a sermon. I entered the packed chapel and gave a sermon that was both powerful and inspiring. The spiritual atmosphere was so high. People were lining up to shake my hand and thank me for my words.

So, with this experience, I learned to never take coincidences lightly because they tell us things that are very important to our lives. I learned coincidences come to us for various reasons. Some come to save us from harm. Others ask us to deliver important messages. Someone out there knows things about us, watches over us and knows what's to come (Mahjoub, 2015).

> "Now the word of the LORD came to me saying, 'Before, I formed you in the womb I knew you, and before you were born I consecrated you; I appointed you a prophet to the nations" (Jer. 1:4-5).

Joseph's story

The story of Joseph is so fascinating. There is so much to learn from his story. Before I begin with Joseph's story, I would like to ask my readers to keep in mind the four points I noted in the earlier chapter. Here, I will repeat them.

1) God does not work at random: God is an organized being. He systematically gives strategic guidance. He selects and prepares his people through a variety of spiritual means, such as dreams, mysterious coincidences, and other psychic gifts. He also synchronizes time, places and events.

2) God sows seeds in people's lives and prepares His people. He gives them profound personal experiences, mysterious occurrences, dreams or "coincidences" that are stored in their subconscious like "seeds."

3) God works with people "Just as They are," as well as their passions and desires, whether they are good or bad. These passions turn into an irresistible lure God uses to guide us down a predestined path.

4) God works in tragic times, as well as with what could be called "bad or sinful" deeds.

Let us now examine how God worked in Joseph's story in the Bible.

Out of all the countless dreams told in the Old Testament, none intrigued me the most for its clarity than Joseph's story and dreams. It relates to my life's story and, I am sure, it relates to your life's story, too. That is, you feel deeply that God has placed in your heart something so powerful that it is pulling you like a magnet, but you haven't discovered it yet. The good news is this thing is in you. It started with a desire within your heart. Something you wanted to do deeply, not only for yourself but also for your family, your community or even bigger. It's an idea that nags at you and won't let go. Joseph had this wish. He had heard the call and pull since his childhood. Joseph was the son of Jacob and the grandson of Abraham. He was Jacob's youngest child. The Bible tells us his father loved him the most. His father protected him and favored him over his 11 brothers. He always got the best clothes and ate the best food. This made his brothers jealous and stirred up hate in their hearts.

Joseph's story is truly fascinating! The Bible refers to him as a dream interpreter. His story was clearly predestined and had so much plotting to it! What do I mean by plotting? When you plan to visit a place that is a long distance away—let's say a thousand miles away – and you've heard so much about it, it is natural that you make plans. What day do you start your journey and how many days it would take to get to there? You create a plan. Which highway do you take? How often do you plan to stop before you reach your destination? Well, believe it or not, God makes plans, too. Here, in Joseph's story, we will examine how God planned and plotted His way to get to what He wanted to accomplish with Joseph. Just keep in mind and remember what I noted earlier: God doesn't work randomly. When God has a claim on you, you better believe it. There is nothing to deter Him from reaching what He has predetermined for you. This is illustrated in God's calling of Jeremiah before the prophet was even born.

> "Now the word of the LORD came to me saying, 'Before, I formed you in the womb I knew you, and before you were born I consecrated you; I appointed you a prophet to the nations" (Jer. 1:4-5).

Joseph's father was always very protective of him. It was as if he knew deep inside his heart that Joseph was special, but he didn't quite understand what. Unlike his brothers, Joseph was spoiled. His father always dressed him in fine clothing like a prince and gave him tasks that were easy to do and close to home, such as shepherding. His brothers, on the other hand, did the hard labor and worked in the fields far from home. Their envy and dislike for Joseph grew greater when, while they were binding sheaves in the field, Joseph fell asleep and had a dream. He told his brothers:

> "He said to them, 'Hear this dream which I have dreamed: behold, we were binding sheaves in the field, and lo, my sheaf arose and stood upright; and behold, your sheaves gathered round it, and bowed down to my sheaf" (Gen. 37:7).

His brothers were infuriated by his dream. Mockingly, they shouted back, saying, "Are you going to be our king?" They knew very well what his dream meant and felt threatened by him.

Not long after his dream, Joseph had another dream that was identical to the first. Beware of identical dreams! You must pay close attention to them because these dreams will most definitely come true. These types of dreams carry important messages that need to be understood and carried out, as we will see in Joseph's dreams. Joseph's second dream involved the whole family. His father, mother, and brothers were together at a family gathering when Joseph stood up and said: "Behold, I have dreamed another dream ... the sun, the moon, and eleven stars were bowing down to me" (Gen. 37:9). This time, Joseph not only had aggravated his brothers but his father and mother as well. His father rebuked him, saying, "What is this dream you have dreamed? Shall I and your mother and your brothers indeed come to bow ourselves to the ground before you?" (Gen. 37:10).

One day, while the brothers were working on a plot land far from home, Jacob sent Joseph to check on them. He was to see how they were doing and return with a report for his father. The brothers were working on a plot of land that required a journey on horseback, which could take many hours or even days. Being young and inexperienced, Joseph didn't know where the plot of land was. The Bible tells us Joseph got lost and had to ask some strangers where the land was. When Joseph finally arrived, his brothers saw his silhouette from far away. They devised a plan to kill him. They said to each other:

> "Here comes this dreamer! Come now, let us kill him and throw him into one of the pits; then we shall say that a wild beast has devoured him, and we shall see what will become of his dreams" (Gen. 37:20).

When Joseph reached his brothers, they stripped him of the special long-sleeved robe his father made for him. Then, they put him in the cistern that had no water. As they started to discuss what they were going to tell their father, they saw a caravan of Arab merchants traveling to Egypt. Judah, one of the brothers who didn't like the idea of killing Joseph, said: "What profit is it if we slay our brother and conceal his blood? Come, let us sell him to the Ish'maelites" (Gen. 37: 26-27). And, they did. Joseph was sold to the merchants for eight ounces of silver. The brothers returned home and told their father Joseph has died. The Bible says Jacob became so consumed with grief, he mourned his son every day.

Meanwhile, when the Arab merchants arrived in Egypt's capital city, they, in turn, sold Joseph to Potiphar, one of the Pharaoh's officers and captain of the guards. Apparently, slavery and human trafficking was the custom in those days. Now, think about how God planned and plotted this scheme of things. The plot of land that Jacob owned and where his sons were working was on the route the Arab merchants always used to travel to Egypt. A modern example of this would be one of the main interstates in the United States people use to travel from state to state. The cistern Joseph was thrown into was by the road, and as the brothers were to throw him in it, the Arab merchants appeared. The merchants sold Joseph to the Pharaoh's captain of the guard. Can all these instances be looked at as mere coincidences? Or were they deliberately predetermined and plotted to happen for a greater reason? Joseph's story can teach us great lessons to apply in life. We can learn to investigate the causes of our own sorrow when we feel we are in the pit (a time of difficulty), and ask if there is a good reason?

There's more. Because he was raised with good religious values, Joseph proved himself worthy, hardworking, smart and trustworthy. The officer was so impressed with him he appointed Joseph head of his household. This included him being in charge of his wife. Beside his cordial personality, Joseph was also very charming and good looking. While the officer was away, his wife tried several times to seduce Joseph. But, he resisted. One day, she forced herself on him, but he tore himself out of her grasp and left part of his shirt in her hand. She tried to blackmail him, saying if he doesn't sleep with her, she will tell her husband about them when he returned. Still, he refused. However, he didn't want to lose his master's trust or be killed for it. Apparently, his good looks were even reported in the Muslim Qur'an's chapter on Joseph.

The story says one day the pharaoh's maids were given potatoes to peel for the pharaoh's meal when, suddenly, Joseph passed by. They were so taken by his beauty, they cut their hands instead of the potatoes!

> "And, when they saw him, they marveled at him, and cut their hands. They said, 'Good God, this is not a human. This must be a precious angel'" (Qu'ran, 12:31).

According to the story, this is why we have lines in the palm of our hands!

Now, back to the story.

When the officer returned home, his wife told him: "The Hebrew servant, whom you have brought among us, came in to me to insult me; but as soon as I lifted up my voice and cried, he left his garment with me, and fled out of the house" (Gen. 39:17-18).

The officer was so shocked by this disturbing news, he immediately ordered his guards to put Joseph into the dungeon to await trial. The punishment for this type of offense could be severe, especially an offense done to the wife of an officer of the pharaoh. He could have been executed. This was another ordeal Joseph had to endure. He escaped death by his brothers and now he's thrown into another pit for something he didn't do. In his prison cell, Joseph got to know the other prisoners: the pharaoh's chief baker and head butler, both of whom were also awaiting trial. These two former servants had also done something to displease their master, were fired and thrown in jail. The story says that while in jail, both men had disturbing dreams, but they had no one to interpret them. When Joseph saw them the next morning, he noticed his cellmates were sad. Because he was a kind person, he was deeply concerned about his friends. So, he asked them why they were sad. They told him about their disturbing dreams, and Joseph listened to them very intently. Each man told Joseph his dream. However, before he interpreted anything, he said there would be one condition. They must remember him when they get out of prison and tell the pharaoh about him. Like his father, grandfather, and great-grandfather, Joseph believed in God and believed in his interpretation of dreams. He thought, "Do not interpretations belong to God?" (Gen. 40:8). Joseph had experience with dreams. His two dreams about his future greatness antagonized his family (Gen. 37:5-11), and he was mocked as the dream interpreter (Gen. 37:19-20). Joseph was confident God would help him understand what the dreams of the butler and baker meant. And, he interpreted their dreams accurately. As their dreams foreshadowed, the baker was executed, and the butler was restored to his former position. Just to help my readers understand how Joseph interpreted their dreams, here are the dreams and their interpretations.

Butler's dream: The Butler's dream as told in the Bible:

> "In my dream, there was a vine before me, and on the vine, there were three branches; as soon as it budded, its blossoms shot forth, and the clusters ripened into grapes. Pharaoh's cup was in my hand, and I took the grapes and pressed them into the Pharaoh's cup and placed the cup in Pharaoh's hand" (Gen. 40: 9-11).

Here is how Joseph interpreted this dream. Joseph said the three branches are three days.

> "Within three days, Pharaoh will lift up your head and restore you to your office, and you shall place Pharaoh's cup in his hand as formerly when you were his butler" (Gen. 40:13).

Let us now look at the baker's dream and see how Joseph interpreted it.

When the chief baker saw the butler's interpretation was favorable, he said to Joseph:

> "I also had a dream: there were three cake baskets on my head, and in the uppermost basket there were all sorts of

baked food for Pharaoh, but the birds were eating it out of the basket on my head" (Gen. 40: 16-17).

After listening to the baker, Joseph said: "The three baskets are three days; within three days Pharaoh will lift up your head—from you!—and hang you on a tree; and the birds will eat the flesh from you" (Gen. 40: 18-19).

Now, back to the story.

It has been two years since the butler was released from jail and returned to his former job with the pharaoh, but Joseph has heard nothing. He is still awaiting his trial. No one knows what Joseph was thinking. The Bible doesn't mention anything, But, you could probably imagine that he must have been wondering: What's going on? God, is this it? Am I going to die here? What about the promise you gave me in those two dreams? I believed you God and believed in my dreams just as my father, grandfather and great-great-father believed in you and their dreams.

Meanwhile, the pharaoh had had disturbing identical dreams that no one could interpret.

Notice! It took God 13 years and many steps to make Joseph's dream(s) come true. There was only one more step to go. All the steps thus far had set the stage for the grand finale: Joseph's interpretation of the pharaoh's dream and promotion to his second-in-command. And, let's not forget his parents and brothers would literally bow down to him before they knew who he was.

Let's now look at the pharaoh's dreams and how Joseph interpreted them (Gen. 41:14-25).

The first dream: The pharaoh dreamed he was standing by the Nile when, out of the river, there came seven sleek and fat cows. And, as they were grazing, seven other cows, ugly and gaunt, came out of the Nile and ate the seven fat cows.

The second dream: Seven heads of healthy grain were growing on a single stalk. After them, seven more heads of grain sprouted —thin and scorched by the east wind. The thin heads of grain swallowed up the seven healthier ones.

The next morning, the pharaoh woke up with a troubling spirit and sent for all the magicians and wise men in the land. He told them his dreams, but no one was able to interpret them. Then, the butler remembered Joseph and said to the pharaoh:

> "I remember my faults today. When the Pharaoh was angry with his servants and put me and the chief baker in custody in the house of the captain of the guard. We dreamed on the same night, he and I, each having a dream with its own meaning. A young Hebrew was there with us, a servant of the captain of the guard; and when we told him, he interpreted our dreams to us; giving an interpretation to each man according to his dream. And, as he interpreted to us, so it came to pass, I was restored to my office, and the baker was hanged" (Gen. 41: 9-13).

The pharaoh sent for Joseph immediately. He was brought quickly from the dungeon, shaved, given a change of clothes and presented to the pharaoh.

Here's an interesting thing to note. Joseph was forgotten by the butler for two years. But, God had a purpose for the delay. After all, if God wanted it, the butler could have remembered Joseph sooner. But, God moved in his perfect time. What can we learn from this? Just as God's thoughts are not like our thoughts, His timing is not like ours. As we have seen, when God felt it was time to get Joseph out of prison, it all happened very quickly. Often when bad things happened to us, we feel there are long periods of time when God doesn't do anything. But, when His timing is right, everything can come together in an instant.

Joseph Interprets the Pharaoh's Dreams

After listening to the Pharaoh tell his dreams, Joseph said,

> "The dream of Pharaoh is one; God has revealed to Pharaoh what he is about to do. The seven good cows are seven years, and the seven good ears are seven years; the dream is one. The seven lean and gaunt cows that came up after them are seven years, and the seven empty ears blighted by the east wind are also seven years of famine.

It is as I told Pharaoh, God has shown to Pharaoh what he is about to do. There will come seven years of great plenty throughout all the land of Egypt, but after them there will arise seven years of famine, and all the plenty will be forgotten in the land of Egypt; the famine will consume the land, and the plenty will be unknown in the land by reason of that famine which will follow, for it will be very grievous. And the doubling of Pharaoh's dream means that the thing is fixed by God, and God will shortly bring it to pass. (Gen. 41: 25-32).

After Joseph successfully interpreted the dreams, the pharaoh put him in charge of the whole land of Egypt. He gave Joseph his signet ring, dressed him in robes of fine linen and put a gold chain around his neck. He made him his second-in-command.

Joseph immediately went about the work to which pharaoh appointed him. As his first act, Joseph went through all of Egypt on an inspection tour. He met with people who managed the agriculture. He became familiar with the locations and conditions of the fields, the crops, the roads and means of transportation, etc.

Because of what he learned from the pharaoh's dreams, during the seven years of abundant harvest, Joseph had the grain stored in reservoirs in cities to prepare for the hard seven years that were to come. And, when those years of drought and famine came, the Egyptian people had grain to sustain them.

It was at this time of drought and famine when Joseph's family came looking to buy grain. And, you know what happened? Well, not knowing who Joseph was, his parents and brothers all bowed down before him. Joseph's dreams, as well as God's plan, were fulfilled! Fascinating, isn't it?

Now, you might have wondered why have I gone to such lengths to talk about Joseph and his dreams? Just as with all the stories in the Bible, Joseph's story has many lessons to teach us. Everything happens for a reason. We are not alone. And, God, as the parent of mankind, is always watching over us. Therefore, the smart thing to do is to trust Him and follow our desires and passions, and just like Joseph, never give up.

As we have learned from Joseph's story, God was so determined to fulfill His will in Joseph that He was willing to do anything. Remember! God works with people just as they are.

Based on the four points I indicated earlier, God does not work randomly. God sows seeds, works with our desires and passions, and works in tragic times

As we can see from Joseph's story, God's plans and timing are different from ours. God thinks and plans far, far ahead because He knows us well. We don't always understand His plan and purpose and, usually, fall short of expectations. God works in steps, laying foundation after foundation across generations until His will is fulfilled.

This is how God worked with the Israelites, his chosen people. Joseph's dream was not only about him and his family. His plan was much bigger. He was chosen to be not only the leader of his family but a leader of the nation of Egypt. And, it didn't stop there. Joseph was God's starting point to create His chosen people and influence Egypt, which leads to Moses. This story has a valuable lesson for mankind today. There is no doubt in my mind these lessons can help us understand our urgent present-day need for attention. Our modern world is not ordinary. We are living in a new era unlike any other in the past.

CHAPTER 3

My Story

How Did It All Begin?

> "You can't connect the dots looking forward: you can only connect them looking backward. So, you have to trust that dots will somehow connect in your future. You have to trust in something—Your gut, destiny, life, karma, whatever. This approach has never let me down, and it has made all the difference in my life" (Steve Jobs, 2005).

I am no Joseph

I am no Joseph, and I am no prophet. But, God seemed to work His plan with me and my dreams in the same way as He worked with Joseph.

As we have observed, God claimed Joseph and selected him out of his 11 brothers before he was born. God had also sowed seeds in Joseph's mind by giving him two dreams foreshadowing his future. He was raised in a devoutly religious family that valued dreams and dream interpretations. Remember what was said in an earlier chapter? God doesn't work at random. In preparation for the special times ahead, God has prepared nations, families, and individuals to carry out his plan. This is illustrated in God's calling of Jeremiah—before the prophet was even born.

"Now, the word of the LORD came to me saying, 'Before I formed you in the womb I knew you, and before you were born I consecrated you; I appointed you a prophet to the nations'" (Jer. 1:4-5).

As mentioned earlier, God works with people "just as they are," and works with their desires and passions. During our life journey, God plants "seeds" and deep desires that turn into powerful passions we cannot stop striving for. We want to make them real. Most of the time, these passions become our visions for the future. It is these desires and passions that started me on the path to search for my calling.

Before I start my story, I would like you to keep in mind the steps I discovered in Joseph's story God used to fulfill His plan for Joseph. I also would like you to remember these four points about God .1. God doesn't work at random. He prepares His people ahead of time. 2. He works with people just as they are. He works with people's passions and desires, whether they are good and bad. 3. When God has a claim on you, He will move mountains to fulfill His plans for you (Isa. 46:11). 4. God also works through tragic and difficult times.

Based on Joseph's story and the four points I mentioned earlier, I would like to tell my story, starting with my upbringing and how I became interested in dreams.

So, without further ado, here is my story.

Family Background

Hometown

I was born in late 1946 to a Muslim family in the tiny Tunisian village of Mellouleche. The people in my village lived very humble and hard lives during World War II. There were no doctors, hospitals or birth records. The closest hospital was 50 miles away, which, to most of the villagers, seemed like a thousand miles. Minor injuries, influenza and stomach-related illnesses were treated by herbal medicine. There was no local public transportation. The exception was a bus that ran once a day to the city of Sfax, the second largest city after the capital, Tunis. It left the village at 6 a.m. and returned at 6 p.m. People of my little village were extremely poor. They didn't travel much, and the methods of transportation were mules, donkeys or horse-drawn carriages. The latter was reserved only for the wealthy.

In the decade after World War II, life in my village became extremely hard. There was a severe drought, and famine was everywhere. Most men, including my father, Mansour, and my uncle, Taib, left their families behind to look for jobs in the big cities. I remember, when I was 6 or 7, wandering up and down the souk, an open-air marketplace, searching for something to eat. I picked up fruit that had been thrown away. These were dates and dried figs covered in sand and surrounded by flies and insects. I would pick up anything I found—nuts, broad beans and pieces of fruit—clean the sand from it and eat it. It was a miracle that I survived. In those days, there was no concept of hygiene in my village. People lived dangerous and hazardous lives.

My family had 13 members. There were my parents, my five sisters and my five brothers. My parents had two other children, a boy and a girl, but lost them a few months after they were born. I was the second child after my sister, Aisha. Because I was the first son, there was a big celebration. Soon, however, I, too, became sick. I developed an allergy to my mother's milk, or so they say. In fact, at 3 months old, I was thought to be dead. Apparently, my parents thought I died because I was too still and not breathing. At that time, it was the end of World War II. There was famine everywhere and add to that the fact our family contained simple peasant farmers with no knowledge of medicine. There were also no doctors or hospitals nearby. So, they tried to see if I was breathing by coming close to my mouth. But, they felt no air coming from my mouth or nose. Also, they felt no pulse, and my stomach was not moving. As a result, they thought I was dead and sent my Uncle Taib to dig a grave for me. Hours later, when my uncle returned home, he was surprised to find people laughing and in good spirits. There I was, alive, giggling and smiling at people gathered around me. This marked me as a miracle baby. The whole family, as well as the neighbors, knew about this incident. It was also marked as a sign of claim by God.

God didn't stop there. He continued reinforcing his claim on me by giving me dreams, visions and many spiritual experiences.

Steeped in religious tradition, superstition, spirituality and dream interpretation, and heavily dependent on weather and rain, our village elders looked for signs of rain in dreams just like in ancient times. My family, too, is very oriented in spirituality and dream interpretation. As mentioned earlier, God doesn't work at random. He plans and prepares His people far ahead of time and sowing seed in their minds.

The village was very quiet during the day. The only sounds you could hear were dogs barking and roosters crowing, waking people up at dawn. Of course, parents would scream for their children to stop playing and come home for dinner. Yes, the village was very quiet, except when it was Wednesday or souk day! On Wednesday, the whole village came alive, with thousands of people filling the marketplace with their goods to sell. They would sell everything from fruits and vegetables to sheep, chickens, cows and camels. Merchants and shoppers came to our village from nearby small towns and farming communities, some from as far away as 30 miles. Souk day was also when people met relatives who lived far away. In addition, it was a time to conduct business. The souk also drew many beggars and fortune-tellers as well. In our village, we called them gypsies.

After my childhood experience when I was almost buried alive, God continued to give me other spiritual signs that are ingrained in my mind.

When I was 7, I had a dreadful dream about a fierce fire that was consuming our house! I woke up and screamed in a panic: "Fire! Fire! Fire!" Lo and behold, to our surprise, a huge fire had already consumed the kitchen and started at our bedroom door. If I hadn't woken up screaming in terror from my dream, who knows what might've happened. Our entire family might have perished. I wondered how a dream could become reality. Did I have the gift of prophecy?

A year or so later, I had another powerful dream that had a great impact on me. This dream seemed very supernatural and was difficult to interpret because it made no sense. It was unexplainable, yet unforgettable. I call this dream the "Flood Dream."

The "Flood Dream"

> *I dreamed there was a mighty flood—like a tsunami—that swept across the Earth. A tidal wave, about one-quarter of a mile high, swept me away. I was riding on the top in the front of it. And, looking down, I saw our home and neighbors, trees, and animals were left behind, underwater! The end.*

Another experience I treasured in my mind is the stunning predictions made about me by a fortune-teller when I was approximately 6 or 7 years old. One day, my father was working in the capital city and we hadn't heard from him for almost a year. At the time, there was no phone or post office to receive mail, and family news was carried by words of mouth. I'll never forget the day a female fortune-teller, who looked like a gypsy, came to our house to sell some items. In my village, gypsies were traveling salespeople, very spiritual and wise, and known to be good fortune-tellers. My mother asked the fortune-teller a question about our family, and, specifically, about my father because we hadn't heard from him in nearly a year. Using a handful of about 30 broad beans, the fortune-teller worked on a mathematical calculation. Among the beans were a black one and a white one. She shook the beans in her hands and tossed them into a large wooden flour sifter. She then measured the distance between the black and white beans and calculated how many beans were between them. She did this three times, and, after the third time, she looked at my mother and said: "Leave some dinner for your husband tonight. He is very close and will be home tonight." To our surprise, my father came home a little after midnight that night! This was my first encounter with spirituality. The second prediction was about me. My mother asked the fortune-teller to tell her about us. The fortune-teller looked at me and asked what my name was. "Ali," my mother said. The fortune-teller said to my mother: "Ali is going to be 'high.' He is going to be famous and travel the world."

My grandfather made the exact same prediction about me.

My grandfather's prediction came during the hard farming season in the winter. There was a lot of hard work to do. Winter would bring nothing but hard labor. Our farm had about 245 acres, but we also owned other plots of land. Some plots were close by and some were 4 to 6 miles away. These also had to be farmed. It took about two hours to get there on foot. They were desolate places; you couldn't see a home for miles. (It reminds me of Joseph's story when he got lost and had to ask passers-by for directions to the land where his brothers were.) Sometimes, when I tilled the land, there was no one there but me, a camel and birds eating worms behind me as I plowed and broke the ground. Every day, I left home at dawn, and, when I returned home late in the evening, I was exhausted. After I unloaded the tilling gear from the camel and fed it, I would go in, greet my parents and siblings, tell them briefly what I did in the field, talk for a while, eat, and go to sleep. While I slept, I sighed a lot, and this worried my father.

At this time, my paternal grandfather was living with us. I recall hearing my father talking to him about me and asking for advice. One night, I heard my father crying: "What can I do? My son is dying on me. He is working too hard, and he is too young to do this kind of job. What shall I do?" My grandfather tried to comfort him. He said, "Oh, my son, don't worry about him. He will grow up and become a successful man, and he will tour the world. I know he will." I liked what my grandfather said about me. He gave me something to hope for, even though the idea of touring the world at that time seemed far-fetched and impossible. It was a great idea, but I couldn't imagine myself even traveling to a city that was 34 miles away let alone traveling the world. Of course, we now know this would later come true. I'm not famous, despite publishing three books, but I have traveled to Russia, the United States and more than 22 countries in the Middle East, Europe and Asia.

Where Hopes and Desires Turn into Passions

Our wishes and desires stem out of hardship and passion. At the age of 10, our family relocated to our home on a farm about 3 miles from the village. Farming was a new experience for my family. I learned later that farming was very difficult because the land was so harsh and dry because there was no rain. When it didn't rain for a long period, the land would be too hard to till. Tilling soil manually by camel in the freezing winter or sweltering heat of the summer is impossible. In the area surrounding our home, we grew all kinds of vegetables—peas, carrots, spinach, broad beans, chickpeas, and onions—in small irrigated gardens. In large fields, we grew wheat and barley. All the work was done manually. Despite the hardship, I pledged I would do my best to make it work. The first year was an experiment. With guidance from my grandfather and our neighbors, we learned the ropes. We had another problem, however. My father was in poor health. For a long time, he had been suffering from an ulcer and was always in pain. Farming was difficult for him. During the two years I helped him, I worked on the farm on the weekends and school breaks. All that changed the year I took full responsibility for the farm.

In sixth grade, I failed the test that would allow me to attend secondary school. Because I was 17, I wasn't allowed to continue my education in public school. I had accepted the fact I would be a farmer. And, this is where the seeds of love and compassion for my father and family began. It was a mixture of great love, adoration and respect for my father. My father was like my God for me. I respected him so dearly. Even when I was in my late 20s, I never smoked cigarettes or drank alcohol in front of him out of respect. Also, as the oldest son, it was my responsibility to help my father with the farming. I loved my father and respected him a lot. It was difficult for me to see him struggle with the pain every day and I felt very sorry for him. My father was the youngest child in his family. He was very handsome, clever, humorous and educated. These qualities could also be seen in my Uncle Taib, the only uncle who I grew to love and greatly respect. The villagers loved to sit in the coffee shops and talk to them. They were very popular in the village and had good reputations. My father was always well-dressed when in public, which made me so proud of him. He was known as the "wise man of the village," and, in my culture, was given the honored nickname, "the serpent." He told many exciting stories about war and the politics of his time. And, he had many hobbies. He also had many different jobs. He had been a fisherman—he had his own fishing boat—a farmer, a store owner and a politician. He even ran for city clerk, but his honesty kept him from being elected. You couldn't be an honest politician. People, however, thought well of him for his wisdom and friendship and sought his help on many subjects.

In the late 1960s, before modern cafes came to our village, tea shops were the only places men could gather. There were no movie theaters or TVs, chairs or tables. In tea or coffee shops, people usually sat on the floor on straw mattresses. The age of television had just begun for us, and only a handful of wealthy families had black and white TVs. There was no electricity in most parts of the village. People used kerosene lamps for light, especially in the country. After dinner, men usually went to tea shops to meet friends, play cards, or talk business. My father could also play shkobba very well. This is one of Tunisia's most popular card games. People loved to play with him because he knew many tricks and signs to identify various cards. By touching his nose or elbow, winking one of his eyes, or sticking out his tongue, cards could be identified, and this helped a person win a game. This game is best played with four people (two pairs of partners). It was very exciting, especially when the players start battling each other and using card signs. The game was usually played to pay for the tea that was consumed by the crowd, which contained mostly friends and neighbors who had gathered to watch the game.

Back to the farm …

CHAPTER 4

Covenant with God

Sprouting Seeds

After my experiences with dreams and other ethereal phenomena, my spiritual development increased rapidly. During my three years of hard labor on the farm—the days I was working on the plots of land far from home—I developed an interesting form of entertainment that helped to shorten my long and lonely days. I produced a script (like a television series) in my head, and every day, I changed the topic. One thing stayed the same, however. Every script was about me. The script was about my going abroad and becoming a success. I would travel to different countries and work in them. Of course, I had lots of money, and I came home with gifts for every member of the family. I would also tell them how much I loved them and cared for them. I made up little stories about each one of my family members.

When I acted out these stories, I would say the words aloud as if I were talking to a real person. I was so passionate when I acted that I often cried real tears. I adored my family and, in some of my plays, I washed my mother's feet. My father loved to have money in his wallet. So, in my plays, in addition to the gifts I bought him, I also had his wallet full of big bills. In my fantasy, my family lived in a large mansion with many rooms, and each person had his or her own bedroom. I also took them to famous places in the country and big fancy hotels and drove them in a luxurious car. I fantasized so well that sometimes I created two or three plays a day. This, I found, made the day go so much faster.

As time passed, the nature of my plays changed its focus. It went from taking care of my family to being a world-famous teacher. In them, I would teach something so noble, such as a philosophy of life that is based on love and truth. Once again, I became so obsessed with the play that I cried real tears during scenes or situations when I tried to help someone.

In my series, I created a play about bad people, like modern-day terrorists. But, at the time, I didn't know they were called "terrorists." I showed how, by true love and caring, they could be changed and become good people. In my imagination, I was able to make myself invisible, and I would appear to them in their homes. I would take these bad people to a place deep in the mountains, where breathtaking landscapes surrounded a beautiful palace. In this palace, I was their counselor. I served and tended them and listened to their problems. I cared for them so much that they became good people and a part of my family.

In my palace, there were no servants. Everybody was family and treated with love and respect. Whenever I left the palace for a few days, everyone said goodbye with hugs. I was like their father and closest friend. I taught them love through caring. Nobody ever wanted to leave. I remember during one play, while I was acting, something so spiritual and profound took over my mouth and spoke through me. I believed I was overcome by a spirit. I was speaking a language I had never heard before. Only much later, after I joined my new faith, did I realize I was speaking in tongues. At that moment, I was speaking and crying so loudly, people could hear me a mile away. As my crying reached its pinnacle, I let go of the camel and the tilling gear, fell to the ground, and cried out: "God! Please help me! Please help me find a good job abroad so I can fulfill these desires and help my family and bring them out of this poverty." I also said: "When all these things are fulfilled, you can have my life. You can do whatever you wish with it. You can take my life. I am all yours."

That day, I went home sad and exhausted. As soon as I got home, I went straight to bed. I didn't eat or talk to anyone. (I believe, on this day, a covenant and promise were made between God and me). From that day on, I believed God had begun a plan for my life, and He worked on it step by step. Another unexplained coincidence, or shall we call it a miracle, happened not too long after. Approximately eight to nine months after I had this experience, a great miracle was about to happen, and it involved my sister's marriage.

Marriage and Tradition

When God predestines, He will move mountains.

What mountains am I talking about here? Surely, I am not talking about literal mountains, such as the Rockies or the Atlas Mountains. I am talking about the mountains of impossibility. Breaking down religion is a mountain. Breaking down a tradition is a mountain. Breaking down bad habits, such as alcohol, drugs and pornography, are mountains. These are the mountains that Jesus in Luke 17:20 talked about when he said if you have faith as small as a mustard seed, you can move a mountain.

Speaking of the miracles of coincidence and the passion and predestination that moved mountains, I have a few. I have no other intention but to tell you that I understood how God has been working in my life. I am no different than any other average person who tries to live a normal life. I was not a religious person. I didn't go to the mosque for Friday prayers. I didn't pray, and I didn't fast on Ramadan. I lived a wild and free life, one that a religious person would call "sinful." But, I had a good heart and I tried to live a peaceful life and be a friend to all.

Having said that, let's continue with my story on the miracles of coincidence and the moving of mountains.

The question asked is how, as poor as I was, did I manage to leave a life of farming and move to the city? How did I manage to even leave the country and travel to Europe? Let's start with coincidences that moved mountains and broke down tradition.

It is really fascinating how systematic God is and how He sees so far ahead. Just as in Joseph's story, in preparing for His next plan, God is even willing to break down heavily instituted traditions, such as marriage, just to pave the way for what's to come. Marriage and family in Tunisia are rooted in tradition. Because of our religion and culture, we marry our cousins. Therefore, the blood lineage stays in the family. My aunt, whose family lived in the same duplex as mine, gave birth to her first child, a son. A few months later, my mother gave birth to my sister, Aisha. So, they were matched with each other. Then, the order changed. My mother had four sons, and my aunt had four daughters. Each of the girls was born within a month of each of the boys. We were all matched with each other. As children, we knew who we were going to marry.

Then something happened. God's providence was at work! The first pairing didn't occur. My father and uncle had a disagreement over marital issues, so the match was called off. Thus, began a competition between my two aunts to see which of their sons would marry my sister. They came with gifts, sang and danced for my father's acceptance. But, one by one, they were dismissed for the same reason. My sister was very beautiful, and our family had a good reputation, so everyone wanted her as a wife. God had a different agenda, though. Shortly after, an unknown relative on my mother's side came to visit. We didn't know her well because she lived in Tunis, which was some distance away. She came with her daughter and son-in-law and one of my uncles who lived in a nearby community. They looked like Europeans. They were very clean and well-dressed and drove a shiny, luxurious and white car. When they drove into our courtyard, all the neighbors came out of their houses to see it. It was a showcase for our family.

They came to ask my father if my sister could marry the woman's older son. There was a festive feeling in the air! The visitors brought gifts, beautifully wrapped candies and delicious pastries I had never seen before. The adults dined and talked. Then, as they stood to leave, the woman suddenly and loudly ululated. This is a sound of joy made by people in my country upon hearing good news. The entire family, as well as the neighbors, knew what happened. God uttered His rejoices, too, and began to prepare the next level of His plan for me.

At my sister's wedding, there were many relatives who we had never met before. Among them was a man by the name of Mr. Komyes. He was related to my new brother-in-law, and it was through him that God worked. He promised my father he would give me a job at his company in Tunis. Mr. Komyes was the manager of the largest mechanic shop in the country, which was owned by the government's largest hotel chain, the S.H.T.T. (Societe Touristique de Tunisie). My new brother-in-law also worked for this company as a tour guide. My brother-in-law, who spoke three languages—French, English and German—drove groups of tourists in beautiful modern coaches to famous historic sites in the country.

When he came to our village, he always came with the latest, and most beautiful, vehicle. People would come out to see it and marvel at its luxury. At times, he took some villagers for short drives, so they could experience the feeling of riding in luxury. It was arranged that I would be an apprentice mechanic in the same shop Mr. Komyes managed, and I would live with my sister and brother-in-law in their apartment, which was above the mechanic shop.

Chain of Miraculous Coincidences

A year later, I traveled to Tunis to start my job as an apprentice mechanic. The day before I left, my father bought me new shoes, pants, shirts and a jacket, and he gave me a little spending money. My mother prepared food for me just as she did for my brother when he left to attend college in Sfax, the second largest city in Tunisia, which was approximately 50 kilometers (37 miles) from our village. She stuffed my suitcase with homemade food and pastries, dates, almonds, and a big container of olive oil to give to my sister as a gift. A few days later, I was at the bus stop with a large group of people who came to say goodbye, just as when my brother left. There were about 20 people, including my parents, brothers and sisters, some close relatives, and neighbors, waiting with me.

Then, another miracle happened. When I arrived at my sister's house, I received more good news. I would not be working as a mechanic apprentice, but in a luxurious five-star hotel, one of the company's best-known, the Amilcar Hotel in Carthage, not far from the presidential palace. Somehow, by God's will, my brother-in-law realized (or God made him realize) that I should be working in a hotel and not in a repair shop. While on one of his visits with a group of tourists to this hotel, something prompted him (God) to ask the manager if there were any job vacancies for me. This manager had been transferred a few months earlier, and just happened to know my brother-in-law. He told my brother-in-law to have me see him. A couple of days later, I was working as a busboy in the hotel's restaurant. This seemed like a miracle to me! This is what I meant when I said that when God chooses you for something, He will move mountains.

And, then, another coincidence occurred. A few days after I started my job, I met an employee who happened to come from the same tribe as I, and whose name was also Ali Mahjoub. He also was from my village, but I had never met him. He had worked in this hotel for about five years. Six months into the job, he decided to quit and left the hotel to be an accountant.

A year or so later, another miracle! The hotel manager called me into his office. Without asking me to sit, he said, "How long have you been working here?"

Nervously, I answered, "A year and six months, sir."

He pulled some papers from his desk and said: "What is this? How could you get such a contract and be chosen for management training in Europe? You have only been working here for only one year and six months! Did you know you have to work for this company for at least five or six years before you qualify for such a contract? Tell me. How did you get this contract?"

I was so nervous and speechless. I tried to think of an answer. Suddenly, I remembered a brief conversation I had with the relative of the man with the same name as me. He once mentioned he had a relative who was a high-level director in the company's head office. So, I gathered all my strength and said: "Sir, I have a relative in a high position in the head office!" The manager looked at me with disgust and disbelief, nodded his head and told me to leave.

Yet, another coincidence, or should I say a miracle, occurred. The hotel manager who called me to his office to tell me about the contract was transferred to another hotel. I didn't know he was only at the hotel temporarily. So, my contract was left in the new manager's hands. A few months later, I was asked to come to his office. After I sat down, he said: "Congratulations, son! You have been selected from a small group of young people for a government-sponsored program to go to Europe for management training. Do you have a passport?"

"No, sir," I replied.

"You will need to leave the country very soon, maybe in two or three weeks!" he said. "Come to my office later this afternoon and I will give you a letter to give to the Department of the Interior, so you can get your passport quickly." I walked out of the office filled with joy and ecstasy.

I did as he instructed. About a week later, after I acquired all the necessary documents, passport photos, etc., I went to the Department of the Interior to apply for my passport. In the 1960s, passports were hard to get. It took months or, perhaps, years to obtain a passport. Also, passports weren't made for travel to communist countries. You could only travel to the 12 or 15 countries that the government approved and listed in your passport.

A few days after I visited the Department of the Interior, I received the news that my passport was ready. The next day, I went to the office where the passports were issued. I greeted the employee, gave the person my name, and was told to wait until I was called. An hour or so later, a man in a uniform called my name and asked me to follow him. He brought me to a room where I was greeted by another man who asked me to sit down. On the desk was a pile of passports. The man asked me my name and where I was planning to travel. I said I was going to Brussels, Belgium, for hotel management training. He congratulated me, picked up a passport and went to the corner of his office where he stamped it. He came back to his desk, opened the passport, and said, "What countries do you want to put in your passport?" I was ready. I handed him the list I had prepared with 12 countries on it. After he finished writing them down, he handed me the passport, shook my hand, and said, "Good luck." I was beaming with joy. I felt like I was floating. I went back to the hotel with so much trepidation. I kept the fact I had my passport secret and didn't tell anyone about it until a week before I left.

Learning a Specific Language

The next step God had me do is learn the right language. I didn't know at the time that God had plans to send me to England. When I first started my job in the hotel, my brother-in-law gave me a German-French dictionary, so I could learn German. At the time, it was one of the most commonly used languages in the tourism industry. Every educated hotel employee spoke German and French fluently, as well as Danish, Swedish, and Italian. I studied German for about a year and learned quite a lot. Then,

I discovered that English is a lingua franca, and the most widely used in the world.

In the early 1960s, most of the tourists who came to Tunisia were German, but there were also some from Switzerland, Denmark, Sweden, France, Belgium, and Italy. Tunisia was like the Bahamas for these European countries. The British tourists began to trickle into our country when a few British families started visiting. But, most British tourists went to Spain or Majorca.

When I discovered English was the language in which the world preferred to communicate, I began to study it. In 1967, British tourists started coming to our hotel. Most of the waiters didn't like them because they didn't spend much money and were lousy tippers. They would order a bottle of mineral water, drink half during their meal, and then ask the waiter to hold on to it until they returned to eat their next meal. The waiters would stick a note with the customer's name and table number on the bottle. The customers usually had the same waiter and table for the entire two weeks. They were not like the Germans or Swiss, who were big spenders. These tourists always ordered wine and left good tips after every meal.

I was different, however. I didn't care much about tips. I loved the English language and wanted to practice it with English-speaking people. I wanted to learn the language faster, so I volunteered to care for the British tourists. Any new British family that came to the hotel would have three daily meals at my station for their entire two-week stay.

After a few months, my English improved. I became the official interpreter between the hotel administration and English-speaking tourists. Any time an English-speaking person wanted something, the administration would assign me to him or her. Even the reception desk asked for me. I had a lot of fun meeting English-speaking families, talking with them, taking them to special places, and showing them all the popular historical sites and famous coffee shops. Every two weeks, four to six families would arrive. Besides having a great time, I discovered that the British did leave good tips, but I didn't tell anyone that. Usually, at the last meal before they left, the families would tip with all the change they had.

Waiters usually knew about their customers' departure about a day or two before they left. On the day they were to leave, waiters would make beautiful flower arrangements on the families' tables. I was well-known for this. Whenever I learned of a client's departure date, I would raid the hotel garden. One day, the gardener, who had had enough of my raids, reported me to the manager. This didn't stop me, though. I waited a while, snuck back into the garden, and resumed my raids.

I loved my British customers and enjoyed their company. Many gave me their addresses and phone numbers in England and made me promise that I would visit them when I traveled to their country. I accumulated a very large list of names and addresses. I longed to travel to England, so, of course, England was on the list of countries that I had on my passport, or so I thought.

There was one event, I remember, that made a heartfelt impression on me. It was the moon landing in 1969, which I was fortunate enough to watch with a small group of hotel guests, four months before I left for Brussels. This event had a big effect on me, and I wished I could live in the United States, the most powerful country in the world. I felt pride as I watched history in the making. It is a futuristic seed that, in time, would become real. You will read about it in later chapters. The preparation is complete, and God is ready for His next plan for me. He is sending me to Brussels!

CHAPTER 5

Brussels, Belgium

On Oct. 23, 1969, I flew to Brussels. At the hotel institute, I took a comprehensive hotel and restaurant management training course that included classes on wines, restaurant service, and a special course on cooking. I practiced at the Brussels Hilton Hotel. While there, I made a few Belgian friends. Most preferred to speak English rather than French because of the bilingual nature of the country—one half speaks Flemish, a form of Dutch, and the other half speaks French.

As usual, when God has plans for you, He has already mapped them out. About a month or so later, I found myself with a burning desire to go to England. This is how God works in people. He works with people's desires, hopes and passions. This was what success-driven young people of my country longed for. They would get a job in a foreign country, such as France, Germany, or Italy, make a lot of money, build a big house, and return home once or twice a year with gifts, money and fancy cars for the holidays. And, this is exactly what I dreamed of doing during my hard years farming behind a camel. I wanted to work abroad and earn a lot of money to help my family, particularly my father, and get out of poverty. This was my desire, my passion, my "seed" of hope that would later come to fruition.

I wanted to go to England so badly I asked my Belgian friends to help me find a job there. A month later, they found an ad in an employment magazine that was published by England's largest hotel chain, the Grand Metropolitan Hotel. The company was looking for people to fill all kinds of hotel and restaurant positions. My Belgian friends and I wrote letters to the hotel asking to be employed. Within a few weeks, I received an answer. I sent the company my resumé, my employment history, a certificate I received from the institute, and a letter of recommendation from the hotel. Within two weeks, I received my contract to work at the Mayfair Hotel, London.

Passport Incident

Desperate times call for desperate measures–
Ancient proverb

It is really reassuring to know that even if we mess up, forget or give up, God is always there. He has ways to remind us of things. Three months before my training program finished in Belgium, my contract, as well as my permit to work in Great Britain, came. Again, I did this without anyone's knowledge. I locked my contract and permit in my suitcase, in which I also had my passport. One day, I had a feeling that something was wrong. I looked at my papers, particularly my passport, and when I looked at the list of countries, I was horrified! England wasn't on the list! I didn't know what to do. One month until the end of my training, and I had a huge problem. After worrying about it for a few days, I began to look for a solution. I needed to add England to my passport. However, I had heard many stories that made my anxiety worse. The Tunisian embassy had very strict rules about adding anything to passports because many former trainees didn't return home after their training period, choosing to go to other countries instead. I agonized over the situation. I was so afraid of being rejected by the embassy and losing this great opportunity, I decided to write "England" in French in my passport.

On my day off, I was determined to fix my passport. I examined it. The list was written in blue ink. So, I bought a container of blue ink and a pen. I went home and locked the door to my room. I sat at a small table, and with my passport and ink pen full, I nervously began to write the word "Angleterre," which means England, in French. To my distress, though, the ink was the wrong shade of blue. Not only that, but I also misspelled "Angle Terre." Again, I panicked. What would I do now? I decided to correct it by "whiting out" the part I misspelled and rewriting it.

I made a list of everything I needed and went shopping. When I found the items, I returned to my room, locked my door, and picked up my passport. It was obvious the ink was the wrong shade of blue and the spelling mistake had to be corrected. I thought I could remove the latter part of the word by scratching it off with the edge of a razor blade. It removed 90 percent, but there was enough left that someone might notice the mistake. I decided to try White-Out. I dipped the sponge in the clear liquid and applied it to the area. To my horror, the liquid spread like a wildfire. It made a hole in my passport the size of a nickel! It was a disaster. I felt like I'd been thrown into a furnace. I was consumed with fear and panic. I was sick for days and went to a doctor. Then, out of the blue, I heard an encouraging voice whisper: "Now what? You must do something about your problem. You are running out of time."

After accepting the situation, I devised a plan. I would say someone had stolen my passport. So, I went to the police station and created a big dramatic scene, completed with tears. I said someone had stolen all my legal papers, money and passport. Seeing how upset I was, a policeman calmed me down: "Don't panic," he said, "it's not a big problem. We will write a report; you take it to your embassy and with it, you will have a new passport issued to you."

While outwardly, I continued to be upset, inwardly I thought: "That's what I want—a police report!" After being interrogated by the police, I was given the report. Then, I went straight to the Tunisian embassy to apply for a new passport. Again, I put on another display, and, this time, I acted very pitifully. I got my passport three days before my training finished.

Even with all this drama, I still managed to keep it a secret. I never told anyone about the job, or what happened to my passport. I didn't even tell my roommate until the night I left.

The evening I was to leave, I invited some people to join me for a farewell party. Around 11 p.m. I stood up and said: "Gentlemen! I have some news! The person you see before you will be heading to London." I held up two things in my hands. "This is my contract to work in London's best hotel and this is my ticket. Thank you for coming, and, now, please excuse me because I must get ready. I must leave in about an hour. I am going to take the train from Brussels to Ostend and then ride the ferry to Dover, England." Everyone, my roommate included, was shocked I was able to get a job like that. Here is a guy many people thought was the least educated, and I had managed to do something those who considered themselves smarter than I had not been able to do. Around midnight, my roommate helped me carry my luggage to the street, and I waited for a taxi to take me to the train station. People who read this story may not think this is intriguing. But, when it is viewed with God's plan, it turns into an intriguing and profound story.

CHAPTER 6

England

The Strange Man at Hyde Park Corner

As I mentioned earlier, I have a special bond with England. I don't know why. Ever since I had the experience of speaking in tongues, I felt an English spirit inside me. I can't describe the joy I felt after arriving in Dover and making it past immigration. I felt like there was so much promise and hope. I felt like an American immigrant.

I'll never forget my first night at a bed and breakfast, which was near Victoria Station, one of London's busiest train stations. Quite honestly, I don't know how I did all of this without spiritual help leading me from place to place. It was so exhilarating to be in one of the world's largest cities. My first week there, I started my job at the Mayfair Hotel.

I rented a nice room from a high-class family in Hyde Park Mansions, near the Marble Arch. I even earned some tips from my first few days of work. I was a sponge, absorbing everything, learning a new lifestyle and getting to know the city. I liked London's black cabs and double-decker buses, as well as its subway stations and parks. It was a long way from my life as a peasant boy living in a mud house in a tiny village in North Africa. I loved the city and country very much. I never thought I would leave it. But, God had a plan for me. This was my calling, and God had planted His seeds.

In England, God planted two seeds in my heart, and these are two very important experiences that were engraved in my memory. The first one is about a strange encounter with someone I met during an event in Hyde Park. About a year after I came to London, I made friends with a Palestinian co-worker. He invited me to go to Speakers Corner in Hyde Park, and I accepted. There were people everywhere. There were four or five pockets of people gathered close to one another in different areas. One person stood on a milk cart; others stood on chairs. They were all talking about different political issues. A crowd was listening to someone speak about African issues. Someone else was speaking about Palestinian/Israeli issues. And, another spoke about India and Pakistan. It was a fascinating and educational place; I walked from group to group listening to the different topics.

When we were ready to leave, my co-worker and I decided to split up. It was my day off, so I wasn't in a hurry. I decided to take a stroll down the road and headed toward Oxford Street, which is the busiest shopping street in Europe. It's a lot like New York's Fifth Avenue. This road stretched approximately a mile along the park. I watched the people traverse the street, and as I approached them, I noticed a man standing by himself. He had a little round table covered with a lace tablecloth. On the table was a black, leather-covered book. The man was talking to a small group of people. He held the book in his hands and said to the crowd, of which I was now a part: "You think you are alive, but you are dead!" He pointed to the buildings that stood along the street. "You are no different than those buildings over there!" This statement got my full attention, and it infuriated me. "What is this guy talking about," I asked myself. "What does he mean, we are dead? And, we are no different than those buildings?"

I was livid. I had spent about two hours listening to different speakers, but none of them affected me as this man's statement had. He repeated it. "Yes, you are dead, even the birds in the air are more alive than you." After a while, I walked away. I convinced myself this guy was just another crazy person. However, I couldn't forget what he said. It bothered me for the rest of the day.

As noted in the introduction, humans sometimes experience unexplained phenomena. These coincidences, dreams, etc., are filed away in our subconscious, influencing our decisions when we least expect it. These experiences are sent by God, however, and are "seeds" that will eventually grow into spiritual instruments and lead people to one of God's divine appointments. The dreams I share here have played a big role in guiding me through my spiritual journey. As mentioned earlier, and forgive me for repeating it, God does not work randomly. Instead, he prepares people step-by-step and perfectly synchronizes time, places and events.

The story about the strange man illustrates that. God sent my co-worker to take me to Speakers' Corner. Then, God put me in the hands of the stranger who so infuriated me. But, I needed to hear that. His statement was a seed that would become a part of the bigger plan God had in store for me.

Marriage: Wars of Cultures and Religions

The second and very valuable lesson I learned in England, and one that would be the guiding light for my entire life, is about religions and cultures. During my earlier years in London, I met a young English lady from Sussex. We worked together at a summer resort hotel in Bude, Cornwall. We fell in love and were soon engaged. At the end of the summer, we returned to London and lived together for a year. Everything was going well until the time of our wedding approached.

Two weeks before the wedding, we moved in with her parents. They were quite wealthy and lived in a huge six-bedroom house. Her father was the director of a big insurance corporation and her mother also had a good job. We began preparing for the wedding and made an appointment with the vicar to talk about what needed to be done. This conversation worried me. As a Muslim, I didn't think I could get married in a church. My fiancée and I had talked about it, but it wasn't a big concern for us at the time. Now, it was a problem.

The day we met with the vicar, I felt an alarming sense of fear and betrayal of my Muslim faith. I was nervous and indecisive. I didn't like the idea of a church wedding, and as we made our way to the meeting, we had a big argument.

The day of the wedding drew nearer, and the pressure increased. I felt like running away. In fact, I thought about it, but I wasn't sure how I could get my suitcase out of the house unnoticed. If I could have managed that, I would have left. There was a spiritual battle occurring inside me between Islam and Christianity! This day was going to be the worst day of my life.

Then, I was overtaken by a spiritual phenomenon.

On our wedding day, as we stood opposite each other at the altar, the minister began to read from a big, thick, black, leather-covered book. I later learned it was called the Bible. A strong wave of panic swept over me, and I began to tremble. Some people noticed how nervous I was and brought me a glass of water. It's normal to be nervous, so no one thought much about it. But, they did not know what was going on inside me. My situation was different. I felt like I was about to die of fear. I had strong feelings telling me not to get married. I felt if I got married in a church, I would destroy everything about my Islamic upbringing, as well as my future. I had never experienced such a fearful and life-threatening phenomenon as this before! I saw my wedding day as my death day, as well as the death of Islam, and the death of my ancestors. Imagine the agony I was in.

As the minister continued to read from the Bible, I was praying desperately to Allah, begging Him to strike me down! In my heart, I was pleading with God, begging Him to let me die. I was in a dire state of mind, and I meant it. I wanted to die to prevent anything from happening to Islam, my ancestors, or my history. Wouldn't that be awful? I was terrified that marrying a person of a different faith would destroy my entire history.

It was too late now. The wedding was over! After the vows and exchanging of the rings, the minister blessed us and pronounced us husband and wife.

Our honeymoon was miserable! We went to a well-known seaside resort where we stayed at the apartment of a couple who were friends with my father-in-law. The entire time we were there, a negative spiritual element kept us at odds with each other. We didn't get along and argued all the time.

After three days, we decided to go home. My wife returned to her family in tears, and, after a couple of days at her parents' house, we agreed to return to London. From that day on, things were different, and we began to realize we made a mistake by getting married.

We began to set rules and conditions, and religion, once absent, became the dominant factor in our lives. We differed in our opinions about having children, and in which faith should they be raised. I, of course, insisted they be raised as Muslims, and my wife argued they be raised as Christians or at least have the option of choosing which faith they would like to be. I disagreed with this.

Three months later, our marriage was over. Surprisingly, 40 years later, the government of Tunisia passed a law in July 2017 that allows couples of different religions to marry. This experience had haunted me for years. I couldn't believe how quickly our relationship deteriorated because of religion. I loved my wife very much, and it pained me so deeply. It felt like my life was soiled and marked by failures. I was a broken-hearted loser and a divorcee. It really bothered me for years. However, approximately 40 years after my marriage experience, it dawned on me that there is a divine reason for my troubled marriage with my British wife and why I had that overwhelming feeling of panic. After all, it was God's plan. He is in charge and knows His plans for me better than I. An explanation on this phenomenon will be addressed in an upcoming chapter., The overwhelming experience I had on my marriage day was a clear protest from God that He didn't approve of it. God wanted my marriage to be part of His Marriage Blessing offered by the Rev. and Mrs. Sun Myung Moon, founders of the Unification movement.

Keep on reading to that chapter.

CHAPTER 7

Iran: A New Beginning

After a fruitless four years in England, I realized I had made a big mistake with God. I had forgotten the promise I had made, and I had forgotten about my family for whom I had pledged to care. Instead, I plunged into the world like a blind man! I went from being a naive country boy raised in the North African desert to someone who relished the faster Western lifestyle. I was a hippie in the early 1970s and a disco/soul man in the mid-'70s.

I asked God for another chance and returned home for the first time in four years. While there, I repented to my family, particularly to my father, and asked for their forgiveness. I made them a new promise that I would never forget about them again and I would continue to help them financially until they no longer needed it. I also promised to build them a nice house. This was expected of young Tunisians when they found a job abroad.

I returned to London with a new determination to carry out my promises to God and my family. I immediately began searching for a job in the Middle East, in either Iran or Saudi Arabia. I realized that England was no longer the country in which I could earn a good income and save enough to help my family. I had heard many stories about the rich Middle Eastern countries. In March 1976, I saw a newspaper ad for a company that was recruiting hotel and restaurant employees in Iran. I applied right away, and, soon, I had an interview with a recruitment agency.

I did very well in the interview and was hired as an assistant restaurant manager at a resort in Iran. A British-born Jewish businessman had opened a casino, the Caspian Casino Club, Old Grand Hotel, on the Caspian Sea, 300 miles north of Tehran. It was a holiday resort that attracted the country's richest and most famous citizens, including the royal family (Mohammad Rezã Shãh Pahlavi).

The Caspian Casino Club, Old Grand Hotel, was once a palace that belonged to the shah. The story said this palace was an

Iranian landmark. One day, the shah stood on a rock upon a hill and saw the sea, which was about 2 miles away, and ordered his palace be built where he stood. He built a magnificent wide avenue with three lanes on either side and, in the middle, there is a wide island with gardens and palm tree-lined walkways that stretched all the way to the sea. At the end of the avenue, near the beach, stood The Chalet, a building used by the royal family for summer vacations. A person standing at the front door of the palace could see The Chalet and be marveled by it. This area became one of the most famous tourist attractions in the country. The shah bequeathed the palace to his grandsons, but they didn't take good care of it. Perhaps, they had more important matters to deal with than this small country village that they only visited in the summer. This is how the British businessman was able to lease it from the royal family.

During my first year in Iran, I kept my promises. I sent money to my father regularly, and I built my family a two-room attachment to the house. I had planned to add more rooms and turn it into a grand villa with front and rear verandas. However, just as before, I lost the vision and returned to the wild life of alcohol and hard living. I was living the so-called high life of the casino world. In this world, you could do nothing without the help of your friends, drugs and alcohol, especially, if you wanted to be in the elite. Otherwise, you would be regarded as a low-class person. At first, I did not associate with those people, but I was humiliated many times. Then, I decided I had had enough, and joined their ranks. It is a sad life that most Westerners get drafted into while working in a different culture, such as those in Islamic Middle Eastern countries. Islamic laws are very strict. There are no public entertainment places, such as pubs, bars, nightclubs, or even movie theaters. So, Westerners tend to hang out together and create their own private entertainment and parties.

It is interesting to note that people's stubbornness and disregard for the law persist even when threatened with death! In Islamic countries, the consumption of alcohol, use of drugs and sexual misconduct are strictly forbidden. The punishments can be very severe. However, all these are plentiful. Despite the strictest rules and harshest punishments, there are people who aren't afraid of death. They smuggle all kinds of forbidden things into the country, and a plethora of alcohol, drugs and sexual-related material can be found everywhere. My second year in Iran, I forgot about God, and, again, I was drawn into the wrong lifestyle.

Then, chaos and revolution brought an end to that!

Iran's Revolution

I thought I would have that hotel job for life. Just before the Iranian Revolution began in 1978, I was promised a great job as the new palace manager for Princess Ashraf, the shah's older sister. I felt I had reached the pinnacle of my career. I had so much pride in my position and a lot of hope. However, a few months after I returned from a short vacation in London, the revolution began. I watched it slowly develop over days and then weeks. We could hear the gunfire in the nearby villages, and there were rumors the rebels might attack the casino, so police and security agents, armed with machine guns, stood guard.

One day, a military helicopter landed in the casino complex. A few hours later, the staff was called together for an emergency meeting. We were told we should get out of the country as soon as possible. We only had three days to evacuate.

On Sept. 9, 1978, the first day of martial law in Tehran, four staff members and I spent nine hours jammed in a small car. We drove through the rugged mountains to Tehran and then were rushed to Tehran International Airport six hours before our scheduled flight. A curfew forbade anyone from gathering in the streets after 6 p.m. There were fears the airport might be attacked. The airport was filled with foreigners trying to flee the country, so they had to add more flights. I left Tehran slightly after midnight and headed to Greece. Once in Athens, I took the ferry to the beautiful island of Mykonos and stayed there a couple weeks. Then, I returned to London.

On the subject of coincidences and spirituality, in early October 2017, an Iranian lady by the name of Shamsi walked into the restaurant I manage in Indianapolis, Indiana, and asked to see Ali Mahjoub. I replied, "I am he." The lady exclaimed, "Thank God, I found you." She proceeded to tell me that she had just visited a

New Age bookstore, just about three city blocks from the restaurant, and found books written by me. "Is it you?" she asked. "Yes, I am the author," I replied. Then, we shook hands again and she asked me for my autograph. As I was signing the books, she told me she knew a famous Iranian poet and writer by the name of Mahjoub and thought maybe he was the author. The interesting part of this story is only a couple days before Shamsi visited the bookstore, I was there and gave the bookstore those two books to sell!

Anyway, going back to Iran Revolution story.

I returned to London, but it wasn't the same as when I had left. Its streets were dirty, and the people were unfriendly. I noticed many skinheads defacing streets with graffiti. I didn't like this London, but I had to stay there and look for another job. I lived in a rented room in Notting Hill Gate. This was the worst and lowest point in my life, I believe. I had hit rock bottom and felt like a loser! There were many times I questioned my purpose in life and why I was living in such poor conditions far away from home. I wished I hadn't left Tunisia. I refused to take any job that I felt was less than I deserved. That usually meant nothing less than a management position. Within six months, I had spent most of my savings.

In desperation, I went to several employment agencies. I found two jobs: one in Gabon, East Africa, and the other in Scotland. I was desperate, so I took the job as a maître d' at the Tay Park Hotel, a small establishment in Dundee, Scotland. I worked there for three or four months. I never visited the city, but choose instead to stay in the hotel's complex. It was like a retreat for me. The hotel sat on a hill and was hidden deep in the forest. After a few months, I realized this job was a no-win situation, and I returned to London to look for a better one.

As luck would have it, during my first month back in London, I saw an ad from an employment agency for jobs in Saudi Arabia! Also, at this time, I met an old Tunisian friend with whom I had worked in a London restaurant. I found out that he, too, left Iran because of the revolution. He offered me the opportunity to open a restaurant with him. While we were working on this project, the agency offered me a job to work as a restaurant manager in a new hotel, the Dhahran International Hotel, in Dhahran, Saudi Arabia. I felt I was a phoenix just raised from the ashes. I could see my future becoming hopeful and promising once again.

CHAPTER 8

Saudi Arabia

God Works with People Just as They Are

Once again determined to fulfill my promise to God and family, I took a job as the restaurant manager at the newly built Dhahran International Hotel in Saudi Arabia. On Nov. 27, 1979, I landed at Dhahran International Airport less than a half-mile away from the hotel where I would work. I readied myself to start a new adventure. The focus was to totally devote myself to completing what I promised my father and family – to support them financially and build them a new villa. I made it clear to myself that I would not do anything that would deter me from fulfilling my promise. There would be no girlfriend, just work. Everything was going fine, until a year later, when I began to run into difficulties with fellow employees in the food and beverage department. But, remember, what I said before, God works in difficult situations. Not that He creates them to make us suffer. We are either to learn from them or realize His intentions. Difficulties arise when our desires conflict with God's plan and timetable.

A perfect example is the following story.

For the sake of argument, the point that follows is very important and needs to be said. First, I must make it very clear that I am not prejudiced against any race or nationality. However, I must say I had a problem with a group of Indians and Pakistanis that dominated the food and beverage department and blocked me from attaining my ideal position as food and beverage director. This was a passion I had developed while I was in England and it got stronger in Saudi Arabia. I coveted this position. I discovered later it was a new "bait" in God's mind that would haunt me later. I had hoped after a year I would be promoted to the assistant manager of food and beverage. Instead, the Indian food and beverage director appointed a new Indian employee as the assistant! This dashed any hopes I had for advancement.

Once again, I had hoped that, maybe, at the end of my second year of the two-year contract, I would be able to renew it, become an assistant director, and, eventually, become food and beverage director. But, again, the Indian manager left the hotel and a Pakistani filled in the position and recruited a young Pakistani as his assistant. I could not believe it! This made me think a lot. Did I question why evil always seems to win over good? I found myself angry at God for allowing it. I remember, one time, I was so upset with God that I pledged I would be as evil as I could. I told God, "I had enough of being a good guy." From that time on, I began to drift slowly away from people and didn't associate with other managers. I began to smoke marijuana frequently. I didn't realize it at the time, but I was developing a new obsession. I couldn't wait for my shift to end so I could go to my room, change into comfortable clothes, lock my door, put on my favorite music and smoke marijuana. I began to ruminate about good and evil. I realized that everything has dual characteristics, i.e., good and evil, left and right, up and down, yin and yang, and that is life. I still couldn't understand, however, why God, who is good, allows bad things to happen. Since He created opposite dualities, did He originally create evil? I became obsessed with finding the answer. I wanted to know more about the universe and spirituality. At the height of my quest to understand the meaning of life, I had two very powerful spiritual experiences that I will never forget. One was a dream about my being sent to the Moon for a scientific study. I call this dream "Moon Mission."

Moon Mission (Dream)

In the dream, I was sent in a space shuttle to the Moon on a scientific mission. It was an unbelievable experience, so dramatic! It was just like a real space mission with a real countdown from mission control. I was in the shuttle, waiting for takeoff, and I could hear the countdown 10-9-8-7-6-5-4-3-2-1-0-lift off! The shuttle began to rattle, and off it went. I was the only passenger on this scientific mission, and it was my job to see what was there. I was afraid not only of what I would encounter but how I was going to live. Despite this, I was ready to face whatever I found.

As the shuttle approached the Moon, I heard mission control telling me to prepare for the landing. And, then, touchdown! I stood, ready to leave the space shuttle. Instead of a space suit, however, I was dressed in a three-piece dark suit and carrying a diplomat's briefcase. The door opened, and there stood two astronauts wearing space suits and helmets. They came forward, bowed slightly, and pointed to the exit like flight attendants do on airplanes. What I couldn't understand was why the astronauts were wearing space suits and I was not. I didn't have difficulty breathing either. It was almost as if their mission was to bring me to the Moon and leave me there. As I stepped to the door and stood high above the Moon's surface, I saw its horizon. It was dark and reddish, just like early dawn on Earth.

Interesting! Speaking of coincidence, during the hotel's grand opening, I attended a management meeting and met the hotel's general manager, Norman Anderson, who was from Scotland. He said that before he came to this hotel, he was the general manager of the New Yorker Hotel before it was sold to a religious group called the Moonies. I was unfamiliar with this group. It wasn't until much later, after I joined the church's movement while I was looking at stuff I had in an old wallet, that the connection between the manager and the group dawned on me.

After the "Moon Mission" dream, my interest in spirituality grew stronger. I had no religious books to read, however. As I stayed alone in my room, I spent many nights trying to understand life's meaning and purpose. I made a painting of my dream and tried to analyze it. I secluded myself, smoked marijuana a lot, and didn't socialize for months. My closest friends worried about me and tried to talk to me, but I was too occupied with my new obsession and ignored them.

One night, I had a very frightening spiritual experience. After I painted a little, I decided to write. Words flowed like a spring in my head. So much information came to me at an amazing speed that I couldn't keep up with it. So, I ended up using a two-hour audiotape. And, that night, I wrote about 20 pages.

It was about 4 a.m., and my body was exhausted, but my mind was overflowing with inspiration. I needed to lie down for a few minutes before I continued. As I threw myself onto my bed, a voice whispered to me, and ordered me to destroy everything I had written! My first thought was, "Ah, it was just a passing thought," so I brushed it aside. The voice returned, but, this time, it was louder. Again, I tried to ignore it. But, when it came back the third time, the voice was frightening. "Destroy the papers or die!" it said. I jumped off my bed, and trembling, took the pages, tore them in half, and threw them away. But, the voice wanted me to tear them up more. At this point, I was wide awake and pacing back and forth, afraid to go back to bed.

After about 40 minutes, I felt a little calmer. So, I went and slowly stretched myself on the bed. The voice returned and ordered me to destroy the cassette tape. This time, without hesitation, I obeyed and destroyed it. That night, I didn't sleep until the Sun came up. What an ordeal!!

This experience, as awful as it sounded, forced me out of my seclusion. Maybe, it was meant to save me, or, possibly, get me out of my obsession. I also quit smoking marijuana. I was so disappointed by the way I had been treated by the hotel's senior management. The food and beverage director's position was the reason I wanted to go to the United States and study food and beverage management at the Culinary Institute of America in Hyde Park, New York.

I believe God gave me this experience, so He could take me away from it and point me in the direction He wanted me to go. God brought me to Saudi Arabia. The question was why? And, before that, he brought me to Iran.

Again, I asked why? Was it because He wanted to show me something about Islam and how my Muslim brothers lived? When I was younger and not so well-educated in religions, I used to believe mine was the greatest in the world. But, later, after God brought me to two of the most important Islamic centers in the world—Iran and Saudi Arabia, which represent the two main branches of Islam, the Sunnis and the Shiites—I discovered Islam is not what I thought it was.

Islam is going through a rough time, just like other religions.

Like Christianity, Islam has many sects or denominations, as well as two clear branches that are at odds with each other. Islamic radical fundamentalist factions, such as Al-Qaeda, condemn the Christian-Western lifestyle as sinful and threaten to destroy Christians if they don't convert to Islam. What kind of Islamic fundamentals have they upheld in their own lives?

It is true that some Christians live sinful lives, but they don't claim to be perfect. They admit they are sinners. Their religion teaches them to be humble, and, in the sight of God, we are all sinners. Westerners believe God is compassionate, loving and forgiving. He is a being who loves and cares about His people and someone who wants to have an intimate and personal relationship with them! He loved His people so much he sent His son, Jesus, to save them! Islam's prophet, Mohammad, revered Jesus. God uses all religions to bring mankind to a higher level of consciousness.

What concerns me is the vicious and hateful spirit that has been spread all over the world by extremist leaders and terrorists who hate Jews, Christians or other religions. In my opinion, the essence of Islam got twisted with politics, and, ultimately, hijacked by militant terrorists fighting geopolitical wars with religion. Islam and politics are now inseparable. Imams in the mosques can't give a message that is free of politics.

I believe Islamic imams have failed in their responsibility to teach faithful Muslims the true teachings of the Qur'an, which God gave to the prophet Mohammed. When I was young, I used to cry when I heard passages from the Qur'an being chanted. I had so much love for Allah and Mohammed. Why can't Islamic imams preach love sermons to the Western world through TV programs like Christian televangelists do? If they care so much about the salvation of the Western world, why can't they do international TV programs and show their true love and concerns to people instead of trying to force people into submission? Is it God's will or theirs? Submission, as defined in Islam, requires sincere and voluntary submission to God's will. Holy books alone cannot help bring people to God. His word must be preached daily by sincere holy men, who live by example and prepare the faithful to receive God.

One day, I felt I need to go on a prayer and meditation walk. I started thinking about the prophet Mohammed, and I saw a vision of him sitting in a sad posture on the ground deep in thought and drawing in the sand. It felt as though he was apologizing to God for all the heartache that Islam had brought upon the world.

This may seem a bit harsh, but I love my Arab Muslim brothers and I love Islam. I also truly love prophet, Mohammed. I know Arabs have a lot to offer to the world. They were known to be the most generous people in the world, and one cannot be generous without also being loving. Muslims have so much love and deep faith in God, clear moral family values, and great cultures and traditions. Muslims endure more personal sacrifices to God than anyone else, such as the month-long Ramadan and prayers with full bows five times a day. God is the only one who knows how faithful Muslims are. Because of their deep faith, Muslims trusted their religious leaders to lead them on the straight-and-true path. Unfortunately, they were misled by hateful mullahs.

I believe this is what God wanted me to understand. That's why he took me to Iran and Saudi Arabia. It was not God who caused me to endure depression while in Saudi Arabia; I did that to myself. I didn't recognize His plan. It was He, however, who got me out of my depression. God had a plan for me. It was not about the food and beverage director position, nor was it about me remaining in Saudi Arabia. His plan for me was bigger. As I mentioned previously when I got the job in Saudi Arabia, I pledged I would do my best to take care of my family. I would allow nothing to deter me from that. In the first year and a half, I sent a lot of money to my father, so he could build a five-room villa. My love and passion to help my family grew so deep, one night, as I was lying on my bed, I asked myself how I could sleep on a comfortable bed with clean sheets and beautiful surroundings while my family slept on an uncomfortable hard stone floor. I remember I cried a lot that night.

Toward the end of my two years in Saudi Arabia, I received letters from my father asking me to stop sending money and urging me to start thinking about my future. He hoped to see me get married and have children. I believe it was also, at this time, that

God confirmed the fulfillment of my promise to my parents and shifted gears in His plan.

After I came out of my depression and accepted my fate, I signed another two-year contract and remained in Saudi Arabia. Then, suddenly, a beautiful American lady came into my life from out of nowhere! She had been secretly in love with me. She was relieved to see me return to my usual jovial personality, which was something she had admired about me. This lady was a nurse and part of a medical team that had come to Saudi Arabia to open a new hospital. About 50 doctors and nurses stayed in our hotel while they waited for their accommodations to be finished. This lady had a contractual marriage with an older doctor. She married him, so she could work in Saudi Arabia. Saudi Arabia law does not allow a woman to enter the country without being accompanied by a man. They lived together in the same room but later decided to separate, and she got her own small apartment in the complex when it was finished. It was during this time that we secretly began to date. There was a problem, however. She was so beautiful; the older man did not want to let her go. He knew she was seeing someone else, but he didn't know who. One day, he asked me to watch her and let him know who it was. Fortunately, because of some problems he had with his company (maybe God's plan), this doctor had to return to the United States.

Love conquers all, or so they say. I am spellbound by love! All the passions and promises I had began to fade away, and a new passion took hold of me—love for my American girlfriend and a promise to go to the United States occupied my thoughts daily. Six months after I signed my new two-year contract to stay in Saudi Arabia, my girlfriend and I decided to quit our jobs and return to the United States. God now has now placed a very powerful bait called "love" in front of me to lure me into quitting my job in Saudi Arabia and bring me to the States for a much greater reason. While she and I were dating, my Moroccan friend, who was also my roommate and assistant restaurant manager, was also dating a girl from the medical group. They planned to go to the United States together.

Six months later, I was preparing for my own trip to the States.

My Moroccan friend and his girlfriend had already left. But, before he left, we agreed to wait until we both were in the United States before we got married and, then, we would be each other's best man.

Interesting to note, I am not sure exactly when I had this dream—I titled it "Chosen"—but I believe it was few months after the "Moon Mission" dream while I was preparing to travel to the United States.

Dream: Chosen

> *Out in an open plain, a gathering of village elders stood in a large circle. In the middle of the circle, three men stood with a powerful untamed black horse; two in front and one in back. The horse reared with so much force, it almost lifted the men into the air. It appeared these elders had held a lottery and a young boy was chosen to ride the horse. Two men walked through the circle, each holding one of the boy's hands, and led him to the horse. The End.*

From what I understood of this dream, God is reminding me I was chosen at 7 years old. As depicted in the dream, the boy who was chosen to ride the wild and untamed black horse was me.

CHAPTER 9

Coming to America

Meeting My Fate and Destiny

Only a week earlier, I returned to Tunisia, so I could apply for a visa to enter the United States. I visited with my parents and told them the good news: I would be marrying an American lady and going to the United States very soon. I promised them I would send pictures of the wedding. After my visit, I obtained my visa from the U.S. embassy.

I flew from Tunisia to Saudi Arabia, then Amsterdam, and finally, the United States.

On the day of my departure, a strange thing happened as I was preparing to take my flight to the United States. After spending the night at the Hilton at Amsterdam Airport Schipol, I boarded a Pan Am flight with a tinge of nervousness and waited for it to take off. As the engines began to rumble and the plane started to pick up speed, a thought ran through my head. Actually, it was more like a voice coupled with a vision of the old doctor. He was telling me "Prepare to die!" Suddenly, I found myself very afraid, and it dawned on me I was about to face a big problem or even death! I was going to face this man sooner than I had thought. I realized my girlfriend lived in the same country as the doctor, and this really troubled me. I spent most of the flight thinking about what to tell this guy if I ran into him.

Had I had this thought before I boarded the plane, I might have canceled the flight. But, it was too late! I was trapped. I was on a plane that was heading to the United States and I had to deal with the confrontation when I arrived.

The flight was pleasant, despite my concerns about the old doctor. The welcome in Los Angeles, however, wasn't so great. After the plane landed, we had to remain seated. The plane sat on the tarmac for two hours before we were able to disembark because there were so many international planes arriving at the same time. We finally got off the plane, but there was another two-hour delay at U.S. customs. When I finally made it through customs, I heard an announcement asking people to stay indoors because of severe smog. I had no idea what smog was, so I asked a fellow passenger. He told me smog is a type of air pollution caused by gasoline fumes.

Despite all this, I was anxious to leave the airport and meet my lady. I was very curious to know what the United States looked like. After leaving the customs area, I met my girlfriend, and we left. I looked up at the sky, and, sure enough, there was a weird-looking yellow haze hovering above me. It didn't look healthy!

Yet, there were more unexpected surprises. As we drove out of the airport on a very big and wide road, I noticed there were rows of tall palm trees lined up along the road. It seemed strange to find palm trees in the United States. It felt like I was still in Saudi Arabia!

Hold on! The next surprise is even weirder and extremely shocking. My girlfriend told me the old doctor had died. She had buried him that very day! It was sad news, but, also a relief! She explained he had gone waterskiing, fell, and hit his head on a rock. He was in bed for more than a week and refused any medical assistance. His brain eventually swelled, and he died from the injury. This had to be one of the strangest coincidences in my life.

My girlfriend lived in Salt Lake City, and, as we took the nine-hour drive from California to Utah, we passed through the scenic Sierra Nevadas. I remember being fascinated by the unusual rock shapes. I had never been this close to a mountain or a forest before.

We finally arrived at my girlfriend's place in the afternoon. Her house was tiny, and it was nestled in a wooded area. While the living room, bedroom and kitchen were small, the yard, which was covered in knee-high grass, was huge. The entire abode sat on 8 to 10 acres of land. My girlfriend and her mom ran a horse farm. I later discovered that everyone in Salt Lake City was horse farmers, and every weekend, there was a horse show. My girlfriend alone owned 12 horses. This is why she went to Saudi Arabia. She needed money to train and feed her horses.

Salt Lake City was a whole new world for me. Everywhere you went, there were horse shows or people talking about horses. Most of the residents wore jeans and cowboy hats and drove big pickup trucks.

The first month I was there, I got to know my girlfriend's relatives, friends and neighbors. I also attended a few horse shows. It was a great experience! I also volunteered to help clean my girlfriend's front yard and mow the tall grass.

As time went by, however, I was getting nervous. I wanted to find a school for hotel and restaurant management training and get a job. After about two months, unfortunately, I realized my girlfriend was not ready to change her lifestyle for me. She was not going to leave everything behind and move to California with me.

We talked about marriage, but there was something I needed to do immediately—file for divorce. With the help of my girlfriend, I hired a lawyer and set a date for a court hearing. In Utah, the law requires a person to be a resident for at least three months before he or she can file for divorce. My girlfriend also helped me write a good resume, crafting it toward my interests in hotel and restaurant management.

Toward the end of the second month with my girlfriend, I found myself overwhelmed by a feeling of despair and had little hope of finding a job or a school. Salt Lake City did not have many quality hotels, so the odds of finding a good job were slim.

After I realized my girlfriend's situation, I also noticed a change in her mood and behavior. Then, the big shock came! I found out she was secretly dating an old boyfriend! I was devastated by this news, to say the least. I couldn't believe she could do such a mean thing! I had no choice but to move. I rented a room in a Motel 6 and felt as though I could die. I was in great pain. My first thought was that I loved her, so how could she betray me so horribly? Next, I was upset at giving up such a great job in Saudi Arabia and losing the $6,000 I had spent to come to the United States.

Then, there was the sorrow and shame my parents and family would feel upon hearing this awful news. I was devastated! I spent three days at the hotel alone with no one to speak to, crying all night and day. The first night was hell. I cried so much, I thought I was going crazy. I was so stressed, I couldn't eat or sleep. Then, late one night, I collapsed with exhaustion and slept until late the next afternoon. I went out for a bit, but because I was extremely depressed, nothing could make me feel better, so I returned to the motel and did another round of crying. Soon, I fell into a deep sleep.

The second night at the motel, I had a powerful lifelike dream. I woke up exactly at 4 a.m.; I touched my face to check whether I was still dreaming. It felt like someone had just left the room. The dream's clear and detailed scenes and deep meaning confused me, so much so I couldn't go back to sleep. I decided to get dressed and look for a coffee shop, so I could determine its purpose. I found one place that would open at 6 a.m. I decided to wait for almost 40 minutes until it opened. I ate breakfast there, and this was my first bit of food in two days. I spent the entire day and night analyzing that dream. Finally, on the third night, I fell asleep. I named this dream "The Funeral Procession."

The Funeral Procession (Dream)

I dreamed I was standing at a road junction near my home and watching a funeral procession. A dead man was being carried in the traditional way on a stretcher. I was amazed by the huge crowd of people, which numbered in the thousands, who were attending this man's funeral and I thought he must be a very important person. Another thing that caught my attention was they were burying him at sunset, which was not part of the traditional funeral service. As I stood watching the scene, wondering who this dead man was, what his real story was, and where these people came from, the dead man suddenly came to live, left the stretcher, walked through the crowd, and headed straight toward me. As he approached, I noticed it was my Uncle Taib. I panicked; I begged him to stop coming closer and not touch me. "I don't want to die. Please don't touch me!" I shouted.

In my village, we believed if you dreamed about a dead person visiting you, it meant that person is coming to take you away. I stood frozen in panic and screamed: "No! No! No!" Too late, my dead uncle grabbed me.

Suddenly, the scene changed, and I was sitting at a table with my uncle and some of my younger brothers and sisters; my uncle sat opposite me. My uncle was holding my hands and screaming at me, begging me to pay attention and take something. It was a life-threatening situation. My uncle kept saying, "Please, my son, take it! Please, my son, take it!" It was as if he was trying to prevent something very catastrophic from happening. I asked: "What? What do you want me to take?" My uncle leaned forward and gave me a strong kiss on my lips.

The scene changed again, and my uncle was now gone. I was clothed in a long white robe. This robe then changed into a uniform similar to something a naval officer would wear. The jacket was white and clean but a bit long. The pants were in the old bell-bottom style. I didn't like it at all. Another thing that troubled me was the outfit came with black high-heel platform shoes that stained my pants with black shoe polish to the knees. And, I complained, saying "How can one wear black shoes with a white suit? The shoes should be white." While I complained about these things, it felt as though someone was taking notes and assuring me these things would be fixed. As I continued, my brothers and sisters were singing and chanting religious songs." The End.

My Interpretation of this Dream

After many years in the church learning about God's truth, spirituality and dream interpretation, one day, as I was analyzing and contemplating this dream, the answer became crystal clear to me! First, the answer validated the teachings of the Rev. Moon on "Returning Resurrection." Spirit people who are in the spiritual world will be able to return to Earth and cooperate with their descendants at the time of the Second Coming of Christ, which I believe this dream indicated to me that my uncle did. I will be talking about this subject at great length in upcoming chapters. However, this is how I interpreted the dream:

1) The people who had gathered for my uncle's funeral were my ancestors.

2) The junction where the funeral procession was occurring became obvious. It was the time, place and occurrences I was facing at the time.
3) The kiss my uncle gave me represented a kiss of "new life."
4) The jacket was a bit longer than what I normally wore. This could mean it was made for a more spiritually mature person, which I wasn't at the time. It suggested I should pay attention to my calling, shape up and be more of a godly person than I was at the time.
5) The pants were fashioned in the old bell-bottom style, and this described my personality at the time: flirty, hippie-like, happy and content. I was too busy living selfishly and disregarding God's laws.
6) The black high-heel platform shoes described how "wild" and wrong the path was I was traveling! They don't portray a godly life, and this told me I had to change!
7) The shoe polish up to my knees emphasized how far I had deviated from morality with my wild, sinful and immature way of life.

My complaints about all the things that were wrong, as well as the feeling someone was watching me and taking notes, meant two things. They are:

(A) God had opened my eyes to all my sins to which I needed to admit.
(B) The person in the dream taking notes, assuring me everything would be fixed or corrected and encouraging me to accept the mission, meant God had forgiven my sins and called me to take my mission in the role like that of a prophet—clothed in a white long robe.

I understood this to mean I was a "new chosen person," and I had to prepare to meet God's new plan for me. I will explain in later chapters. It is amazing how God reaches out to people through dreams. We are truly living in the Last Days! God declared:

> "And in the last days, it shall be, God declares, that I pour out my Spirit upon all flesh, and your sons and your daughters shall prophesy, and your young men shall see visions, and your old men shall dream dreams" (Acts 2:17).

After evaluating my dream, I began to understand its very significant and spiritual message. However, its entire meaning eluded me because I was depressed about my life. Nevertheless, I felt the dream offered me some hope and gave me comfort.

Like in Joseph's dreams, God gave me an identical dream. On my third night at the motel, another significant dream woke me up at exactly 4 a.m. I felt as light as a feather, which was just how I felt in the previous dream. This time, however, I was excited and full of life! Once again, I couldn't go back to sleep, so I got dressed and went to the same coffee shop I had gone to the previous morning. This time, in addition to waiting for the coffee shop to open, I also waited for a nearby bookstore to open. I knew I was changing, but I couldn't quite comprehend it. At 9 a.m., after the bookstore opened, I bought four books; they cost me $100. They were Carl Sagan's *Cosmos* (1980); Gustavus Hindman Miller's *10,000 Dreams Interpreted: A Dictionary of Dreams from Abandon to Zodiac* (1988); a book about the Zodiac; and an ethics book. I wanted to know everything about life and the universe, so I could find an answer to my dreams. This dream is called the "Outdoor Concert."

Outdoor Concert (Dream)

> *I dreamed I was standing on a hill, watching a musical concert in the valley. Below, there was a huge crowd of people that numbered in the thousands. It was a huge event, such as the Woodstock concert that occurred in 1969. People gathered around the stage to listen to music. On the stage, two musicians poured their hearts and souls into their songs. However, I noticed the people seemed to be glued to the ground as if they were drunk or high on drugs. The audience wasn't responding; they were trying to get up but could not. I couldn't believe how rude these people were by not showing their appreciation to these singers. I started to applaud loudly, and, suddenly, the*

entire crowd began to move. They clapped monotonously as if they were machines. People ran up the hill toward me.

Then, the scene changed. The two singers came to me first and shook my hand. I thought these singers were the prophet Mohammed and Jesus Christ. The one who I thought was Jesus said: "Ali, in the sixth of something (It wasn't clear— "sixth" of what month), you will receive something so precious, more precious than life! Go out and look for it." While he was instructing me, the other person stood humbly on my left.

The person who talked to me was strong and bulky with short dark hair and a short and nicely trimmed beard. This is a different description of what Hollywood says Jesus looked like than what you might see in the Christian traditional description of Jesus. The End.

Eager to start reading these books immediately, I went out and found another coffee shop. I was there for two hours, thumbing through all four books, and trying to find a quick answer. At around noon, I returned to the motel, still excited, but physically and emotionally exhausted. I tried to read more, but I was tired, so I threw myself on the bed. I slept until the next day!

It was important to me that I find an answer. The books I bought were too complicated and I needed more time to study and understand them. I felt an overwhelming desire to make an action plan. I got dressed, went for a walk and meditated. I was thinking about the meaning of these dreams and what I needed to do next. Suddenly, I was inspired to visit my Moroccan friend in Memphis, Tennessee. As I noted earlier, Mohammed was a Moroccan friend and my assistant manager at Dhahran Hotel in Saudi Arabia. He, like me, got engaged to one of the nurses and came to the United States. We planned to be each other's best man. I couldn't believe I hadn't thought of this before. I was really moved by this idea. I was uplifted and excited! I went immediately to the Greyhound bus station and bought my ticket to Memphis. I was so relieved to finally know what to do, and I was looking forward to seeing my friend.

After a day and a half of traveling on the bus, I arrived in Memphis around 9 a.m. I called my friend to let him know of my arrival, which, of course, was a surprise to him. I told him I was at the bus stop. He was very happy I had come to see him. He, too, had something rather urgent news to tell me.

Twenty minutes later, as we drove to his apartment, he poured out his heart to me. He said God must have sent me to him. He told me that just when I called, he was walking out the door. He's leaving his wife! When the phone rang, he dropped his suitcases right by the door and ran to answer it. And, when we arrived at the apartment, the two suitcases were indeed right by the door. It was strange the day I arrived, my friend's wife had left him after they had had a big argument. She went to stay with her parents for the weekend.

We spent two days talking about our problems with our unfaithful women and compared our lives in the States with our lives in Saudi Arabia. There we had free accommodations, no income tax, free airline tickets and two weeks of paid vacation every six months. Here, we had to pay for everything. But, our biggest problems were our girlfriends. This was truly strange! My friend was bitterly complaining and cursing himself for making a big mistake and marrying his wife. I, on the other hand, was complaining just as bitterly about how my girlfriend betrayed me and I didn't get the chance to marry her. My friend said he had already decided to leave his wife and go back to Morocco and, then, eventually, head to Saudi Arabia.

The Search for My Dream Promise

After spending five days with my friend, I began to feel the need to decide my next move. I felt overwhelming pressure to come up with a quick plan to move on and recalled all the unfortunate events I had experienced since I had come to the States.

After reasoning with myself, I finally accepted my fate. I looked very closely at the few positive things I had. One was my divorce from my wife, for which I had already started the process in Salt Lake. I felt that even if this were the only thing I accomplished, I could free myself. I was in a great nation, and I planned to take advantage of this opportunity. I would find a way to build a future. I also had the compelling promises of my dreams, but I still needed to clarify them.

Then, suddenly, as if a dark veil was lifted from me, and I came up with a plan! I decided that while I was waiting for the court date for my divorce case, I would take a bus tour of the United States and do three things: See the country's most famous cities—Las Vegas, Los Angeles, San Francisco, Chicago, and, finally, New York—and take pictures; visit the headquarters of all the large hotel chains and apply for jobs there or in foreign countries, such as Saudi Arabia or Bahrain; and search for the promises of my dreams. My dreams had dual meanings. One was abstract and rather spiritual; the other was a promise of something physical, which I took to mean a job opportunity. I decided to do as I was told in the dream and "go out to look for it." So, I printed my resume, bought a Greyhound bus 30-day pass with the option to add a 10-day extension, and planned to leave early the next day. My friend was also happy because it cured my depression.

The next morning, my Moroccan friend took me to the bus stop, and off I went on the first part of my journey, heading from Memphis to Las Vegas.

Las Vegas is a magical city, flooded with colorful and glittering lights. It is a city filled with wonders, vibrating with sounds from slot machines, music and activities. This is excitement like I had never known! There were hundreds of big hotels and casinos with live shows and plenty of gambling! This was my kind of city, I thought!

For the first three or four days, I just enjoyed myself. I went sightseeing, hopped from one hotel/casino to the next and got to know them all. At the Star Dust Resort and Casino, which was closed in 2006, I watched an exciting live show. I also had the chance to help out a group of croupiers with whom I had worked. They wanted my help testing a system they developed for the American roulette game.

However, a few days later, I realized Las Vegas was not for me. After entertaining myself for few days, I tried to find a job. I visited a few hotels and applied in person, but none offered me a job immediately, and I felt it was time to move on to the next city. I was taking so many pictures, I looked like a tourist or a freelance journalist. The next morning, I took the bus to San Francisco.

Once I arrived in San Francisco, I checked into a nearby motel, freshened up, and headed for the busiest side of the street. I didn't do much sightseeing in the City by the Bay. I didn't even visit the famous Golden Gate Bridge. For some unknown reason, I didn't feel comfortable there, and it didn't seem like this city had anything to offer me. So, after three days of visiting a few hotels and applying for jobs, I decided to head to Los Angeles. I only spent two days in Los Angeles, and, soon, I found myself moving on to my next destination, Chicago. I checked into a motel, as usual, and bought a map of the city. I was only in Chicago to visit the headquarters of Hyatt and apply for a job. My "guardian angel" had already directed me to move on to the next city and let me know that time was running out. I bought my bus pass 20 days ago. So, with only 10 days left, I decided to quickly return to Memphis and apply for a job at the headquarters of Holiday Inn. I hadn't thought about doing this while I was visiting my friend.

CHAPTER 10

From Memphis to New York

My Mysterious Lady Friend from Chattanooga

Before I continue with the story, I must point out that I had no plans to visit any other cities after Memphis.

The day after I arrived in Memphis, I went to the corporate headquarters for Holiday Inn and applied for a job there and at the famous Peabody Hotel in downtown Memphis. I didn't hear from either one immediately, so I was losing hope that I would ever find a job. I only had one week left on my Greyhound pass. After two days in Memphis, I was at a complete loss. I didn't know what to do next. The next morning, I was sitting in a café and making plans over a cup of coffee. Maybe I would return to Salt Lake City and wait there for the divorce court case, which was scheduled for Oct. 27, 1981. Suddenly, a voice whispered, "What about New York City?" The voice began to tell me how great New York City was. It's the city that has captured the world's attention, with its beauty, high-rise skyscrapers, and the best shopping in the world. The voice finished by saying, "How can you not visit New York? What if your promised dream is in New York? You need to go there and try. You still have a week left on your pass. Why not go there for just two days?" The voice really did its job and convinced me to take the bus to New York. Amazing indeed! What a great salesman God is!

That very day, about 1:30 p.m., I boarded a bus for New York City. I walked toward the back of the bus, looked for a good seat by the window, and found an empty one in the sixth row. I placed my bags on the seat by the window, and I sat in the aisle seat, hoping to have both for myself, and, allowing me room to sleep. But, just as the bus started to fill up, a beautiful young blonde girl in her mid-20s boards. She looked like a model! She walked up the aisle, looking for a vacant seat. There were a few empty seats toward the back. But, as she approached the area in which I was sitting, she stopped, dropped her bag on the floor, looked around, and then asked "Do you mind? Could I sit with you?" I was glad to let her have the window seat!

There was something special about her. I was very relaxed with her sitting next to me and I felt some attraction toward her. As the bus drove out of the city, we exchanged a few smiles and looks, but no words. About a half-hour later, we started a conversation. The young lady told me she was visiting her parents in Memphis, and, now, she was returning to Chattanooga where she lives. She worked in a beauty salon as a hair stylist and she told me a lot about Chattanooga and its historic places, such as Lookout Mountain and the Great Smoky Mountains. She commented on how beautiful my accent was and asked where I came from. I told her my entire story. I told her about the trip I'd been taking on the Greyhound bus, and how I was finishing it with a trip to New York. Our conversation was so fulfilling and amusing, and after about three hours, we were holding hands as if we had known each other for a long time. Coincidence? Continue reading. There is more...

As the bus drew closer to Chattanooga, she wrote down her address and phone number and handed the paper to me. She made me promise to visit her for a few days in the near future. The bus stopped at Chattanooga's main bus terminal, and the driver told the passengers who were not getting off to remain in their seats. Most passengers, including the young lady, got off. It felt weird and empty without her. I stood on the bus and waved to her as she walked into the building. She turned and waved back. As the bus began to fill with new passengers and drove away, it felt like some piece of me had been left behind with the girl. I thought about her a lot. But, I had to soon suppress my feelings and focus my attention on New York. I occupied the time by planning my itinerary until I finally fell asleep.

New York

What can I say about New York?

I arrived early in morning and checked into a motel about a block away from the bus depot at 42nd Street and Eighth Avenue.

I was so excited; I spent the entire day just walking from street to street, from 42nd Street to Fifth Avenue to Central Park, until I was exhausted. For the first couple of days, I took a lot of pictures. A few stuck in my mind. I couldn't believe that in such a great city as New York, in one of the richest countries in the world, you could see homeless people sleeping on the streets and eating out of trash cans! In another part of the city, I saw a homeless man relieving himself in the middle of the street with cars and people ignoring him as they passed. This scene also shocked me.

New York is a very big and busy city! I was unsure of where to go to look for a job. I was desperate and was slowly starting to give up and accept my fate. On my third day in the Big Apple, I had the most shocking experience of my life. For safety reasons, I decided to store my cameras and briefcase with all my legal documents and passport, in one of the storage lockers at the bus depot. I didn't want to leave them in my motel room, and I wanted to have a relaxing day and not have to carry anything. So, I put everything into a locker and toured the city. I planned to pick them up the next morning. However, when I returned to the terminal the next day, I opened my locker and found … nothing! I panicked! What else could happen to me? I lost the girl I loved, lost a good job in Saudi Arabia, almost spent all my savings, and now this! What was left except my life? Am I going to die?

Out of desperation, I looked inside the locker again to see whether I could find a note or something. All I found was a tiny piece of paper that looked like half a ticket. I almost threw it away, but something told me to hold on to it. Panic-stricken, I ran with the piece of paper to the luggage claim office and presented it to a man behind the counter. The man looked at it and said, "Oh, yes, give me a minute." He disappeared into the back of the office. A minute later, he came back with my belongings! Oh, what a relief! The man explained to me what had happened. The depot regularly checks the lockers, and, at a certain time, personnel will remove the items for safety measures.

Shaken with fear from this experience, I walked out of the terminal and tried to find a coffee shop, so I could have a cup of coffee. Not far away was a place at which I had breakfast a few days earlier. I went there. As I drank my coffee, I tried to find a meaning for what had just happened. I made plans to leave New York as soon as I could. I decided New York was not the place for me. I also realized I had only three days left on my Greyhound pass, and I needed to move quickly.

As I was making my plans, a faint voice whispered, "Aren't you forgetting something? What about that girl from Chattanooga who you met on the bus? Could she be your dream promise?" Suddenly, I went from hopelessness to excitement! I began to realize if there was any hope for me to remain in the United States, I had to see the girl from Chattanooga again. I thought about how we met. It wasn't a coincidence that she asked to sit next to me! I decided to visit her for a few days. Overwhelmed by this idea, I went back to the bus depot and called her to tell her I was coming for a visit. She shouted with joy and asked, "When?"

"Soon," I said. "Maybe tomorrow."

She was overjoyed by this news and said she would wait for me to call as soon as I arrived. That same day, I went back to my motel, packed, checked out, and returned to the bus depot in time to catch the next bus to Chattanooga. On my journey, I contemplated my situation, including the looming divorce hearing, which would be in Salt Lake City. I wondered again if this lady could be the answer to my dream.

Hold on! There is more thrilling stuff ahead.

CHAPTER 11

Encounter with My Destiny

After arriving in Chattanooga early the next morning, I called the girl. After we exchanged pleasantries, she told me she was getting ready for work and asked if we could meet at a restaurant that wasn't too far from the bus station. She was going to bring a friend with her, she said. I took down the information and agreed to meet her. However, something came over me. I couldn't stop thinking about this friend she said she was bringing with her! Who could this person be? For some strange reason, I thought it could have been a boyfriend.

Knowing how hurt I felt when the one I loved hurt me unreasonably, I decided then and there not to meet her. I just couldn't do it. I could not inflict pain on someone the way it had been inflicted on me. The girl was so beautiful, and there was no way she couldn't have a boyfriend. So, it was obvious this person would be her boyfriend.

Now, you might think what I did was crazy and made no sense. But, for reasons that defied human logic, I did what I had to do. I came to Chattanooga to meet my destiny. What I had prepared for all my life was coming to fruition on Oct. 6, 1981.

After deciding not to meet my lady friend, I thought since I was in Chattanooga, I might as well stay a couple days and look at this historic city. I checked into a hotel about 8:30 a.m., rested and freshened up. Something prompted me to put on my good suit. I left my hotel, looked around and headed straight for the busiest part of the street. There, I saw a library and a restaurant where I ate some breakfast. At around 11 a.m., I noticed the street getting busier. I decided to take a walk along the busy street to familiarize myself with the city and what it had to offer.

I walked slowly, looking at everything like a tourist. After a while, I found myself feeling pretty good about the city. The street was busy. People were eating lunch on the grass, in restaurants, and at hot dog stands.

What happened next will blow your mind. Just keep reading.

President Anwar Sadat Assassination: My Link to the Unification Church

Speaking of coincidences, as I continued to walk down the street and check out the city, I came upon a large department store. For some reason, I decided to go in. As I approached the entrance, I saw a newspaper stand. The headline on one of the stories caught my eye: ASSASSINATION! Since leaving Iran at the beginning of its revolution and then hearing about the Iraq-Iran War, I had become more interested in politics and read newspapers quite frequently. This headline immediately made me reach into my pocket for a quarter. But, a voice whispered: "Why are you buying the newspaper now? Go into the store first, shop and buy it on your way out." So, I put the quarter back in my pocket and walked into the store. I didn't even notice who had been assassinated. You see, we need to respect and obey the faint voice that speaks to us every day. It's none other than God's voice.

Once inside, I heard the horrible news: President Anwar Sadat of Egypt was the one who had been assassinated. Sadat had been my greatest hero, my role model. I had so much love and respect for him. I felt I knew him because I had met him at a private banquet in Iran, which was hosted by the shah in 1977. I was among the few selected to serve at the head table where the shah and all the heads of state sat. I felt so proud to have had the opportunity to talk with him and serve him.

There were two Arab presidents who made great impressions on me, and more importantly, on Arab history in general, for their heroic contributions to peace in the Middle East. They were Sadat and President Habib Bourguiba of Tunisia.

Bourguiba, known for his dynamic, but long-winded speeches, had won the hearts of his people. He addressed his people as if they were his sons and daughters. He liberated Tunisia from French occupation and made some daring reforms that affected the country's religious and family traditions. He was a strong proponent of women's rights. He expanded women's right to divorce, raised the marrying age to 17 and prohibited polygamy. He also allowed women to remove the veils Muslim women traditionally wore and encouraged them to get an education. He was concerned about the country's economic state during the month of Ramadan – one month of fasting from dawn to dusk that prevents men from working. This usually put the nation's economy at a standstill. To save the economy, the president ordered men to not fast, and told them he would take the responsibility upon himself. Because of this, he incurred the ire of all the Arab nations.

Marriage and family were steeped in Arabic religious traditions. The dowry, for instance, was a big issue. There were so many monetary conditions the bridegroom's family was often left penniless. Bourguiba changed that! After he divorced his French wife, he married a Tunisian named Wassila. On national television, he offered one dinar (about $1) as a dowry and encouraged people to keep the tradition going, but not to go broke! I really loved this president and had great respect for him!

Despite the fact he was imprisoned under French rule because he was fighting for Tunisian independence, Bourguiba stood with the West during World War II and supported the Allies against Nazi Germany. He was eventually released by the Germans because they hoped to get him to join their side. After he was released, he told his people not to side with the Germans because they were going to lose the war and the freedom of Tunisia rested on the shoulder of the Allies.

President John F. Kennedy also had a lot of respect for Bourguiba. When he visited the United States in 1961, Kennedy said:

> Like President Washington, President Bourguiba is a revolutionary, and like President Washington, he also, when the revolution was won, had the sense of judgment, self-discipline, and strength to attempt to bring good will and peace among his people and to the people of the former occupiers of his country and his surrounding neighbors (Kennedy 1964, 350).

Truly, Bourguiba was a great statesman. He was prepared by God to not only save his country but also to provide the Allied forces with the means to defeat Hitler and Mussolini. It is interesting to note there were ample reasons for Bourguiba to oppose the Allies—the enmity between them and the occupying French forces are just two—but he knew the Allied forces would win and pushed his countrymen to join and fight side by side with them.

Truly, Bourguiba should have received the Noble Peace Prize.

My adoration for Sadat was as great as it was for Bourguiba. What Sadat did for peace was remarkable! His achievement ultimately cost him his life. He was the first Arab leader to sign a peace treaty with Menachem Begin, prime minister of Israel, during President Jimmy Carter's administration. This was done against the wishes of all the Arab states, and against the wishes of various Islamic radical movements in his own country. I could not understand how a peasant boy with humble origins kept witnessing these events. Sadat was my final link to God. I had been delivered to my destiny at the right place and time!

But, enough digressing for now.

Upon hearing the radio announcement, I literally ran out of the store and headed straight for the newspaper stand! Without paying attention to anything, I stood in the middle of the sidewalk, opened the newspaper and began to read. Before I had read the first line, however, a female voice with an accent said, "My, my, my. It must be terrible, terrible news or good, good news!" At this moment, I was about to explode. I lowered the newspaper to have a look at the person talking to me, and there, a few inches away from my face, was a young lady with red hair. She had a big smile on her face and waited for my response. I expressed my disappointment about Sadat's assassination.

After talking for a while, the young lady said her name was Jacinta Setherly, and the young man standing quietly next to her was John Weiman. They asked me whether I would like to have a cup of coffee, and I accepted. We bought coffees and walked to a nearby park where we sat on the grass and talked. They invited me to their home for dinner that evening so I could meet more people of different nationalities. She was from New Zealand. They were very hospitable, and the idea of meeting new people from other countries sounded great to me. So, I accepted their offer.

Upon entering their home, Jacinta and John introduced me to a lady named Sarah, who was from England, and two other men, Kenzo Endo from Japan and Richard, an American. The group was very friendly, and they seemed to be involved in religious activities on the nearby campus. One room contained a blackboard and rows of chairs had been set up for lectures. After a while, I was led to the dining room table. There were whispered exchanges among the members of the group, and I thought that meant there might be something wrong. As we sat at the table, Sarah dished out a humble meal that was not sufficient for everybody; some had no food. However, the food wasn't the most important thing to me at the time. I was enjoying myself with this very friendly group of people.

My dinner companions were a branch of an international student group known as CARP (Collegiate Association for the Research of Principles) and were based on the campus of the local college. Sarah asked if I would like to hear about what they were teaching. I said yes. I sat in the front row with Jacinta and John and listened as Sarah talked. She gave a religious overview of their teachings, which was reasonably educational and inspiring. Everything sounded fascinating. But, what stuck in my mind was a presentation about the three growth stages. I have never forgotten this.

Just as humans pass through three stages of growth, she said, so, too, does everything else in creation. You plant the seed, and it takes time to sprout. Second, once it sprouts, it takes time to grow into a plant. Finally, at the plant's third stage of growth, it blossoms. This description seems simple to anyone, like me, who had spent years as a farmer. This part of the lecture also taught me that nature, like humans, had feelings and a purpose for its existence. This was fascinating and new to me. I never suspected that plants had feelings, purpose, or a sense of direction.

Finally, I was asked whether I would like to hear more. They mentioned that, on weekends, a group of 30 or more people would gather for a two-day workshop in a large log house deep in the mountains. Would I be interested in joining them? Excitedly, I said yes. I left these friendly people, and John accompanied me to my hotel. We agreed he would pick me up in the morning.

Early the next morning, John came to pick me up. He put my large suitcase in the trunk, and my traveling bag, briefcase, and two cameras went into the front of the car with me. The workshop was held in Flowery Branch, Georgia, in a spacious log house nestled deep in the woods, close to a river and the mountains. I love the mountains and forests, so I was excited when we drove down a winding dirt-covered road that passed through the incredibly picturesque scenery.

When we finally arrived, we were greeted by a group of people. People were hugging each other. I could feel the excitement in the air. John and I were among the first to arrive. The group had received exciting news that the Rev. Chong Goo (Terry) "Tiger" Park, who was CARP's national leader at the time, and Howard Self, who was the church's southeastern regional leader, were going to be the guest speakers. I realized then this meeting was a regional gathering to meet these men.

By late afternoon, there were more than 40 people crowding the place; they came from the surrounding states. They were happy, bright and energetic people. Their motto was "Bright, Light and Exciting." One leader announced it was time to prepare for the arrival of the special guests and ordered everyone to take his or her bags to his or her room.

Men stayed in the brothers' rooms and the women stayed in sisters' rooms. There was one big lecture room with a blackboard, a spacious living room and two smaller rooms. One was used as a prayer room and the other was for special guests. At about 7 p.m., which was dinnertime, everyone gathered in a circle and sang a few songs, which were accompanied by two people on guitars. There was an official welcome, and then all the new guests introduced themselves. Each person was welcomed with enthusiastic applause. The group leader then announced the schedule for the two-day workshop: Wake up at 6 a.m., prayers at 7 a.m., breakfast at 8 a.m., and the first lecture session would be at 9 a.m. At the end of the announcement, the group leader had a person say grace, and, then, we lined up for a buffet dinner and sat wherever there was room on the living room floor.

During meal time, we were told the special guests would be late, and, once they arrived, the national head would speak.

After dinner, people dispersed. Some went for a walk in the heavily wooded area, some went to the river, and others stayed in the house and watched videos. The girls were whispering and seemed excited about a new video that came from the church's main office, but I somehow got the impression these girls were trying to hide something. They were whispering to each other and seemed to be waiting for someone to leave the room. I suspected it was me they were whispering about.

After a while, the girls decided to watch the video, which featured a speech from the group's founder. They were concerned about me watching the video and worried I would not like it. They politely said if I didn't like it, I could go for a walk and come back later. I, however, chose to watch the video. I really liked what I heard.

I stayed and watched the second video about a recent mass wedding—people of different races and nationalities getting married together. It was awesome! I was moved by the idea of the interreligious and international mass wedding—a God-centered marriage, the primary purpose of which was for salvation and resolving problems among races, cultures and religions.

Looking back at how I was led to this group, I was intrigued! The way was purely providential; there was nothing coincidental about it. The burning desire to search for my dreams was fulfilled from the moment I met this group. I could clearly see how I was miraculously delivered to them! I felt so comfortable with these people and felt totally at home! Nothing was keeping me from staying with this group as long as I wanted. I didn't have a job or a girlfriend. I was not upset the bus pass had expired. These people welcomed me. And, as I entered their world, everything stopped. I felt the processes of rebirth and resurrection through their teachings. It was as if I had just boarded a ship that was ready to leave port. I was no longer on land, and so I shifted my attention to the immediate need for the ship's rules. There was relief from everyday activities. I felt free, and it was an awesome feeling. I felt relieved from my stressful life journey. It was as though my search had ended!

The special guests arrived around 10 p.m., so we gathered in the lecture room. The atmosphere was very uplifting, and the young people were excited and happy. Even though it was getting late – they had been on the road for nine hours—the speaker wanted to talk to the group. So, we went to the lecture room, and, a few minutes later, Park appeared with a big smile. He looked like a fearsome fighter but was filled with a bubbling enthusiasm. His speech was filled with drama, laughter and seriousness. As he talked, he bounced and stamped on the floor and made loud noises like a tiger. He talked about the rally where he and 70 students had a counter-demonstration against the 180,000 angry, leftist, antiwar demonstrators in West Germany in 1981. He told how he and his small group were squashed in the center of this rally and were dragged into fistfights.

Park talked about terrorist involvement and how that was connected to the antiwar demonstration. Later, I learned someone told him about me because this person was afraid I might be a spy from a terrorist group. So, there was an air of caution during his talk. It also didn't help that I hadn't shaved for several days. As far as I was concerned, I loved this man and was very inspired by him. He was a powerful speaker. Apparently, he had just returned from West Germany and was on a speaking tour. I was fascinated by this powerful, tiger-like man, whose nickname was appropriate. However, because of the guests, the two days to which I was invited was postponed to the following week. And, instead of it being a two-day workshop, they changed it to a seven-day workshop. I returned to my motel room in Chattanooga and promised John I would return with him for the seven-day workshop. My search was over! The force that kept me moving from state to state in search of an answer had suddenly vanished. My last hope, the girl I came to see, had disappeared.

At this moment, I had no idea how long I would stay in Chattanooga. I also didn't have any plans. I was looking forward to returning to the workshop and meeting more people. I prepared myself for the workshop and packed extra clothes to last me for a week in a small carrier bag. That week, while in my hotel room, I had a scary, dramatic and vivid dream, which I labeled "Submarine Invasion."

Submarine Invasion (Dream)

I was walking on a beach a few miles from New York City. As I faced the ocean, I could clearly see Manhattan and its beautiful skyscrapers to my right. Suddenly, I saw a submarine surfacing and submerging; it was apparently spying on America. I realized the seriousness of this. I began to scream and wave frantically to the residents of the city, trying to wake them up. No one was paying attention. About a minute later, a military helicopter hovered over the spot where I saw the submarine. It submerged and hid as the helicopter passed over the area. The sub resurfaced, this time closer to the shore, and soldiers began to emerge. Thousands came ashore.

At this time, I was in total shock. Suddenly, I noticed the presence of an army camp inland, a few hundred yards from me. I sensed the presence of a very important general of Asian descent waiting to ambush them. Before I realized what was happening, I became a participant in the dream. A young Asian man in civilian clothes was pointing a gun at my head, and I felt like he could shoot me at any moment. Stricken with fear, I desperately covered my head with my hands and tried to recite the Surah Yasin from the Qur'an for spiritual protection.

My father taught me that whenever I was in danger or felt threatened, the best way to protect myself was to recite the Surah Yasin. I had seen and heard my father do this many times when we went camping. To protect us from scorpions and poisonous snakes, my father would draw a circle around us with a stick, reciting the Surah Yasin. [It is commonly known as the heart of the Qur'an. This name emphasizes the great importance of this surah in the Qur'an. Therefore, true believers say reciting this surah brings many great benefits or rewards]. This way, we slept peacefully without fear, and if anything tried to come our way, it would stop at the line.

Now, I'm going to continue the dream. I tried to recite the Surah Yasin, but I couldn't remember it! I was unable to recite any surahs. When that didn't work, I began to look for a way to free myself. I thought, perhaps, that I should jump on the man and grab his gun or grab a handful of water and throw it at his eyes. Millions of thoughts flooded into my mind faster than I could deal with.

The picture changed again. At the shore, a few feet from the ocean appeared an open staircase. The man with the gun gestured for me to go down the stairs. I obeyed. I was relieved when I realized this man had been sent by the Asian general to protect me. After a while, I was ordered to come out. As I walked up the stairs, the young man with the gun was waiting at the top. I looked at his hand; he had a shiny silver gun in his hand. I didn't feel threatened by him at all. I looked toward the ocean to see where the submarine had gone and saw it had been trapped by a mysterious bright, shiny, extraterrestrial like silver ship. I looked to the right and saw what looked like a military truck parked about two blocks away, and I, again, felt the presence of the Asian general.

I understood the dream was very significant, but I didn't think about it too much because I was so focused on the trip to the workshop. But, years later, after I joined the church, I reread this dream. I thought about, analyzed and asked who the Asian man with the gun was and who the Asian general was who ambushed the Russians when they came to the shore. I thought it might have been an incident that had happened a couple weeks after I had it. A Russian submarine S-363, which became famous under the designation U-137, ran aground 6 miles from one of Sweden's largest naval bases on Oct. 27, 1981 (Interesting! This day was the same day of my divorce court date). I tried to see whether there was any connection to the Russian submarine in my dream, but I found none. Then, as if someone lifted the veil off my head, the answer came. I was astonished by the clarity of the content revealed, and I realized what the dream was all about. Here's my interpretation:

A). "Tiger" Park was the man who pointed the gun at my head and led me to safety down the staircase. B). The mighty Asian general who sent the young man with a gun to save me was none other than the group's founder, the Rev. Sun Myung Moon. C). The huge and mysterious silver ship catching the submarine could only be interpreted as a "divine" force from the spiritual world that God sent to Moon. D). In the dream, I desperately tried to recite a special surah in the Qur'an, but I couldn't remember a word. To my understanding of this dream, the Qur'an had reached its highest peak and it could not teach me anything more. The teachings of Islam had delivered me to a higher stage of salvation and reconnected me with Jesus through Moon's teachings. To some religions, this may sound like blasphemy, but this is my honest belief! Perhaps, the rest of my story will corroborate this.

Late Friday evening, John came and picked me up for the seven-day workshop. The trip to the workshop took about three hours, and, by the time we'd arrived, it was dark. There were a few people and John took me to the brothers' room. There were no beds and John got me a sleeping bag. This time, I was so excited to meet more people, I didn't care much about what I was sleeping one. By noon the next day, the place was jam-packed with people who came to the workshop from five neighboring states. For the rest of day, as well as on Saturday, there was nothing to do but fun and games, including basketball, volleyball, baseball, fishing and camping. This weekend was a regional retreat for these young people. It was so much fun meeting them, and they welcomed me as one of their one. But, the real workshop began on Monday. I now knew what the workshop was about, and I was looking forward to learning more. There were so many lectures, and a lot happened during this workshop, so I can only share some of the most fundamental teachings of this group, which I grew to like deeply. Having said this, before I go on with the next chapters about the New Truth I discovered in the teaching of the Unification Church, I would encourage you to read the Divine Principle on your own and discover the truth for yourselves. There is more profound truth! Continue reading.

Part Two

Best-Kept Secrets of the Bible

CHAPTER 12

Biblical Illiteracy

Before introducing the truth I learned in the workshop, I must first say a few words regarding scripture illiteracy. Based on what I have experienced from many years of debates and discussions about God's word in the Bible and in the Quran, I doubt most professing believers, whether they are Jewish, Christian, or Muslim, thoroughly know what their scriptures say, nor do they understand them. I, for one, must confess I had no clues as to what the Quran says apart from hearing the Quran "chanted." Even when I read the Quran on my own, most of the time, I don't understand it. Some of the words are written in an old Arabic language, possibly Saudi Arabian Arabic, that is hard for a farm boy from North Africa like myself to understand. It's funny, buts the following incident is a perfect example of the differences in the Arabic languages. While I was working in a hotel in Saudi Arabia, a prince came to stay in the hotel with a large group of his family and wanted to order room service. Of all the employees in the food and beverage department, I was the only person who spoke Arabic. I was sent up to the prince's suite to take his order. The prince asked me a question about the menu. Politely, I tried to explain it to him in my poor broken North African Arabic. Listening to me for few seconds, the prince interrupted and said, "What is this? I don't understand a word you said." Then, he waved his hands and said, "Go and send me someone who speaks Arabic." Not only is the Qur'an written in an old Arabic language, I am embarrassed to say most of what I learned about it was from my many years of debates on Facebook and the Internet. It's quite embarrassing. I didn't even know the greatest Quranic Surah, "The Night Journey!" To add to this, the debate about theology or about the life of the prophet is not only discouraged but, in fact, forbidden. So, from what I, as a little farm boy, understood about the Quran, the stories were mostly chronological accounts about the prophet Mohammed and how he fought his enemies. This is the same for

Jews and Christians. Like Muslims, most Jewish and Christians are Bible illiterate. It is clear to me many Americans—including confessing Christians—don't know their Bible. According to studies made by George Barner, 60 percent of self-proclaimed Christians can't name half the Ten Commandments or the four Gospels of the New Testament, let alone know what is inside of them (https://www.barna.com/research/six-megathemes-emerge-from-barna-group-research-in-2010/?). Add this to the 80 percent, including "born again" Christians, who believe "God helps those who help themselves" is a direct quote from the Bible! I noticed this problem myself. Many times during a debate, when Christians were confronted about a verse, they would ask, "show me where that is in the Bible," or they would say, "which Bible are you quoting from?" Believers, whether they are Jews, Christians or Muslims, rely heavily on what their religious scholars and spiritual leaders tell them. Having said this, it's time we learn some of the new truths from the teachings of the Rev. Sun Myung Moon. Christians opposed him and felt threatened by him simply because of his controversial declaration—proclaiming himself as the returning Messiah—and for his thought-provoking concept on major fundamental Christian beliefs, such as the Fall of Man, The Last Days, the Second Coming of Christ and the life and mission of Jesus Christ. All these topics will be addressed at greater length in the following chapters.

I would like to start with the Last Days.

CHAPTER 13

Last Day: End of Covenant

Could Last Days Prophecies Be Misinterpreted?

In John 16:25, Jesus said, "I have said this to you in figures; the hour is coming when I shall no longer speak to you in figures but tell you plainly of the Father." Also, in John 16:12-13, Jesus said:

> "I have yet many things to say to you, but you cannot bear them now. When the Spirit of truth comes, he will guide you into all the truth; for he will not speak on his own authority, but whatever he hears he will speak, and he will declare to you the things that are to come."

One would ask, what did Jesus mean by this? In these Bible verses, Jesus is clearly indicating in the Last Days, Christ, at his Second Coming, will give new truth. One would also ask, why would we need new truth if the Last Days is the end of life as we know it? What good is a new truth if all mankind is to be destroyed at the Second Coming? There will be no Earth and no people. These Bible verses could only tell us that at the Second Coming, Christ will bring a new covenant with new sets of truths and heavenly laws. This is what the End Times means. Surely, the prophecies of the Last Days have been misunderstood and, therefore, misinterpreted? The Last Days could only mean the beginning of a New Covenant for the present day, and not the destruction of Earth and the end of life as we know it. It is worth your time sticking with me and discovering a wealth of new, inspiring, eye-opening and, often, shocking truths. I promise by the time you have finished reading this book, you will not only become a Bible expert, but you will also discover your own calling and what God had planned for you. It is extremely important for us to understand the true meaning of the Last Days because, and I must point out, the key theme of the Last Days is the Second Coming of the Messiah, with whom God will establish His New Covenant for the present day. The best explanation I found on the Last Days is in the teachings of the Rev. Sun Myung Moon. In the introduction of the Divine Principle, the Unification Church refers to it as the "completed Testament." It says.

> "God is a living and active God. Both throughout history and in the minds of people, God's active providence has left its mark. Then, what of man, the object of his living God's dispensation; what has man been like throughout history? At each stage in history, God has had to deal with man according to man's spiritual state and intellectual level. Has man always remained the same internally, or has he been progressing and constantly improving?" (Divine Principle Green Book, 3).

In another remarkable explanation, "the sun will be darkened, and the moon will not give its lights, and the stars will fall from heaven" (Matt. 24:29). The Divine Principle says the following, "Then what is the meaning of these predictions?" Gen. 37:9-10 gives us an insight. There we find the interpretation of one of Joseph's dreams, in which the Sun symbolizes the father, the Moon symbolizes the mother, and the stars, their children. Jesus and the Holy Spirit give rebirth to fallen man and, thus, stand in the position of father and mother (referred to "Christology").

Therefore, in the New Testament (Matt. 24:29), the Sun and Moon represent Jesus and the Holy Spirit, who are the sources of the light and truth that illuminate the spirits and hearts of mankind. The stars represent the believers (Christians), who are the "children" of Jesus and the Holy Spirit. To say the Sun and Moon will be darkened is to say the light of a new expression of the truth will outshine that of Jesus and the Holy Spirit. One would question, how is this possible? Just as the Old Testament was outshone when Jesus and the Holy Spirit came with new words of truth, when Christ comes again with a new expression of the truth, the words of Jesus and the Holy Spirit will be outshone.

We need to understand when evangelical Christian preachers deliver fiery sermons on the End Times, they usually start with the Olivet Discourse (Matt. 24, Mark 13 and Luke 21) or the Book of Revelation. For centuries, the End Times sermons and discussions have been centered on the New Testament. However, warnings and sermons on the Last Days were given in the Old Testament as well. Christian teachings on the End Times, unfortunately, resulted in giving us the end of the story. It makes more sense to start at the beginning rather than at the end and try to figure out the story from there.

The following are a few Old Testament passages that are crucial to understanding the Last Days. You will rarely hear Christian preachers, Jewish rabbis or Muslim imams mention these in today's churches, temples or mosques:

A- Noah's Days were Last Days: Jesus said, "As were the days of Noah, so will be coming of the Son of Man" (Matt. 24: 37-39).

B- Jacob's prediction of the Last Days: Would you believe the first mention of the Last Days is in Gen. 49:1? "Then Jacob called his sons, and said, 'Gather yourselves together, that I may tell you what shall befall you in days to come.'"

C- Ironically, the first mention of the Last Days is in the first book of the Bible and not the last. This passage speaks of the last days of the 12 tribes of Israel.

Let's look at another prophecy by the prophet Isaiah:

"The word which Isaiah, the son of Amos, saw concerning Judah and Jerusalem. It shall come to pass in the latter days that the mountain of the house of the Lord shall be established as the highest of the mountains, and shall be raised above the hills; and all the nations shall flow to it" (Isa. 2:1-3).

This segment of the scripture is full of descriptions about the Last Days that can be traced through the New Testament to the Book of Revelation. In the same context of Isa. 2, is the parable of the vineyard (Matt. 20: 1-16). The vineyard is the house of Israel! (Matt. 20: 7). It is a vineyard God said produced worthless grapes! Jesus quotes the same parable in Matt. 21:23-46. In verses 40 to 45, Jesus describes what is to come upon the Jews in the

Last Days. The Pharisees, being familiar with the prophet Isaiah's words, knew exactly what Jesus was saying, and that Jesus spoke the parable about them. The end of the Old Covenant system ended at the cross, yet the final destruction of the temple system came in 70 A.D.

I hope you find the chapter on the Last Days insightful.

But, wait! I have more exciting information to give you.

In the next chapter, I will be introducing you to the full description of the meaning of the Last Days and how the prophecies are explained in the Divine Principle. Just get yourself ready and have a Bible on hand so you can read for yourself and verify every verse I've discussed. We will examine all the Last Day prophesies verse by verse. I am certain you will be amazed at the wealth of knowledge you gain. I am sure you will be delighted. Read on and enjoy! I present to you the Unification Church's perspective on the prophecies of the Last Days and how the church has interpreted them.

Let's now continue with our topic on the Last Days prophecies based on Christian concepts, what they say and what was understood.

Christians Take on the Prophecies of the Last Days

The Last Days are a fascinating subject for all religions, as well as to those in the secular community, particularly since 9/11. In preparation for the millennium, there were many books written about Bible prophesies and dark predictions of the Last Days. Most were written in the two decades before and after the events of 2001. These books include *Nostradamus and the Millennium* (1987), by my favorite author, John Hogue; *Decoding the Bible Code: Can We Trust the Message* (1998) by John Weldon; *The Da Vinci Code* (2003) by Dan Brown; *The Harbinger: The Ancient Mystery That Holds the Secret of America's Future* (2012) by Jonathan Cahn; *The Zealot* (2013) by Reza Aslan, and *Killing Jesus* (2013), by Bill O'Reilly and Martin Dugard. There have also been many movies, such as "The Passion of the Christ" (2004), TV documentaries and radio talk shows on this subject.

As the year 2000 approached, there was a dire feeling in the world. People had a sense of dread as to what the first year of the new millennium would reveal. After the events of 9/11, some people felt panic and were afraid the world could be entering the End Times. But, even with all the books, movies, documentaries and radio programs, I found nothing with a better or clearer understanding of the Bible's prophecies than the Divine Principle, which are the teachings of the Rev. Sun Myung Moon.

Honestly, while researching the subject, I recalled I had a tough time starting this chapter. It was very challenging. But, as I have consistently stated throughout this book, when God calls, He also provides. God has been with me from the start and has led me to many great books that could answer almost every question I had for this chapter. It was not easy to write because of its topic. It deals with supernatural and apocalyptic elements, such as the Last Days and the Second Coming of Christ, which are hard to interpret. But, I persevered, and things began to happen.

After approximately three months of trying to write this chapter, a thought came to me like a whisper. It suggested maybe I should examine how Christians view the Last Days.

Excited about that idea, my daughter, Alisa, and I went to a library in Noblesville, Indiana, hoping to find books written about the Second Coming of Christ and the Last Days. I found a handful of books and two DVDs with captivating titles, "The Seventh Sign" (1988) and "The End of Time" (2012).

Anxious to see what I would find on these DVDs, I dashed home to watch them. Although I had an idea about how most Christians believed the Second Coming would happen, I found, to my disappointment, the contents of these DVDs to be very disturbing. Their views on the "rapture," which projects the Last Days will come as a Judgment by Fire and the destruction of the Earth (2 Pet. 3:12 and Mal. 4:1), were particularly disturbing, as were their depictions of the destruction of heaven and Earth and creation of the New Heaven and Earth (Rev. 22:1, 2 Pet. 3:12, Isa. 66:22, Gen.6:13). In addition, I was bothered by the depictions of the meeting the Lord "in the air" (1 Thess. 4:17), and the Sun and Moon will darken, and stars will fall from heaven (Matt. 24:29). All these catastrophic phenomena would supposedly happen in a split second with no warning!

No offense to any religion, but I am very stunned that Christians interpreted these biblical prophecies as literal doom and gloom! These DVDs reminded me of a poster I had seen a few years earlier on the wall of a church describing the "rapture." The rapture is the Christian's teaching that at or before the return of Christ (Matt. 24:30; Acts 1:11), the Christians who are alive on the Earth will be transformed into resurrected bodies and be, literally, caught up into the clouds to meet Jesus. I didn't think of much at the time. But, for some reason, it appears to be important to me now as I write about it. In the poster, there was a scene of chaos: a city on fire with demolished buildings and car crashes. It also showed the spirits of the dead and the living heading up to the sky to meet the Lord, who was standing on a cloud with a myriad of angels and saints surrounding Him. This video tells it all: www.facebook.com/christianhome11/videos/1189057204542134/. It is a wonderful depiction of the second coming of Christ.

Although the group that produced these DVDs had some insights on the signs of the times that were prophesied to happen before the appearance of the Messiah and the destruction of the Earth, in my view, when I compared them with what I learned in the Divine Principle, they sounded like they were taken from an elementary school textbook. These Christian groups seemed to be so excited and even looked forward to these destructive phenomena happening in their lifetimes!

I must admit what I had believed about religions and God in the past had been vague. After I learned the truth from Moon's teachings, my belief in God and the scriptures changed dramatically. I can't understand the reason why God would choose to wait all those years(Six thousand years) and allow bitter wars to go on, only to destroy the Earth in a split second at the Last Days? What about His unconditional love and humanity's free will?

If God is almighty and could do anything He wanted, why didn't He destroy everything after the fall of mankind and start over, thus eliminating thousands of years of suffering? Could there be a reason why God had to wait? Was it not because God was waiting for humans to fulfill their "portion of responsibility," as the Divine Principle refers to it?

This is what intrigued me about the Divine Principle. It was the idea that God created human beings as "copartners" and endowed them with a certain portion of responsibility to realize God's purpose for creation.

If we don't fulfill our portion, the will of God won't be realized.

This is why it has taken God so many years. The religions deny that human effort is needed. They rationalize that God is Almighty and He, alone, can do anything. Therefore, He does not need man's help!

Jews, Christians and Muslims have lived in fear of the Last Days because they believe it would be a time of supernatural calamities or doomsday. In Islam, the Qur'an gives a similar description to the Christian's concept of the rapture, or "Judgment Day," calling it the Day of Resurrection or Youm al-Quiyama.

Muslims believe the entire world will come to an end on one appointed day, and everything will be destroyed. The Qur'an describes it as follows: "When the sky bursts apart, when planets are dispersed, when the seas spill forth when graves are overturned, then each soul will know what it sent forward and what it left behind" (Qur'an 82:1-5).

At the moment of the final hour, a trumpet will call the people to assemble. This trumpet will be blown by the Archangel Raphael (Israfil in Islam) to tell everyone Judgment Day has arrived. Every living creature, both past and present, will gather before God. Mass panic will ensue because everyone will begin to worry about judgment. "Then, when the trumpet is blown, there will be no more relationships between them that day, nor will one ask after another" (Qur'an 23:101).

After this, Judgment Day will begin. God will then revive the dead to be judged for their deeds. A person's deeds will be put on a scale, the good ones will be on one side; the bad on the other. Whichever side tips the scale determines that person's fate.

But, the world does not need to end for people to face God's judgment. An individual faces judgment when he or she dies! In other words, an individual's death is his or her End Time. The good news is, according to the Divine Principle, this is not going to happen. Rather, the Last Days will be a time of great rejoicing because it is the time when God's ideal of creation (Kingdom of

Heaven) will finally be realized!

Another point I also found very remarkable was the idea that God had an original plan, or "blueprint," for the creation. Had this plan been realized, human history would have been replete with goodness, happiness and joy. There would have been no need for religions or houses of worship and no need for a messiah.

Because of God's love, compassion and grace for humans, God set up religion to return humans to His plan for creation. As He said in (Isa. 46:11), "I have spoken, and I will bring it to pass; I have purposed, and I will do it." Thus, the Last Days is the period when the evil world is finally transformed into the ideal world. This is the true meaning of the Last Days.

The Bible indicates there have been two attempts to bring about the Last Days. The first was during the time of Noah. God said, "I have determined to make an end of all flesh; for the earth is filled with violence through them; behold, I will destroy them with the earth" (Gen. 6:13). This suggests that God telling Noah to build the ark and that He would bring a flood was an attempt to bring about the Last Days.

The second example occurred during Jesus' time. The Israelites were eagerly awaiting the Messiah. Jesus came to lead the Israelites closer to God and build the Kingdom of God. This is why Jesus referred to himself as coming to judge everyone (John 5:22) and why Malachi prophesied:

> "For behold, the days come, burning like an oven, when all the arrogant and evildoers will be stubble; the day that comes shall burn them up, says the Lord of hosts, so that it will leave them neither root nor branch" (Mal. 4:1).

Unfortunately, by not believing in Jesus, the Israelites failed in their responsibility, and this delayed the fulfillment of God's will. It is for this reason that Jesus said, "As it was in the days of Noah, so will it be in the days of the Son of Man" (Luke 17:26). This is also why, in Matt. 24:20, when there is a prediction of the Second Coming of Christ, humanity will experience many supernatural calamities of wars, earthquakes, tsunamis, etc., like those predicted during Noah's time and Jesus' time (Gen. 6:6-7 and Isa. 24:29).

From what we can tell, most of the prophecies have come to pass. Yes, there were many wars, natural calamities and plagues, but the Earth and the solar system were not destroyed or affected as predicted! They continue to spin on their orbital axes as they have done for billions of years.

So, what then do these predictions mean if they are not to be taken literally? From my understanding, the destruction of the solar system is not God's plan, even though some Bible verses express God's dissatisfaction with humanity and His threats to destroy mankind. For example, in Gen. 6:13, God expressed His frustration and threatened to destroy the Earth during Noah's time. "A generation goes, and a generation comes, but the earth remains for ever" (Eccles. 1:4);"He built his sanctuary like the high heavens, like the earth, which he has founded for ever" (Ps.78:69); and, "Thou didst set the earth on its foundations, so that it should never be shaken" (Ps. 104: 5). As explained in the biblical quotes, Earth is not the problem. It is the evil and spiritual entity that has dominated human souls since the Fall of Mankind that God is determined to end.

The following section is by far the greatest and clearest interpretation of biblical prophecies on The Last Days I have ever heard. It is taught in the Divine Principle.

Phenomena Prophesied in the Last Days

Heaven and Earth Destroyed by Fire

You might ask why do Christians believe in the biblical prophecies found in the Book of Revelation, which foretell these supernatural calamities and the destruction of heaven and earth? If these prophecies are not literally going to happen, then what do they mean? First, to make things clear, we must understand it was Jesus who dictated the revelation to John. Second, the revelation is a repetition of ancient Judaic beliefs, which were formed hundreds of years before the destruction of the first temple and go further back to ancient Egyptian beliefs.

There are many Old Testament prophecies repeated in the New Testament, such as Dan. 7:13 and Matt. 24:30, which predict the Messiah would come on the clouds of heaven; Isa. 65:17

and Rev. 31:1, which speak of the coming of a new heaven and earth; and Joel 2:28 and Acts 2:17, both of which speak about the Last Days phenomena.

Let us now look closely at these prophecies from a new perspective and discover for ourselves their real meanings.

Judgment by Fire

In 2 Pet. 3:12, it says "… the heavens will be kindled and dissolved, and the elements will melt with fire!" As we have learned, the destruction of the Earth and the heavens were not God's plan. If this were to happen literally, then God's dispensation of salvation would not be fulfilled.

There is a prophecy that Jesus' days would be a day of destruction by fire (Mal. 4:1). It is stated in John 5:22 and John 9:39 that Jesus is the master of judgment. In Luke 12:49, Jesus said he came to cast fire upon the Earth, but He never literally brought about judgment by fire.

So, what do these Bible verses mean? They must be symbolic. In Jer. 23:29, God says His word may be likened to fire. "Judgment by fire" really means judgment by words of truth. In John 12:48, Jesus said, "he who rejects me and does not receive my saying has a judge; the word that I have spoken will be his judge on the last day."

Also, 2 Thess. 2:8 says, "… the lawless one will be revealed, and the Lord Jesus will slay him with the breath of his mouth." Similarly, Isa. 11:4 says, "… and he shall smite the earth with the rod of his mouth, and with the breath of his lips he shall slay the wicked." John 5:24 says: "… He who hears my word and believes him who sent me has eternal life; he does not come into judgment, but has passed from death to life."

From these verses, "judgment by fire" means judgment by the words of truth.

Meeting the Lord on the Clouds

In 1 Thess. 4:17, it says: "Then we who are alive, who are left, shall be caught up together with them in the clouds to meet the Lord in the air; and so we shall always be with the Lord."

This prophecy also cannot be taken literally. Many Christians are waiting for Jesus to come from the sky on a cloud, but this is not what is predicted to happen. Christ will be reborn on Earth just as He, Jesus, was 2,000 years ago. In the Bible, Jesus said He "came from heaven" in his first coming (John 3:13), yet we know He was born in a manger. No one saw Him coming from the sky.

Based on what I learned, heaven, in the Bible, usually means the holy, exalted and sinless realm. Judaism, Christianity and Islam mistakenly believe that God lives in the sky, and the Earth is the unholy place, a realm dominated by sin and evil.

So, 1 Thess. 4:17 refers to the development and elevation of heavenly characters and spiritual perfection to a higher realm where they can serve Christ in an ideal world until He returns to establish His kingdom on Earth.

Sun and Moon Darkened. The Stars Fall from Heaven

Matt. 24:29 says: "Immediately after the tribulation of those days, the sun will be darkened, and the moon will not give its light, and the stars will fall from heaven."

Should these calamities literally come to pass, then the Earth would be obliterated and uninhabitable, and God's providence of salvation could not be fulfilled. Then, what do these predictions mean? Gen. 37:9-10 gives us an insight. In this verse, we find the interpretation of one of Joseph's dreams. His father interpreted it to mean the sun symbolized the father; the moon represented the mother, and the stars were their children.

Let us now proceed to Joseph's dream:

> "Then he dreamed another dream, and told it to his brothers, and said, 'Behold, I have dreamed another dream; and behold, the sun, the moon, and eleven stars were bowing down to me. But when he told it to his father and to his brothers, his father rebuked him, and said to him, 'What is this dream that you have dreamed? Shall I and your mother and your brothers indeed come to bow ourselves to the ground before you?" (Gen. 37:9-10).

Later in Joseph's story, we find that, indeed, Joseph's father, mother and brothers all bowed before him when he became the prime minister to the Egyptian pharaoh. Joseph set the pattern for Moses, who became prime minister of Egypt about 1,000 years later. Jesus, had he been accepted and not crucified, would have risen to a high government leadership position and possibly become Israel's king.

As the Divine Principle states:

> Viewed in this manner, the sunlight symbolizes the light of truth of Jesus' words, and the moonlight symbolizes the light of the Holy Spirit. To say that the sun and the moon will be darkened is to say that the light of a new revelation that gives a new expression of the truth will outshine that of Jesus and the Holy Spirit (i.e., the New Testament). Just as the Old Testament was outshone when Jesus and the Holy Spirit came with the new words that were to fulfill the Old Testament, the "father" of the Old Testament age is Moses and the "mother" is the Law and the "Children" are the Chosen People of Israel.
>
> When Christ comes again with a new expression of the truth, the words of Jesus and the Holy Spirit will be outshone. For truth to lose its light means that the period of its mission has ended with the coming of an age for a new expression of the truth. The "Stars" falling from heaven represent those Christians in the Last Days who do not accept the truth from the Lord, and thus lose their position as the children of God" (Divine Principle Green Book, 70).

Having explained the meaning of the Last Days based on Moon's teachings, let us now move on to our next topic, the Fall of Man. What happened to Adam and Eve in the Garden of Eden? What are the Tree of Life, Tree of the Knowledge of Good Evil and the forbidden "fruit?" And, who is the talking serpent?

CHAPTER 14

The Fall of Man

Fate and Destiny—Our Free Will

The Bible teaches that Man was created with the ability to make moral choices and is responsible for those choices. The Fall of Man was not a predetermined event in which Adam and Eve were hapless victims of a puppetmaster God. On the contrary, Adam and Eve had the ability to choose obedience (with its attendant blessing) or disobedience (with its consequent curse). They knew what the result of their decision would be, and they were held accountable (Genesis 3).

By reflecting on what was taught in the Principles of the Creation chapter of the Divine Principle about God's original plan for mankind, we can assume the Fall of Man means something created to be good and wonderful suddenly became evil! God created man to have a completely functional body with extraordinary capabilities. But, somehow, by eating a seemingly simple piece of fruit, the forbidden fruit, mankind lost its divine nature and was separated from God. This is the doctrine accepted by Judaism, Christianity and Islam. The belief in the fall of man also has abstruse and far-reaching implications, so much so that humans will never be able to placate themselves until they can restore their divine natures.

Because of the fall, humanity must now grapple with the conflicting natures of good and evil. When we look at ourselves, we see two opposing contradictory natures or minds within ourselves: an "original" mind, which can find goodness and repel evil, and a "fallen" nature, which is subconsciously driven toward evil. In Christianity, the being that controls this "fallen nature" is Satan. This chapter examines how mankind fell. It also clearly exposes the identities of the forbidden "fruit" and the serpent and explains the meaning of the Tree of the Knowledge of Good and Evil and the Tree of Life. Let's begin with the forbidden fruit. Is it literal or symbolic as are many things in the Bible?

The Fruit: Literal or Symbolic?

Jews, Christians and Muslims have believed the original sin and root of all evil was because Adam and Eve ate the fruit from the Tree of Knowledge of Good and Evil. This is what the Book of Genesis says. However, it is necessary to ask whether the fruit is literally a piece of fruit, or is it symbolic, as so many other things are in the Bible. According to Moon's teachings, the fruit is symbolic.

So, then, what is the fruit? Was it a test? How could something edible cause a man to fall? It is hard to believe that God would create something to test mankind to see whether humanity would obey His word. He declared they would die if they did so. But, Adam and Eve didn't die. They lived very long lives. As I will explain in a later chapter – the resurrection chapter—the "death" that is mentioned in this verse is also symbolic. Still, this verse indicates the fruit represents something so stimulating that Adam and Eve's desire to eat it was stronger than their desire to live. What is this attractive, but deadly, fruit? (Gen. 3:6). In a nutshell, the "fruit" symbolized Eve's sexual love organ! The fall was caused by a sexual act that was enticed by the serpent against God's commandment.

Wow! As you know, I was raised a Muslim. But, for some reason, after I heard this story for the first time, it really made sense to me. So, I thought about it. As the Divine Principle explained, If Adam and Eve were, as the Bible said, at first, naked and unashamed, then why would they feel ashamed of their nakedness right after they ate the fruit? Why would they also cover their sexual organs with fig leaves? If you take the fruit literally and eat it, human nature would require you to hide the parts of the body that were directly involved in the act; i.e., your hands or mouth, not your lower parts. I thought a lot about this new concept. If God is truly a being of love and emotion, as Christian scripture teaches, then He must have grieved deeply following the loss of His intimate relationship with His children. You don't find this concept taught in Islam, Judaism or Christianity, and this idea nudged me closer to God and the Unification Church.

The Identity of the Serpent

The story of Adam and Eve, in the third chapter of Genesis, tells us it was the serpent that caused the fall of Adam and Eve. It was the talking serpent that tempted Eve to eat the forbidden fruit, causing her to commit the first sin. This serpent, which could talk, knew God's plan and knew He forbid Adam and Eve to eat the fruit, could not literally have been a slithering reptile, so it must be symbolic. This talking "serpent" must have been a spiritual being. According to Rev. 12:9, which says, "And the great dragon was thrown down, that ancient serpent, who is called the Devil and Satan, the deceiver of the whole world—he thrown down to the earth, and his angels were thrown down with him," the serpent was not only a good angel who once lived in heaven but also an archangel, a leader of a high angelic order. He was like the archangels, Gabriel and Michael. But, for some reason, he lost his position and was thrown out of heaven and into Hell with his minions.

How could an angelic being with a high-ranking title possibly fall out of God's grace and then do horrendous things to God and humanity? The only answer is this angel must have been created like human beings, with a nature that needs to go through the three stages of growth to reach maturity to the level of perfection. So, this now brings us to the real meaning of the word fruit. There are two kinds of love: principled love and unprincipled love. Very simply, this archangel was jealous of Adam and Eve. Before God created them, this archangel received spontaneous and uninterrupted love from God. However, after Adam and Eve's creation, this archangel saw God was ecstatic with love for them. This archangel felt like he was receiving less love from God. God appointed him to be the personal caretaker for Adam and Eve, but the archangel found Eve so beautiful and got too close to her. Soon after, he found he was infatuated with her beauty. The archangel seduced Eve, they had sex, and this was the beginning of unprincipled love. It was unprincipled because this spiritual being, disguised as a serpent, broke the laws of heaven and had sex with a human being. It's possible this was the origin of all kinds of unnatural sex, including homosexuality, incest or any other kind that goes against God's standard.

Could Spiritual Beings Manifest Substantially?

One might think this is absurd, but how could a spiritual being have a sexual relationship with a human being? Yes, you better believe it! There are myriad stories written throughout history that mention spiritual possession, spirits engaged in sex with and married to human beings. There are also numerous stories in the Bible mentioning angels/spirits that manifest themselves substantially and have sex with humans. For instance, in the story of Sodom and Gomorrah (Gen. 18:16-19), two angels disguised themselves as men to investigate the wickedness occurring in those cities. They stopped at Lot's house, talked with him and ate supper with his family. The people of the village demanded Lot let these two visitors leave so they could have sex with them. Lot tried to protect his guests by offering them his two daughters with which to have sex, but they refused. The angels now understood how evil the people of these cities were, so they set fire to the two cities and destroyed everything and everyone, except for Lot and his daughters.

Also, if we are to take the Bible as truth, there is a story in Gen. 6:4, that mentions the Nephilim, children born of the sons of God and the daughters of men. This can also be found in the Book of Enoch, a Jewish religious work mentioned in Gen. 5:24 and discovered with the Dead Sea Scrolls. In it, watchers, or fallen angels, are the angels who fathered the Nephilim. Perhaps, the best story reported in the Bible is from Jude 1: 6-7, which says it clearly:

> "And the angels that did not keep their own position but left their proper dwelling have been kept by him in eternal chains in the nether gloom until the judgment of the great day; just as Sodom and Gomor'rah and the surrounding cities, which likewise acted immorally and indulged in unnatural lust, serve as an example by undergoing a punishment of eternal fire."

The Result of the Fall

As stated in the Divine Principle, there are four major aspects of fallen natures (sins) mankind inherited from Satan, which can be perceived in human nature: (1). Failure to see from God's viewpoint. Satan could not accept and love Adam and Eve as God loved them. In fact, he was jealous of them because he thought himself superior to them. The best example of this is when a student feels jealousy toward a teacher's favorite instead of appreciating him or her as the teacher does. (2). Leaving one's own given position. An example of this can be found in the family or at work when a person feels he or she is more qualified than anyone else and begin to criticize and correct others as if he or she is their supervisor instead of performing his or her own assigned job. (3). Reversal of Dominion. The angel was created to be under man's dominion, yet he dominated Adam and Eve. The perfect example of this aspect of Fallen Nature can be found at work or in a religious community when a member disrespects his or her supervisor/leader's direction and tries to dominate. (4). Multiplication of Sin. This aspect of Fallen Nature can be found in a peer group or workplace when a bad person begins to spread false rumors and tries to push his or her own bad thoughts and habits onto others and make them join his or her rank.

In analogy to a tree, these fallen natures have been passed down to humankind, like DNA, since the fall of Adam and Eve and are classified as follows: (1). Original Sin: a sin that is derived from the spiritual and physical fall of Adam and Eve. When using an analogy to a tree, this sin is seen as the root of all sin. (2). Hereditary Sin: sin that is inherited from one's ancestors through the blood lineage, as mentioned in the Ten Commandments (Exod. 20:5). This sin is analogous to the trunk of a tree. (3). Collective Sin: sin that is neither one's own sin nor hereditary sin but is the sin for which everyone is partially responsible as a member of mankind. For example, the faithlessness of John the Baptist, the chief priests and the scribes toward Jesus was responsible for his crucifixion. Although a relatively small group of people was directly responsible for the crucifixion, Christianity and mankind have had to bear the responsibility for that sin. Collective sin is like the branches of a tree. (4). Personal Sin: sin that is committed by everyone. Such sin may be compared to the leaves of a tree. All sins originate with Original Sin. Thus, man cannot be finally cleansed of any sin without first being cleansed of Original Sin. Therefore, a messiah is needed.

This brings us to the next few chapters that focus on Jesus' tragic death, which was considered by Moon to be as disastrous as the fall of man itself. We will also examine a controversial take on his birth, mission, death and resurrection.

Please note! The following chapters are by far the most thought-provoking teachings Moon ever uttered in the history of Christianity. Please have a Bible on hand to verify every point discussed in these chapters.

CHAPTER 15

The Cross: God's Will or Man's Failure?

"He came to his own home, and his own people received him not" (John 1:11).

The Story of Jesus

I have heard many stories and read many books about Jesus, including recently published books, such as *Zealot: The Life and Times of Jesus of Nazareth* (2013) by Reza Aslan and *Killing Jesus* (2013) by Bill O'Reilly and Martin Dugard. I have also seen many movies, such as 2004's "The Passion of the Christ," which caused a huge retaliation from Jews all over the world because it portrayed them as vengeful and "Christ Killers," and "Son of God," which was released in 2014.

No story has ever touched me more, with its clear-cut new truths on Jesus' life, than the one told by Moon in the Divine Principle chapter, "Mission of The Messiah." It has the most thought-provoking truths on Jesus' story, and it is so shocking that many Christians consider it as blasphemy. Why? I gave the answer. It was because what Moon was preaching was seen by most as unorthodox and a threat to the validity of their traditional teachings.

As a Muslim, it was hard for me to hear Jesus' story for the first time. It was so painful and powerful that I found myself weeping uncontrollably and drenched in tears. As I recall, even the lecturer, Jim Garland, was so involved in the story, that he also broke into tears and made everyone weep. Jesus was truly misunderstood by the very people who were being prepared to receive him. No one understood his messianic mission, not his mother, half-brothers or disciples. Even John the Baptist, who was the greatest prophet who ever lived, didn't truly believe in Jesus.

This lecture revealed an important new truth that was hidden in the Bible: there was a conflict between John the Baptist and Jesus. The problem was regarding Jesus' crucifixion. In the next chapter, we will examine closely the ardent role John the Baptist came to fulfill. Before we move on to the Christian's views on the Messiah's mission, let us first understand the Jewish concept of the Messiah and the role he was expected to fulfill.

According to Judaism, the word "Messiah" in Hebrew means "the anointed one," and usually signifies a king. The chosen people of Israel believed in the word of God as it was revealed through the prophets. God promised them he would send them a king and savior. This was their messianic expectation. God sent this Messiah in the form of Jesus Christ. "Christ" is the Greek word for Messiah.

However, the Jews misunderstood the messiah's role and what He was meant to fulfill. They thought only about their own suffering, struggles and wars. They only thought of the Messiah as a warrior king who would lead them in a final war that would destroy their enemies once and for all, and make them the rulers over all the nations on Earth. But, the Messiah came not as the powerful warrior king the Jews had hoped for, but as a simple uneducated man from a humble family from Nazareth.

Christians, on the other hand, have traditionally believed Jesus was the expected messiah God promised to send to the chosen people, and His sole mission was to die on the cross to save mankind from sin. This is what God originally planned.

No, it was not! According to Moon's revelation, crucifying Jesus was a tragic mistake. The crucifixion was caused by the sheer ignorance of the Israelites. In a sense, both the Jews and Christians have misunderstood the messiah's true purpose.

God truly loved his chosen people, the Israelites. They were to be the foundation for the coming of the Messiah. Many times, God prophesied the coming of the Messiah, and he warned the people to prepare for his coming. God even sent the prophet, John the Baptist, to prepare the faithful for the imminent coming of the Messiah. John was to submit himself to Jesus and lead his followers to accept and follow him.

Tragically, however, the much-prepared people, including John, failed to recognize Jesus as their messiah. Jesus did everything he could to convince the Israelites he was the Messiah, but his words fell on deaf ears. He was mocked, sneered at, had stones thrown at him, branded a blasphemer and, ultimately, crucified. Ironically, the Roman rulers of that time knew he was innocent (Luke 23:14-16; John 18:38; Matt. 27:19-23; Matt. 15:10-14), and those who found him guilty were the Jewish leaders and his own people. They were the ones who insisted Jesus must die. Why? First, Jesus said in the Bible that God's will was clearly for the chosen people to accept and believe in Jesus and receive salvation (John 6:29, 10:37, 38).

The Bible said, "He came to his own home, and his own people received him not" (John 1:11). The Apostle Paul testified that "none of the rulers of this age understood this; for if they had, they would not have crucified the Lord of glory" (1 Cor. 2:8). Also, the night before Jesus was betrayed, He spent several agonizing hours in the Garden of Gethsemane, praying desperately: "My soul is very sorrowful, even to death; remain here, and watch with me." "... My Father, if it be possible, let this cup [death] pass from me" (Matt. 26:38-39). Who could have known God's will for the Messiah better than Jesus himself? From this Bible verse, it's very clear that death on the cross was not God's plan for Jesus.

Again, if Jesus' death on the cross was predestined, why would Jesus say to Judas Iscariot: "Woe to that man by whom the Son of man is betrayed? It would have been better for that man if he had not been born" (Matt. 26:24). Again, how can we explain Jesus crying out on the cross: "My God, my God, why hast thou forsaken me?" (Matt. 27:46).

If the crucifixion was truly God's original will for Jesus, then Jesus should have felt a sense of joy and victory on the cross, having successfully completed his mission. One question remains: If the Jews were wrong to sentence Jesus to death and Christians were wrong to believe his death was God's plan, then how can Moon's new revelation explain the mystery of Jesus' death? If it was not God's will, then whose was it? According to the secret Moon decoded in the Bible, Jesus' death is related to three main issues:

1. The Israelites saw Jesus as a heretical zealot and a rabble-rouser, who was bent on destroying Jewish law. This was the main point of Aslan's book. As he noted in the introduction:

> First century Palestine, an age awash in apocalyptic fervor. ... Scores of Jewish prophets, preachers, and would-be messiahs wandered through the Holy Land, bearing messages from God. ... Jesus' time was the age of zealotry—a fervent nationalism that made resistance to the Roman occupation a sacred duty incumbent on all Jews" (Aslan 2013, xxiii-xxxi).

2. Jesus' unknown biological father. Many Israelites of his time questioned whether his birth was legitimate.

3. John the Baptist and the return of Elijah. The most damning issue was John the Baptist's failure to support Jesus' mission and join his flock. In the upcoming chapter, we will examine John the Baptist and the role he was sent to fulfill.

Resurrection

If we were to take everything in the Bible literally, then we would have to believe that, at the Second Coming, the buried and decomposed physical bodies of all past believers will be restored to their original state of life in the flesh (1 Thess. 4:16, Matt. 27:52). But, can we believe this? To resolve this question, let us first investigate the meaning of resurrection.

In Luke 9:60, the Bible gives us a hint about the true meaning of resurrection. We read that one of Jesus' disciples asked Jesus to let him go home for his father's funeral and Jesus said, "Let the dead bury their own dead, but as for you, go and proclaim the kingdom of God." In these words, we find two different concepts of life and death. One concept is related to the function of the physical body. The other is related to the people who were gathered for the burial of the disciple's deceased father. The question asked is, why did Jesus indicate that those who were attending the funeral were dead when they were alive? Interesting! Remember the story I told about the man at Hyde Park Speakers Corner and his statement that infuriated me? As the Divine Principle explains, the people who are physically alive gathered to bury the dead were, in fact, spiritually dead: "It was because being under Satan's dominion, they were ignorant of the purpose of life and did not know God, who is the source of life" (Divine Principle, Green Book, 75). Rev. 3:1 says, "you have the name of being alive, and you are dead." These words sum it up and give new light to the meaning of life and death. The word "resurrection" means passing from death to life. With Jesus' view of death, life would then mean to be within God's dominion. In John 11:25-26, Jesus says, "I am the resurrection and the life; he who believes in me, though he died, yet shall he live, and whoever lives and believes in me shall never die." This tells us that whoever is connected to God's dominion through Christ is alive, regardless of whether that person's physical body is dead or alive. This brings us to the Christians' concept of the Last Days and the rapture.

The Rapture

As explained in the Resurrection section, the rapture is the preconceived idea that, at the end of time, all those who believe in God, whether alive or dead, shall meet Jesus in the sky and go with Him to heaven. However, the rapture has an important meaning that is different from what Christians understand it to be. Its true meaning is the resurrection of good spirits—of people who served God's will throughout the ages—would be resurrected at the time of Christ. In the air isn't a literal place. It is the elevated spiritual maturity level to that of the Messiah. They are to serve as witnesses to their own descendants of their religion and connect them to the Messiah. The rapture can only happen when the Messiah appears.

Another specific task the rapture created is to serve as a witness to God's plan of salvation for all humankind. Matt. 27:52 says when Jesus died on the cross, many saints rose from their tombs. This is also a phenomenon of the resurrection. As the Divine Principle states, "By cooperating with those on Earth who believe in and attend the Lord of the Second Coming, and by helping them to become divine spirit selves," they themselves become divine (Divine Principle, Green Book, 84). By doing this task, the returning spirits would gain the same benefits. Maybe the following Bible verse will make it clearer. "And all these, though well attested by their faith, did not receive what was promised, since

God had foreseen something better for us, that apart from us they should not be made perfect" (Heb. 11:39-40).

Thinking of this, I couldn't help but think of my deceased uncle, Taib, and my brother, Mohammed. I wrote about them in the "Funeral Procession" dream. Their spirits were resurrected and witnessed to me about the Lord of the Second Advent. I believe both are in a good place in heaven!

CHAPTER 16

John the Baptist: Saint or Sinner?

"Are you he who is to come, or shall we look for another?" (Matt. 11:3)

Excuse me for making in such a blunt statement. No offense to any religion, but when you finish reading this chapter you will know why. Before beginning this chapter, I must first emphasize how extremely important John the Baptist's total unity with Jesus was in God's plan for salvation. John was sent by God not only to witness to Jesus and follow him, but to play a crucial role in fulfilling the older brother/younger brother pattern that God had started with Cain and Abel. As we will examine in an upcoming chapter, God set up the pattern in the Old Testament—the older brother must serve the younger brother. This pattern must also be fulfilled on a national and world level by John the Baptist and Jesus. John was sent ahead of the Messiah "to make people ready for the Lord." John's total unity with Jesus is necessary for God's plan of salvation.

There is one matter that we must delve into deeper, and that is God's dispensation of having Jesus go the way of the cross. As clarified earlier, it wasn't God's original plan that Jesus die on the cross. It was because of the failure of the chosen people to recognize him as the Messiah. So, it became God's painful secondary arrangement, which was necessary because of the people's faithlessness. The Jewish people failed to believe in him and demanded he is crucified.

Why couldn't the Jewish people recognize Jesus when He came to them? Why did they fear him so much they allowed him to endure such a horrible death? There were several reasons. Aslan, in his book, described Jesus as a zealot who was so threatening to the Roman way of life that he was captured and executed as a state criminal. But, this is not it! There were two issues that prove to be the most significant reasons for the Jews' disbelief:

The return of the prophet Elijah, which is mentioned in Mal. 4:4-6, the last Book of Prophecy in the Old Testament; and the issues that concern John the Baptist.

This is what Malachi's prophecy said:

> Remember the law of my servant Moses, the statutes and ordinances that I commanded him at Horeb for all Israel. Behold, I will send you the Eli'jah the prophet before the great and terrible day of the Lord comes. And, he will turn the hearts of fathers to their children and the hearts of children to their fathers, lest I come and smite the land with a curse (Mal. 4:4-6).

Who was Elijah? He was one of the prophets God sent to Israel 900 years before Jesus. In 2 Kings 2:1-11, there is a tale about him ascending into heaven on a chariot of fire. The Israelites, who were longing for the Messiah, were focused on the second arrival of Elijah. The Old Testament did not foretell when the Messiah would come. In Mal. 4: 4-6, however, it clearly says Elijah would precede him. Here, we must understand how crucial the Second Coming of Elijah was for the Jewish people. This prophecy was the chosen people's greatest and, perhaps, most accurate sign that God had given them. Elijah was to be sent ahead of the Messiah to prepare the people for the coming of the Lord. Malachi also warned if people didn't receive him, God will strike the land with total destruction. So, the Second Coming of Elijah was so vital to God's dispensation and to serve as a sign that the Lord is coming.

Why didn't God send Elijah in the way the Israelites expected, descending from heaven on a chariot of fire? God didn't forget to do this. There was no literal chariot of fire! We must remember that, according to Malachi's prophecy, there was no information on how Elijah would come, nor was there any information about Elijah's purpose. Jewish scribes, Pharisees and those who interpreted prophecies, made a huge mistake when they expected Elijah to return that way. This misconception about Elijah's literal return to Earth is the same misconception Christians have of Jesus' return on the clouds from the sky. This is also the same misconception held by Muslims. It is extremely important that we learn the lessons of history. God never works the way these religions suggest.

The same thing can be said about their views of the Last Days and Armageddon! It is because of a misinterpretation of what is to come that often drives extremist and fundamentalist religious movements. It is like what happened with the Essenes during Jesus' time. They, too, were expecting the end of the world and were preparing for the final war. They thought they would win the war against the Romans and even against other rival sects—the Pharisees and the Sadducees. In the end, however, they, along with the rest of the Jews and the Second Temple, were destroyed by the Romans.

Returning to Jesus' story, Jesus' problem with the Israelites began when He appeared and proclaimed Himself to be the Messiah, telling the people they should believe in and follow him. Since they considered him to be a simple man from Nazareth, and there was no evidence that Elijah had returned, they questioned how he could be the Messiah? One day, Jesus' disciples went out among the Jewish people to testify. The people, doubting that Jesus was the messiah, asked them where Elijah was. When they returned to Jesus, they asked him: "Then, why do the scribes say that first Eli'jah must come?" (Matt. 17:10). Jesus replied: "Eli'jah does come, and he is to restore all things; but I tell you that Eli'jah has already come, and they did not know him, but did to him whatever they pleased" (Matt. 17:11-12).

It was then the disciples understood He meant John the Baptist.

When Jesus said John the Baptist was Elijah, his disciples had no problem accepting it. But, the Israelites could not. John did not come from heaven, and he himself denied he was Elijah (John 1:21). Jesus knew people were not ready to accept it and said: "if you are willing to accept it, he is Eli'jah who is to come" (Matt. 11:14). Christians have traditionally believed John the Baptist was a great saint, but new studies have disproven that. John the Baptist turned out to be the greatest failure! So, who shall the people believe, Jesus or John the Baptist? Naturally, it depends on how these men were compared with the people of that time.

Jesus

Let us take Jesus first. How did Jesus appear to the Israelites of His time? The Bible says Jesus was an obscure young man who was brought up in the house of a humble carpenter. He had no formal education and was not schooled in spiritual discipline. There were questions about his paternal legitimacy (John 8:41). Yet, Jesus claimed himself "Lord of the Sabbath" (Matt. 12:8), known as one who abolished the law (Matt. 5:17), was a friend of tax collectors and sinners, and known to be a glutton and drunkard (Matt. 11:19). He put Himself on an equal status with God (John 14:9-11) and told the people they had to love him more than anyone else (Matt. 10:37). Because of this, the Jewish leaders labeled him a blasphemer and claimed He worked by the power of Beelzebub, the prince of demons (Matt. 12:24).

John

On the other hand, how did the Israelites see John the Baptist? He was the son of a prominent rabbi and the miracles that surrounded his birth were known throughout the country (Luke 1:5-66). John had a formal education, and, when he was older, he lived like a beggar in the wilderness.

In the eyes of the Jews, John led an exemplary life as a man of faith. In fact, John was held in such high regard that people even asked him if he was the Messiah (Luke 3:15; John 1:20). Given this evidence, it seems the Israelites believed more in John the Baptist. The Jewish people decided Jesus only said John the Baptist was Elijah, so people would believe he was the Messiah.

Unfortunately, by denying he was Elijah, John the Baptist made Jesus look like a liar. Had John the Baptist truly understood his mission and fulfilled what God had wanted—to completely unite with Jesus—the prophecy of Zech. 8:7-8 and 20-23 would have come true. The Jews would not have suffered the way they did, and human history would have been different.

The Mission of John the Baptist

Why did Jesus say John the Baptist was Elijah? In Zech. 8:7-8 and 8:20-23, there is a prophecy about God and His plan for His people, which was to be accomplished during the time of John the Baptist and Jesus. It says:

> Thus says the Lord of hosts: Behold, I will save my people from the east country and from the west country; and I will bring them to dwell in the midst of Jerusalem; and they shall be my people and I will be their God, in faithfulness and in righteousness (Zech. 8:7-8).

Zech. 8:20-23 says:

> People shall yet come, even the inhabitants of many cities; the inhabitants of one city shall go to another, saying, 'Let us go at once to entreat the favor of the Lord, and to seek the Lord of hosts; I am going.' Many peoples and strong nations shall come to seek the Lord of hosts in Jerusalem, and to entreat the favor of the Lord. Thus says the Lord of hosts: 'In those days, ten men from the nations of every tongue shall take hold of the robe of a Jew, saying, 'Let us go with you, for we have heard that God is with you.'"

By reading the above prophecy, we can see Zechariah received this vision approximately 500 years before Jesus. In his vision, Zechariah emphasized the restored Jewish community that was to come. These visions revealed God's plan to bring a great blessing to the Jewish people. God clearly told his people of the great blessings He would bestow on them. They will be His most special people. People of other nations will be begging to have a Jew in their midst so they, too, could be blessed. The Jewish people were meant to be the most precious, most blessed and advanced people in the world. Had they listened and obeyed their God and believed and accepted Jesus Christ, they would have been blessed. But, instead, they were caught sleeping! They were so occupied with other matters and political issues the messiah's imminent coming wasn't a priority at the time.

It is like Christianity today! The United States, which is considered the center and leading nation of Christianity, has been asleep as well. The country is in dire straits. Americans are so busy, occupied by wars and divided politically at home and abroad there is hardly any concern for Jesus' return or the End Times.

Christians are also divided in their views about God and the return of Christ. They, too, are occupied with competing at home and abroad over denominations and spreading the gospel to other nations, just as the Israelites did. The priority focus of Christians is on matters other than the return of Christ. They don't think the Messiah will return anytime soon!

After Zechariah, God sent the prophet Malachi. The 400 years between Malachi and Jesus' birth was the period God used to prepare the chosen people and the world for the Messiah's arrival. During Jesus' time, the world was prepared and had become polarized between a godless Cain-type Roman Empire in the West and multiple developing religious cultures in the East. Jerusalem stood in the middle of these two worlds.

God sent Malachi with another prophecy, informing the Israelites of the coming of the Messiah and the return of Elijah.

> Remember the law of my servant Moses, the statutes and ordinances that I commanded him at Horeb for all Israel. Behold, I will send you Eli'jah the prophet before the great and terrible day of the Lord comes. And he will turn the hearts of fathers to their children, and the hearts of children to their fathers, lest I come and smite the land with a curse (Mal. 4:4-6).

Malachi, in the above quote, reminded the Israelites of God's promise to them that the Messiah would soon arrive. He also gave them a clear sign when and how He would send the Messiah. He would send the prophet Elijah back to Earth to help prepare for His coming.

How could John the Baptist miss the most important point of his mission and not recognize Jesus as the Messiah!? Despite everything God did, what happened to Zechariah's testimony? Wasn't he told by the angel that his son, John, will be given the mission of Elijah?

> And he [John] will go before him in the spirit and power of Eli'jah, to turn the hearts of the fathers to the children and the disobedient to the wisdom of the just—to make ready for the Lord a people prepared (Luke 1:17).

Read Mal.4:5-6 again and notice how identical it is to Luke 1:17.

Let's look at Zechariah's own prophecy regarding his son, John. "And you, child [John] will be called the prophet of the Most High; for you will go before the Lord to prepare his ways" (Luke 1:76).

Even though John flatly denied he was Elijah, we can see through his choice of clothing that he completely imitated Elijah's lifestyle. Let's look at the following two biblical verses.

> Now John wore a garment of camel's hair, and a leather girdle around his waist, and his food was locusts and wild honey (Matt. 3:4).
>
> "They answered him, 'He wore a garment of haircloth, with a girdle of leather about his loins.' And he said, 'It is Eli'jah the Tishbite" (2 Kings 1:8).

It seems rather odd, that despite all the signs and miracles that were invested in John the Baptist, and despite the fact he once confessed he was sent to make straight the path for the Lord, he still refused to accept he was Elijah! "For this is he [John] who was spoken of by the prophet Isaiah when he said, 'the voice of one crying in the wilderness: Prepare the way of the Lord, make his paths straight'" (Matt. 3:3).

What happened to John? Why did he deny being Elijah when he dressed like him, lived like a beggar in the desert and did the work of Elijah? What more does John need to convince himself that Jesus was right about him?

Malachi warned God would "strike the land with a curse" if Elijah was not heeded. Jesus indicated the people did not recognize John as Elijah, and, as a result, Jesus was going to suffer at their hands. By denying he was Elijah, would not John bear the burden of the responsibility for that circumstance?

Many Christians, when they heard about John, said: "But John was a good saint. He had already testified to Jesus, what more could he have done?" They point to the biblical verse where John gave his testimony:

> "And John bore witness, 'I saw the Spirit descend as a dove from heaven, and it remained on him. I myself did not

> know him, but He who sent me to baptize with water said to me, 'He on whom you see the Spirit descend and remain, this is he who baptizes with the Holy Spirit.' And I have seen and borne witness that this is the Son of God'" (John 1:32-34).

Also, John the Baptist, when speaking about the Messiah, said, he, himself was "not worthy to untie" His sandals (John 1:27). Despite the spiritual vision, he heard God's voice telling him who Jesus was and saw the dove descend and remain on Jesus. John testified to it all, but, in the end, he lost his faith and became one of history's worst failures!

As John moved away from his responsibility, Satan came and invaded him! He pushed John out of his mission's priority and got him involved in a political controversy, which, eventually, got him in trouble with King Herod. He was put in jail and later beheaded (Mark 6:14-29). Because of John's failure, Jesus had nowhere to go. John also made Jesus appear to be a liar and turned the people of Israel against Jesus (Matt. 17:10-11 and Matt. 17:12-13).

Let's look at John 1:19-23:

> "And this is the testimony of John, when the Jews sent priests and Levites from Jerusalem to ask him, 'Who are you?' He confessed, he did not deny, but confessed, 'I am not the Christ.' And they asked him, 'What then? Are you Eli'jah?' He said, 'I am not.' 'Are you the prophet?' And, he answered, 'No.' They said to him then, 'Who are you? Let us have an answer for those who sent us. What do you say about yourself?' He said, 'I am the voice of one crying in the wilderness: 'Make straight the way of the Lord,' as the prophet Isaiah said.'"

We must understand John created a big problem for the Israelites when he denied he was Elijah. This only tells us that John, despite all the confessions he made about Jesus, didn't really mean the things he said. It's as if the Holy Spirit pushed him to testify about Jesus against his will! John would not have testified otherwise! This shows John must have struggled with the same problems as the Israelites: How could Jesus be the Messiah if

Elijah had not come? And, worst yet, John, like the scribes, judged Jesus externally and accused him of being all sorts of things.

John had a great national impact on the people of Israel. In Matt. 16:13-14, the Israelites saw him as a great prophet. Some saw him as Elijah and others thought he might be the Messiah. John's influence and power had even reached King Herod (Mark 6:19-20).

Had John done his mission effectively, he would have influenced the Jewish people and persuaded them to follow Christ. Jesus would not have died a merciless death on the cross. God's plan would have been completed successfully and the Jewish people would have scattered all over the world! What's more important is the Kingdom of God would have been established on Earth and the world today would be a joyful and peaceful place.

When John was in prison, he sent his disciples to Jesus to ask the following question: "Are you he who is to come, or shall we look for another?" (Matt. 11:2-3).

From this verse, we understand that John was confused. Jesus was offended by John's question and answered in the following manner:

> "'Go and tell John what you hear and see: the blind receive their sight and the lame walk, lepers are cleansed and the deaf hear, and the dead are raised up, and the poor have good news preached to them. And blessed is he who takes no offense at me'" (Matt.11:4-6).

After the disciples left, Jesus began to talk to the crowd that gathered around him, saying:

> "Why then did you go out? To see a prophet? Yes, I tell you, and more than a prophet. This is he of whom it is written, 'Behold, I send my messenger before thy face, who shall prepare thy way before thee.' Truly, I say to you, among those born of women there has risen no one greater than John the Baptist; yet he who is least in the kingdom of heaven is greater than he. From the days of John the Baptist until now the kingdom of heaven has suffered violence, and men of violence take it by force. For all the

> prophets and the law prophesied until John; and if you are willing to accept it, he is Eli'jah who is to come. He, who has ears to hear, let him hear. (Matt. 11:9-15).

Christians have held the strong belief John the Baptist is one of the greatest saints because they only looked at his testimony to Jesus: "Truly, I say to you, among those born of women there has risen no one greater than John the Baptist; yet he who is least in the kingdom of heaven is greater than he" (Matt. 11:11).

In truth, John was the greatest of all the prophets. Why? Because he was the one who would not only testify from the other side of the street, causing friction between his and Jesus' disciples (John 3:22-30), but he should have been Jesus' right-hand man and chief disciple. Other prophets could only prophesy from a long time before him, which is why John was greater than a prophet.

Christians conveniently overlooked the rest of Jesus' statement about John, which says, "yet he who is least in the kingdom of heaven is greater than he" (Matt. 11:11). I am shocked that even my favorite talk show host, Bill O'Reilly, former political commentator and host of Fox News Channel's "The O'Reilly Factor," missed that point. In his book, *Killing Jesus* (2013), he seemed to deliberately stop in the middle of that verse and skipped the part that states the above phrase. This is how he quoted it: "I tell you the truth: among those born of a woman, there has not risen anyone greater than John the Baptist" (O'Reilly and Dugard 2013, 150).

Period. He moved on to another topic.

What did Jesus mean when he said these words about John? How does one qualify to be placed in such a position? Jesus explained it this way: "Whoever then relaxes one of the least of these commandments and teaches men so, shall be called least in the kingdom of heaven" (Matt. 5:19).

Unfortunately, because of John's failure, the Messiah's mission was incomplete and was postponed until the Second Coming of Christ.

Now, this is important. I want to clarify something. The reason I mentioned Jesus' birth and mission at great length is not to demean or disqualify His divinity. I believe with all my heart that Jesus is my savior and the savior of all mankind. My purpose for presenting this seemingly controversial, yet thought-provoking, idea is to offer a greater understanding of God's work. Had Jesus remained alive, he would have brought the complete salvation that was foretold, and His return would not be necessary. Jesus said a new truth would be given, and he hinted this truth would not be easily accepted. He said:

> I have yet many things to say to you, but you cannot bear them now. When the Spirit of truth comes, he will guide you into all truth; for he will not speak on his own authority, but whatever he hears he will speak, and he will declare to you the things that are to come (John 16:12-13).

CHAPTER 17

Hidden Patterns in the Bible

Thousands of years have passed since the books of the Bible were canonized and became the Bible we know today. Little do we know, however, that the Bible contains hidden truths. These truths are encoded in the Old Testament, and no one knows what they are except for Christ who will reveal them at His Second Coming.

This may not be the case, however. During Moon's early years of intense Bible study, ardent prayers and anguish questions to God, one of the many revelations he received were two significant providential patterns or modal courses God used repeatedly within Old Testament stories. These patterns could only be hinting at some extraordinary clues that can be applied as lessons of some sort. I must add, Moon did not study theology or philosophy in school or with any teacher. God chose him to reveal the new expression of truth in the forms of revelations. God answered his prayers, revealing to him these repeated patterns were indeed being used by God to resolve an issue related to each of the providential families. The first is the "Three Blessings" found in Gen. 1:28, which is repeated in every providential central figure. The second is the older brother/younger brother, or Cain and Abel, pattern. We can find this pattern repeated in Adam's family between Cain and Abel; Ham and Sham in Noah's family; Ishmael and Isaac in Abraham's family; and Jacob and Esau in Isaacs' family. Genesis 38 reported a very fascinating story on Tamara, which I will talk about in an upcoming chapter, but the interesting part is her twins. While she was in labor, the two brothers, Zerah and Perez, began to wrestle within her womb to determine who would come out first. Zerah sticks his hand out of the womb and a red cord is tied around his wrist as a mark he came out first. Suddenly, Zerah was pulled back inside the womb and Perez emerged before Zerah. Yet, the best example of the younger brother/older brother pattern is found is Rebecca's story, told in Gen. 25:21-26. Rebecca's twins, Jacob and Esau, were wrestling in her womb. When Rebecca asked the Lord why this is happening, the Lord said, "Two nations are in your womb, and two peoples, born of you, shall be divided; the one shall be stronger than the other the elder shall serve the younger" (Gen. 25:23). This pattern was carried out in Abraham's family between Ishmael and Isaac, extended to Isaac's family between Jacob and Esau, and believe it or not, continued to Zechariah's family between Jesus and John the Baptist. One would ask, why is this pattern repeated throughout the Old Testament if not to teach us something important? In the upcoming chapters, I will be talking at great length on these subjects. However, before I talk about these patterns, I would like to present to you the first and most important pattern, the Three Blessings.

CHAPTER 18

The Three Great Blessings

The Blueprint of Creation

Gen. 1:28: God's Most Important Commandment for Humanity

It is extremely important we understand the true meaning of Gen. 1:28, which talks about the three great blessings God bestowed on Adam and Eve before their fall. It answers questions about what caused their fall and changed their bloodline from what supposed to be God's bloodline to that of Satan's bloodline. Therefore, we must understand why the Bible, in both Matt 23:33 and John 8:44, implies we are a brood of vipers and children of Satan. In this chapter, I will speak about the meaning of the three blessings as they were revealed to the Rev. Sun Myung Moon. These are meanings no Christian, Jew or Muslim had ever noticed before. The story of the fall is the story of what had happened to Adam and Eve, God's children.

For thousands of years, Jews, Christians and Muslims believed in the story of the Garden of Eden, but it never dawned on them to ask, "What if not? What if Adam and Eve did not disobey God and did not eat the forbidden fruit? What kind of a story would it have been?" Surely, Adam and Eve, as well as the archangel, would not have been thrown out of the garden and would have remained one with God. There would have been no religions, churches, temples or mosques, and no need for a Messiah. Adam and Eve would have consummated their marriage, with God at its center, and would have formed God's "first" family, thus filling the Earth with children of goodness. This is what God had envisioned for Adam and Eve. Think about it. If we, as human beings, live purposeful lives, have hopes, dreams, visions, and plans for our lives, what about God? God, too, must have had a plan and a vision he wanted Adam and Eve to fulfill. God, too, must have had planned to have a substantial "family" on Earth to give him everlasting joy and happiness, just as a married couple would have hoped and desired to accomplish from their marriage: a loving family with good children. The Three Great Blessings are the hope and plan God had desired from Adam and Eve.

> "And God blessed them, and God said to them, 'Be fruitful and multiply, and fill the earth and subdue it; and have dominion over the fish of the sea, and over the birds of the air, and over every living thing that moves upon the earth'" (Gen. 1:28).

Gen. 1:28 was God's primary "plan," and the commandment God clearly instructed Adam and Eve to fulfill. The "Three Great Blessings" were God's blueprint. In other words, before building a house, one must have a blueprint to follow. What then is the blueprint of the creation God revealed to Moon? The Principles of the Creation chapter in the Divine Principle gives detailed explanations of this blueprint of the creation, answers the fundamental questions about life and the universe, and how and for what purpose God created the universe. As the chapter stated:

> "The fundamental questions about life and the universe cannot be finally resolved without understanding the nature of God, the creator. This is so because in order to understand and solve the problems concerning any resultant being we must first understand the causal being. So, in order to answer the most basic questions about all resultant beings, we must first understand the nature of God, the Creator, and the principles (blueprint) by which he created the world" (Divine Principle Green Book, Page 3).

This chapter gives a thorough scientific study of nature very much like a forensic investigation in search of clues. It begins by studying and observing nature.

Two thousand years ago, one of Jesus' disciples, Saint Paul, was debating with a group of atheists who demanded he show them God. He replied: "Ever since the creation of the world his invisible nature, namely, his eternal power and deity, has been clearly perceived in the things that have been made. So they are without excuse" (Rom. 1:20). As we examine the creation, we find there are two different dual characteristics in the creation. This may sound simple, but if we dig deeper, we find more interesting things. The first set is Plus and Minus/Male and Female, or positivity and negativity. The second set is the invisible internal character-nature and external forms, such as shapes and structures. These characteristics exist in all creatures. However, Man was God's favorite of all creations. Gen. 1:27 tells us we, human beings, were created in the image and likeness of God. Since God is the first cause of all beings, and each being has dual characteristics (Rom. 1:20), God, too, must have these dual characteristics within Him. Having discovered these dual characteristics in the creation, the question that is asked is do these beings exist as individuals, separately and unrelated to one another, or do they have a reciprocal relationship? Although everyone seems to exist independently, the entire creation originates from the Ideal of God, who is the being of harmonized dual characteristics. Therefore, each created being does not exist independently but is created to exist through a reciprocal relationship. How do reciprocal relationships function and what drives them? The Divine Principle call these forces "Universal Prime Force—Give and Take Action." In God's Ideal Formula, these dual characteristics are sorted into Subject and Object positions. The Subject takes the upper position to the Object. The ideal reciprocal relationship is established when the subject and object have a good giving-and-receiving relationship. This is initiated by the Universal Prime Force and is called a give-and-take action. When the subject and object aspects within a being and between beings are engaged in give and take, all the forces necessary for its existence, reproduction and action are generated. The creation was to be a perfect object to God, who is the subject. In Matt. 5:48, Jesus commanded us to be perfect as God is perfect. How then can an individual grow to perfection? What was God's plan for perfection? When an individual engages in a reciprocal relationship of give and take with God, he or she becomes a perfect object to God and one with God's will. God, therefore, becomes the center of his or her thinking (John 14:20). The fact God gave the first human beings (Adam and Eve) his commandment (Gen. 2:17) means Man was created to respond to God by keeping that commandment. Let us consider the following few examples on the principles of Subject-Object and Give-Take forces. In the individual, the mind is the subject and the body is the object – the body cannot function without proper give and take with the mind. In the family, the husband is the subject and the wife is the object. Important! This is not a value judgment. It is set this way by God's Principle (although in certain conditions, the wife can stand in the subject position). In the family, the parents are the subjects and children are the objects. In school, the teacher is subject, and the student is the object. In employment, the employer is the subject, and the employee is the object. Why is it important to understand these dual characteristics? When an ideal man and an ideal woman enter a reciprocal relationship of love that is centered on God's ideal, they form an eternal foundation of power. This foundation is called the *Four Position Foundation*. The *Four Position Foundation* is the foundation upon which God can operate. It is also the foundation of goodness through which the purpose of God's creation is accomplished. Now, you might ask, why am I speaking at length about this subject? It is because this is God's original plan and formula. God has a fundamental purpose for all these dual characteristics and how they should function to realize his ideal. God created Adam and Eve with a mind and a body for a greater purpose than themselves. Adam and Eve were meant to have a proper vertical give and take with God individually.

Now, let us continue with our main topic on the Three Great Blessings.

Unfortunately, established religions misunderstood the proper meaning of this Bible verse. Judeo-Christian and Islamic educators of the scriptures have overlooked this verse, and, oftentimes, have misinterpreted its meaning. All the problems in the world have occurred because we did not realize this plan. If you look at the world today, it's situation is dire. We long for peace and harmony but can't keep away from conflict and war. We long for love and affection but keep getting tangled up in selfishness, jealousy, greed and materialism. Free sex and false love have saturated the world, and the breakdown of families and divorce has become the norm in many Western countries. Even the Earth has suffered great abuse. We have overused its bountiful resources to the point of polluting it and damaging the ozone layer. The result is climate change, which is the main source of most of the natural disasters the planet has endured over the last three decades. This is the reality of our world today. We need to take a closer look at the meaning behind each of the blessings of Gen. 1:28. As we have learned from what is written in the verse, there are three blessings God bestowed upon humanity: Be fruitful, multiply and take dominion.

Let us take the first blessing: "Be fruitful." What does it mean? Generally, Jews, Christians and Muslims understood it to mean "have children." But, this is not the true meaning. The Divine Principle explains the true meaning of the first blessing "is "Be perfect," or, for a better word, be mature. As we read the Bible verse, after God created the world and saw it was good, He created his masterpiece—humans. He created them in His own image and blessed them. His first commandment to Adam and Eve for each one to grow to perfection and reach spiritual and physical maturity by having a united mind and body centered on God's will and direction. There is a reason God created humans with the dual characteristics of mind and body. As explained earlier, for any human to reach maturity, his or her mind and body must engage in a reciprocal relationship of give and take. The mind is the subject because it directs the body. The mind is also God's command tower and the temple of God. It is where God dwells and where He communicates with humanity. In a way, our consciousness is God! "Do you not know that you are God's temple and God's spirit dwells in you?" (1 Cor. 3:16).

The first blessing was the "model formula" and system by which humans should develop their spiritual maturity, character and individual perfection. It is the foundation on which God can build His ideal—a God-centered family. Simply speaking, had Adam and Eve fulfilled this first blessing, the other two blessings, "Multiply and Take Dominion," would have been automatically fulfilled and the world would have been totally different. It would have been the most wonderful and joyful world one could imagine.

Adam and Eve were each meant to maintain a proper give and take between mind and body. Because uniting their minds and bodies centered on God, which meant becoming one with Him in heart, they would have fulfilled God's first plan. They would have become mature individuals with a divine nature and be as perfect as God (Matt. 5:48). When a person achieves God's first blessing, he will naturally share God's feelings as his or her own. He or she reaches perfection and becomes the temple of God (1 Cor. 3:16) and one with God (John 14:20). The perfect example of this is Jesus Christ (Matt. 5:48). Therefore, the first blessing was God's first and most important commandment for Adam and Eve before marriage. The whole idea behind the first blessing is to enable Adam and Eve to reach maturity in body and in character to understand and fulfill their portion of responsibility before marriage.

Not long after God blessed Adam and Eve with the three great blessings, He commanded them to not to eat from the "tree of the knowledge of good and evil ... for in the day that you eat of it you shall die" (Gen. 2:17). Traditionally, Jews, Christians and Muslims have believed "be fruitful" meant to have children, and their views on the second blessing, "to multiply," meant they were to "have more children." As noted earlier, the true meaning of "be fruitful" is to reach perfection.

No wonder God gave his three blessings to man, not one, but four, times: First to Adam and Eve (Gen. 2:18); then Noah (Gen. 9:1); then Abraham (Gen. 22:17); and, finally, Abraham's grandson, Jacob (Gen. 26: 24). The pattern is clear. God wanted Adam and Eve to multiply righteous offspring for him. Had this happened, God would have been able to fill the Earth with good and sinless people capable of taking dominion over creation with God's love and care, thus fulfilling the third blessing. Unfortunately, as we can see from the circumstances of our world today, we don't have a peaceful world because mankind is not perfect (Matt. 5:48) and did not become God's Temple (1 Cor. 3:16).

CHAPTER 19

The Miracle of the Human Body

The Human Body Is an Engineering Marvel

I am baffled by how so-called educated people, such as scientists, could say that humans evolved from monkeys. I don't think any of the human systems we will examine evolved or were added after birth. According to the Bible, humans were created in God's image, with no organs to be evolved or added. While researching the miracles of the human body, I stumbled upon a very interesting documentary video. It featured Dr. Mark Reisman, a cardiologist at the Swedish Medical Center in Seattle and was coproduced by BioMedia Associates in South Carolina and NASA. According to the video, there are seven vital systems in the body: cardiovascular; digestive and renal; nervous; reproductive; respiratory; sensory and skeletal. If one of these systems is not functioning properly, the body cannot fulfill its purpose. As we shall see, each system plays a major part in keeping the body healthy.

1. **Cardiovascular system**: At the center of the cardiovascular system is the heart. The heart is a muscular organ that is a bioengineering marvel. It works flawlessly, 24 hours a day, seven days a week, over the course of an individual's life. The heart delivers blood to all parts of the body through a vast network of arteries and veins.

2. **Digestive and renal systems:** The body needs food and water, and through an almost miraculous sequence of mechanical and chemical processes, it converts food into the nutrients that will eventually sustain everything the body does.

3. **Nervous system:** The nervous system starts with the brain, extends down the spinal cord, and connects to every part of the body through a vast network of nerves called the peripheral nervous system. At the heart of this system is the neuron, a specialized cell that carries electrical impulses along neural pathways.

4. **Reproductive system:** One of the body's major systems, the organs and structures in this system are different in men and women. There is no greater miracle on the planet than creating a new life. In the video, Reisman explains each stage of this miracle, including the genetic basis of life, development of sex organs, the formation of sex cells, conception, the emergence of the embryo, growth sequence of the fetus, and, finally, birth.

5. **Respiratory system:** Breathing brings oxygen into the lungs. Deep inside the lungs, the oxygen is transferred into the bloodstream and used to power the muscles, including those that produce breathing. Reisman takes the viewer through the structures of the air passageway, the anatomy and physiology of the lungs, and, in the end, reveals the mechanism of the gas exchange between the respiratory and cardiovascular systems.

6. **Sensory System:** The human body has five senses: touch, taste, smell, hearing and sight. They have evolved independently over millions of years and are brought together by the central nervous system to allow us to interact with the planet's environment. Reisman provides a look at the anatomy and physiology of each of these senses and explains how the brain uses each to its fullest.

7. **Skeletal System:** The 206 bones of the human skeleton are a miracle of bioengineering. Lightweight, but incredibly strong, our bones give us the ability to walk upright, which frees our hands for precise manipulation of objects.

Human Body: A Model for an Ideal Society

On the spiritual side, we also found a profound spiritual functioning system that governs the inner aspect of human life, such as ethics, love and morality. As we have learned in the previous section, all the organs work together to keep the body healthy. Looking deeper into the seven systems, we also discover there is a hierarchy of systems. As I researched the human spiritual aspect, in addition to the Holy Scriptures, I discovered CAUSA International (Confederation of the Associations for the Unification of the Societies of the Americas), an anti-communist educational organization created in 1980 by the Rev. Sun Myung Moon. CAUSA was founded to give Latin Americans an ideological framework in their struggle against communism. Chapters were formed in 21 Central and South American countries, and there are several chapters in Europe, Asia, Africa and the United States. Its headquarters is in Washington, D.C. By comparing the body's systems to that of the model for an ideal society, CAUSA presents the best explanation for the spiritual aspects of man.

No one has seen the original world that God intended because it was never realized. Therefore, it is difficult to envision. Yet, we find this model in the human body. As we read earlier, the body is composed of many organs and billions of cells. Each cell works harmoniously toward a common goal, and there is no conflict. A right arm does not quarrel with the left; the legs move the body wherever it wants to go. Although the mouth enjoys the taste of food, it is a hand that brings the food to the mouth without any complaining. Why do all the parts of the body work in harmony? There are two important factors. The first, which was mentioned earlier, is the entire body has one purpose: Every part is working for the body's well-being, while, at the same time, benefitting from the whole. The second factor is there is one center of coordination: the brain. It gives proper communication and coordination, so the body can function accordingly. If you see the body in this way, it provides an example of how an ideal society could function. In a God-centered ideal, the whole society functions like the body. First, there is a common purpose, which is the very intention of God's creation—joy, peace and happiness for all. Everyone works for this goal and reaps its benefits (CAUSA 181, paraphrased).

CHAPTER 20

Christian-Muslim and Jewish Struggles

Cain and Abel Struggle—Favorite Son

The Muslim, Jewish and Christian struggles cannot be understood nor resolved without understanding its original cause. This is so, because, throughout history, mankind only looked at the conflict externally, for example, through politics, economics and religious and racial disparities. As we will explore in the coming pages, the chapter on Cain and Abel will answer the question about the origin of conflict in the three Abrahamic religions. The real issue of division and misunderstanding started back in the Garden of Eden. The struggle between Cain and Abel – the older brother/younger brother scenario—continued into the families of Noah and Abraham, and, eventually, into Zechariah's family with John the Baptist and Jesus.

As noted earlier, the commonalities between these faiths are as numerous as the divisions. However, when it comes to the Holy Scriptures, they diverge somewhat. According to Islam, the Bible is, in fact, a misrepresentation on the part of the Judeo-Christian tradition of God's exact revelation. Muslims argued the exact revelation is in the Qur'an.

The difference of opinion is related to which of the two sons Abraham had almost sacrificed to God. Is it Isaac, as the Bible said, or is it Ishmael as the Muslims claim?

According to the Muslims, it was obvious is the son who Abraham was willing to offer to God was Ishmael. As we learned in the chapter on Cain and Abel, the problem of sibling rivalry became the formula for how God dealt with this issue by setting a "pattern" to resolve it. It is important to understand this issue has been the chief cause of conflicts among the religions. Therefore, I believe the explanation on the Cain and Abel Formula Course in the following chapter, if understood, will solve this problem.

The question of which son is God's favorite is strongly expressed in each religion's theology: Isaac for the Jews, Ishmael for the Muslims and Jesus for the Christians. Whoever is chosen as the favorite will be the automatic heir and become God's most beloved.

As we will learn from the Cain and Abel chapter, the position of the younger son, who would inherit God's blessing, is extremely important. This is why Christian and Jewish fundamentalists demean Islam, saying Ishmael is the illegitimate son of Abraham, not the real heir. Hagar, a slave woman, bore Ishmael. Little did Jews and Christians realize that God bestowed His blessing on Ishmael, too!

I don't know why Jews and Christians do not recognize this because it is clearly expressed in Gen. 17:20. Although the Bible does state it was Isaac who Abraham almost sacrificed, and it would be he who would inherit Abraham's blessing, God did not discriminate. "As for Ish'mael, I have heard you; behold, I will bless him and make him fruitful and multiply him exceedingly; he shall be the father of twelve princes and I will make him a great nation" (Gen 17:20).

I feel like O'Reilly, arguing the case of the "favorite son." When Abraham said to God in Gen. 17:18-19, "O that Ish'mael might live in thy sight! God answered, 'No, but …" This does not mean that God wanted Ishmael and his descendants to vanish from the Earth. If that were the case, God would have said, "No," or He could have chosen not to interfere and let Ishmael die of thirst in the desert. That way, He would have saved Himself and humanity from enduring so much pain and suffering, and Islam would never have been founded.

Obviously, the conflict between Muslims, Jews and Christians is a "family" problem that had to do with God's younger brother-older brother restoration pattern. Because of a misunderstanding, however, it turned into bitter jealousy and envy! Which son would inherit God's everlasting covenant?

Cain and Abel Formula Course

Remember the older brother-young brother pattern I spoke about earlier? Well, this it!

From the dawn of history, there have been stories of sibling rivalry, and those mentioned in the Old Testament have never been fully understood. For Jews, "salvation" is not what Christians understand it to be: believe in Jesus and you will be saved. The Jewish idea of salvation contains two elements, purity of the bloodline and birthright.

Theologians, religious leaders and devout believers have read these Bible stories many times without discovering anything different than from what they knew and understood: Cain committed the first murder by killing his younger brother, Abel. Some theologians even questioned why these passages were included in the Bible. No one seemed to have an answer to that question. Except for the Rev. Moon. He said key Bible codes, which had been kept hidden for centuries, had been revealed to him in form of revelations during a period of vigil prayers. The new revelation decoded a pattern, or formula, that God had used many times to try and resolve two significant, but distinct, spiritual "dysfunctional orders": family dysfunction and sibling rivalry between the younger brother and older brother and the change of blood lineage from Satan to God.

In this chapter, we will examine how God used this pattern, starting with Adam's family and Cain and Abel and continuing with Jesus and John the Baptist.

Large parts of the Bible contain secrets that God revealed to Moon. Every event and every bit of narrative not only tells us what happened at a time in history but also how God intervened! Stories, such as Adam and Eve in the Garden of Eden, Cain and Abel, Noah and the Flood, and Abraham and his family, contain clues to hidden meanings and how God worked His formula to resolve issues with these families.

The Pattern in the Cain and Abel Formula Course

Before I begin talking about the topics of the new revelation, I would like to ask readers to have a Bible in hand and read the verses mentioned in these next sections.

The Divine Principle unveiled a Bible secret that pertained to God's providence of salvation to resolve the Cain/Abel struggle.

Because God could not work directly with Adam—he embodied both God and Satan—God promised in Isa. 46:11: "I have spoken, and I will bring it to pass; I have purposed, and I will do it." Right after the Fall of Adam and Eve, God symbolically divided Adam into two sons and placed them in two positions, one representing good and the other representing evil. Cain, the older son, represented evil, and Abel, the younger son, represented good. Important! These positions (Cain and Abel) are not to be taken literally as a value judgment.

As we read the Bible, we question God's intentions for the seemingly unjust events that were reported in the Old Testament, such as when God chose Abel over Cain, and why God loved Jacob more than Esau, even while they were still in their mother's womb. People would read these stories and wonder why. But, because of their faith and love for God, they did not question God's supremacy. God began his pattern immediately after the Fall. After setting up this arrangement, God had the two sons offer sacrifices separately. Then, he decided which should represent good, and which should represent evil. If we re-examine their situations carefully, we discover both sons, Cain and Abel, were the results of Eve's fall, and the question of who would represent good and who would represent evil depended on the Fall of Eve.

If you remember from the Fall of Man chapter, the fall was caused by a sexual act. Eve was involved in two forbidden sexual acts. The first was her relationship with Lucifer, which caused the spiritual fall. The second was her relationship with Adam, which caused the physical fall. Both were crimes against God. However, if we were to take a deeper look at each and question which one was closer to God's plan and, thus, more easily forgivable, it would have to be the second one.

In Gen. 3:3-7, the Bible says Eve's first fallen act was motivated by her desire to enjoy what she was not ready to enjoy. This desire led her to consummate a relationship with Lucifer, who was never going to be Eve's spouse. The second fallen act was motivated by Eve's desire to return to God's side after she realized what she had done. Moreover, even though the act was committed before the time God had set, it was a relationship with Adam, who in God's plan, would have been her spouse.

As noted in the Divine Principle, Cain and Abel were both fruits of Eve's illicit love. God "labeled" them based on Eve's illicit acts. Cain, being born of Eve's first sexual act, was chosen to represent evil. Because Abel was born of Eve's second sexual act, he represented good. This was the reason why the Bible mentions the conflict between firstborn and second-born sons. Cain and Abel's story can be found in Gen. 4:7. Gen. 9 contains the story of Ham and Sham, Noah's sons.

In Gen. 21, we find the stories of Ishmael and Isaac, and, in Gen. 25, there is the story of Jacob and Esau.

The Pattern in Noah's Family

God also attempted to use His pattern of good and evil in Noah's family. According to the Bible, approximately 10 generations after Adam, the Earth was filled with so much evil and violence God decided to send a flood. "And God said to Noah, 'I have determined to make an end of all flesh; for the earth is filled with violence through them; behold, I will destroy them and the earth'" (Gen. 6:13).

God called Noah and bestowed His blessings upon him. Just as He told Adam, he told Noah: "Be fruitful and multiply, bring forth abundantly on the earth and multiply in it" (Gen. 9:7). God also asked Noah to build an ark. As noted in the Divine Principle, Noah worked on the ark for at least 100 years (www.gotquestions.org/Noahs-ark-questions.html) in absolute obedience to God's instructions. In this sense, the time of Noah could be the "Last Days" and the second beginning of humanity!

Upon Noah's absolute obedience to God's instructions, God sent a flood to cover the entire Earth, and after 40 days, only Noah and his family were saved, along with two of every type of animal. Then, the test came. Noah's sons, Ham and Sham, were expected to re-enact the offerings made by Cain and Abel. Because Ham was Noah's second son, it was his job to restore the position of Abel and make the symbolic offering. Therefore, for Ham to stand in Abel's position, he had to become inseparably one in his father's heart. Let's examine this.

Some days after Noah completed the ark, he must have been so excited that he celebrated his accomplishment by drinking some wine, got drunk, and fell asleep naked. The Bible says Ham saw his father lying naked in his tent, felt ashamed, and was offended. Not only that, Ham managed to get his brothers, Sham and Japheth, to feel the same way. Swayed by Ham to feel ashamed, they turned their faces away. They walked backward and covered their father's body with a garment. This may seem like a righteous act, but, according to the Divine Principle, this act constituted a sin, so much so Noah rebuked Ham, cursing his son to be a slave to his brothers (Gen. 9:20-25).

One would ask: Why was it a sin to be ashamed of nakedness? To understand this, let us first understand what constitutes a sin. According to the Divine Principle:

> "Satan cannot manifest his powers—including the power to exist and act—unless he first secures an object partner with whom he can make a common base and engage in a reciprocal relationship of 'give and take.' Whenever a person makes a condition for Satan to invade, it means that he allowed himself to become Satan's object partner, thereby empowering Satan to act. This constitutes sin" (Divine Principle, Green Book, 126).

Because Ham was ashamed of his father's nakedness and covered him up, he opened the door for Satan to enter. Consequently, Ham did not pass his test. Since he could not establish the required task God had for him, the providence of restoration in Noah's family ended in failure and was prolonged until the next central figure appeared in the Bible.

The Pattern in Abraham's Family

Gen. 15:9-13 says that, after approximately 16 generations, God called Abraham and asked him to make a special offering. He gave Abraham detailed instructions on what the offering will be and how it should be prepared. God asked Abraham to sacrifice a heifer, a goat and a ram, each of which should be 3 years old, a dove and a young pigeon. Abraham brought all these animals to the altar as he was instructed. He cut them all in half except for the bird. Apparently, Abraham must have gotten tired and wasn't too concerned about it. He fell asleep.

Then, birds of prey came to feed on the carcasses, but Abraham drove them away. As the sun was setting, Abraham fell asleep and had a frightening dream-vision, a thick and dreadful darkness came over him. God must have been so displeased with Abraham. As a result, God punished him by having his descendants, the Israelites, enter Egypt and suffer slavery for 400 years. "Know of a surety that your descendants will be sojourners in a land that is not theirs, and will be slaves there, and they will be oppressed for four hundred years" (Gen. 15:13).

Why was it a sin to not divide the offering? Was it because the offering was not killed and (Satan's) blood was not shed, and because not dividing them into halves could mean he was not dividing good and evil? Without being divided, the offering could not be accepted by God because it did not provide Him with an Abel-type object partner, which He alone could accept.

Not long after Abraham failed in the symbolic offering, God called him again. This time, He commanded Abraham to sacrifice his only son, Isaac (Gen. 22:2). Abraham had a new commitment to God and his faith was absolute. Isaac was completely loyal to his father. The two of them formed the foundation for Jacob's victory over his brother, Esau.

In this way, God began a new consignment to restore Abraham's failure through "indemnity." With great and absolute faith and obedience to God's command, Abraham was about to kill Isaac. But, God intervened and told Abraham not to. "Abraham's zeal to do God's will and resolute actions, carried out with absolute faith, obedience and loyalty, lifted him up to the position God had intended (as if already having killed Isaac)" (Exposition of the Divine Principle, 1996).

Therefore, Satan was completely separated from Isaac. We must also understand when God said, "Now I know that you fear God" (Gen. 22:12), He revealed both his reproach to Abraham for his earlier failure and His joy over the successful secondary offering.

If Abraham had not failed in the first offering, Isaac, and his half-brother, Ishmael, would have stood in the position of Cain and Abel. It would have been up to them to fulfill the indemnity (restitution) condition to complete God's plan of salvation.

But, since Abraham failed, Isaac was put in Abraham's position, and Isaac's sons, Jacob and Esau, took the place of Ishmael and Isaac. So, it became their destiny to fulfill God's intended plan.

It is important, therefore, to understand the significance of Abraham's offering. It was a spiritual condition to separate good and evil. When Abraham didn't perform the symbolic offering, it was changed to human sacrifice. Burnt offerings, prayers and fasting are not what God wants to accomplish. They were only conditional.

I also want to clarify the Divine Principle's meaning of indemnity. According to the book, indemnity means restitution, suffering offered in submission and obedience to God's commands. This is why all three religions fast, pray and perform other rituals as part of their routines.

The Pattern in Jacob and Esau

The Bible tells us that Jacob and Esau began fighting while still inside their mother's womb (Gen. 25:22-23). Even then, God loved Jacob and hated Esau (Rom. 9:11-13), but we must understand this was for a reason: They were supposed to fix the mistakes Cain and Abel had made.

The story of Jacob and Esau is very significant because, for the first time, after a long and agonizing period, God finally fulfilled his long-awaited and cherished hope. He restored the proper order of things. As we will examine later, God was able to form His "chosen people," renew a covenant with them and set the foundation to send the Messiah.

Now, you might ask, what did Jacob and Esau do to give them this status? After all, Jacob, in particular, was a skillful manipulator. As seen in Gen. 27:1-14, he cheated his brother and stole his birthright. But, God's ways are not our ways! In God's view, Jacob was the root of the chosen people and in the lineage from which Moses, King David and, later, Jesus, would come.

Many theologians and religious leaders find fault with Jacob.

But, the truth was Jacob did not steal his brother's birthright. The only thing Jacob had in his heart was the burning desire to serve God and preserve his birthright.

Unlike Jacob, Esau didn't care about God or his birthright. As most of us know from the story of Jacob and Esau:

> "Esau said, 'I am about to die; of what use is a birthright to me?' Jacob said, 'Swear to me first.' So he swore to him, and sold his birthright to Jacob. Then Jacob gave Esau bread and pottage of lentils; and he ate and drank, and rose and went his way. Thus Esau despised his birthright" (Gen. 25:32-34).

Again, as we can see, in Gen. 27: 5-14, the plot to give the birthright to Jacob was devised by their mother, Rebecca. Rebecca has been misunderstood by religious scholars and put into the same classification as Tamara, Rehab, Ruth and Bathsheba.

As we will see in the coming chapters, each of these women was mistreated by the religious leaders of their time. However, through examination of their lives and deeds, we are amazed by their faith and determination to do what God had instructed them to do.

Men need to humble themselves and repent for our arrogant attitudes. Men were not the only ones to have sacrificed and served God. Women and men have contributed equally.

We read in Gen. 27: 8-13 that Jacob was worried about being caught by his father when Jacob said to his mother:

> "Behold, my brother Esau, is a hairy man, and I am a smooth man. Perhaps my father will feel me, and I shall seem to be mocking him, and bring a curse upon myself and not a blessing.' His mother said to him, 'Upon me be your curse; only obey my word, and go, fetch them to me."

Rebecca never forgot God's words when he instructed her:

> "The children struggled together within her, and she said, 'If it is thus, why do I live?' So she went to inquire of the Lord. And, the Lord said to her, 'Two nations are in your womb, and two peoples, born of you, shall be divided; the

> one shall be stronger than the other; the elder shall serve the younger.'" (Gen. 25:22-23).

Rebecca was extremely confident in saying, "Let the curse fall on me." She was not afraid to do what she had to do to make sure her younger son received the blessing.

Rebecca's victory in fulfilling God's instruction became a model that all mothers follow. As author Kevin McCarthy noted, Rebecca had set the standard of two major responsibilities. The first was keeping faith in the vision that God gave her pertaining to Jacob's future even before he was born, and the second was maintaining a close mother-son cooperation that prevented Cain from murdering Abel. That way, Satan could not do any harm to Jacob because of the bond between Jacob and his mother, Rebecca.

This mother-son cooperation was followed by Moses' mother. She helped maintain Moses' allegiance to God during the 40 years he spent living in Egypt. This pattern also was fulfilled by Mary, Jesus' mother.

CHAPTER 21

Change of Blood Lineage

The Lineage of Jesus

The Making of a New Adam: The Five Notable Women of the Bible

If we follow the biblical clues about Jesus's conception, birth and early life, we discover two obvious missing links in Jesus's life. The first is the missing 30 years. Scholars believe Jesus was born around 5 B.C. and he was crucified around 30 A.D. But, one thing to keep in mind is there is a huge gap missing in his biography. We know absolutely nothing about Jesus from the time he was 8 days old until he was in his early 30s. There is one exception, however. According to the Gospel of Luke 2:41-51, when he was 12, Jesus traveled with his parents to Jerusalem to celebrate Passover. That's it. That's all we have. Otherwise, 30 years of absolute silence. Here is arguably the most influential individual in human history and we know nothing about him until after he started his public ministry, at most, three years before his crucifixion. Something is wrong with this. As for the second missing link, this has to do with his (Jesus') parentage. Was Jesus conceived by the Holy Spirit as Christians held or did he have a biological father who is shrouded in mystery? Thus, because of this chapter's controversial content, before I begin I must say that in no way I am being disrespectful to Christians nor I am devaluing Jesus' status. In fact, I believe in Him and love him more than any prophet. Having said this, I would like to talk about the astonishing new thought-provoking concept I learned from the teachings of the Rev. Moon. I would like to talk about the hidden stories in the Bible, very much like the story of Cain and Abel we just read in the previous chapter. And, like the explanation about the Cain and Abel pattern, this chapter is a revelation received by Moon in which it explains Jesus' conception and whether he was conceived without sexual intercourse, born into the flesh sinless and pure, as Christians and Muslims held, or something else.

Many Christians, including Catholics, who are not prepared for this new provocative chapter, may, perhaps retaliate and have a hard time accepting this truth. However, when we look closely at the stories in the Bible regarding Jesus' linear background, what was revealed might be extremely shocking!

The most significant story of this nature is the one in Matt. 1:1-17, in which five notable women in Jesus' lineage are mentioned: Tamara, Rahab, Ruth, Bathsheba and Mary.

In this chapter, we will examine the pattern that God used throughout the Old Testament to purify the one who would eventually give birth to a sinless "New Adam." We will take a closer look at these clues and explore the secrets that have been hidden in the stories of the Bible's five notorious women. The entire 38th chapter of the Book of Genesis is devoted to the story of Tamara.

Among these women, there is a commonality in each of their stories. Each apparently performed questionable and immoral sexual activities. Tamara had an incestuous relationship with her father-in-law while engaged to another man. Rahab, who was a prostitute in Jericho, protected the Israelite spies from the king who sought to kill them (Josh. 2:1-6). Furthermore, Rahab is the mother of Boaz, who was a part of Jesus' lineage (Matt. 1:1-5). Ruth tempted Boaz on the bedroom floor while she was engaged to a close kinsman. From Ruth and Boaz's marriage came Obed, father of Jesse, who was King David's father (Ruth 4:1-22). Bathsheba was involved in an adulterous relationship with King David while married to Uriah (one of King David's generals), and she gave birth to Solomon (2 Sam. 11:2-4), who was in Jesus' lineage (Matt. 1:1-6). Finally, there is Mary, who became pregnant with Jesus while engaged to Joseph.

One would ask: Why would the scriptures preserve only the names of the women in Jesus' lineage involved in what appears to be decadent and immoral behaviors? Why would an entire chapter of Genesis be devoted to the story of a woman who deceived her father-in-law into having sex with her? These stories could only support the Divine Principle's new revelation on how God worked

His pattern to purify the lineage of Jesus. Let us not be mistaken! These women did what they had to do because they were influenced by a source beyond them. That source was for providential reasons, which manifested to re-create a new, sinless Adam.

Tamara

The story of Tamara is a very remarkable and exemplary story of how God performed his pattern of purifying the blood lineage. In Gen. 38, we read that Tamara married Judah's oldest son, Er. However, the Bible said Er "was wicked in the sight of the Lord" (Gen. 38:7), so God puts Er to death. Then, Er is never mentioned again. In response to Er's death, Judah gave Tamara to his next oldest son, Onan. According to tradition, the closest relative of the deceased would take the widow as his spouse.

Onan accepted Tamara as his wife, but he seemed rather reluctant to have children with her (Gen. 38:9). Onan knew the offspring would not be his. Therefore, whenever he would have sex with his brother's wife, he would spill his semen on the ground to keep from producing offspring that would be his brother's children. God was very disappointed with Onan's behavior. What he was doing was wicked in the Lord's sight, so He also put him to death (Gen. 38:10).

One would ask why God punished Onan so severely for spilling his semen. According to Kevin McCarthy, this verse has served as an admonition from God for all those men who were tempted to commit such a sin. However, the verse's meaning is far more significant. If the truth is known, there have been many "wicked men" in history, yet God did not put them to death as swiftly as he did Onan. Obviously, God had a very intense interest in cultivating a ripened "seed" from the tribe of Judah, which would develop in the fertile womb of Tamara.

God spent countless generations trying to create a "true seed" and worked hard to prepare the good fertile ground. As McCarthy noted, God's primary will was to produce His own uncontested lineage. It will spring forth from the tribe of Judah through Tamara's womb. As noted in Matt. 1:1-17, from Tamara's womb, Christ will come 40 generations later.

Tamara's story is very remarkable. Her undivided passion to fulfill what God had planted in her heart was so powerful. Nothing deterred her from accomplishing His will. Even the fear of death would not stop her! After Onan's death, the next person in line for Tamara's hand is Judah's youngest son, Shelah. Judah told Tamara, however, she would have to wait until Shelah became a man before they could marry. Gen. 38:11 reveals that Judah is secretly concerned about the fate of his last son. Apparently, Judah was suspicious of Tamara. He was concerned his son's deaths were Tamara's fault.

As time passed, Tamara realized Judah was never going to give Shelah to her. Desperate, she hatched a plan. Tamara was getting old—she was probably in her late 40s—and the chance of getting pregnant was getting slimmer. She decided she had one last chance to receive the providential seed. She also knew she would have to risk her life because if she became pregnant and people found out about it, she would surely face a horrible death!

So, Tamara disguised herself as a prostitute and waited for Judah, who was on his way to visit a friend. Judah approached her and suggested they have sex together. Tamara agreed. The price she asked for required him to leave some sort of identification until he returned with the payment (a young goat). She asked for his cord, seal and his staff, which were the equivalent to modern-day documents of identification. She said she would hold these items until he returned.

Months later, Judah discovers his daughter-in-law is pregnant. Judah immediately condemns her to be burned to death. Tamara sends a message to Judah saying, "'By the man to whom these belong, I am with child,' she said. And, she said, 'Mark, I pray you, whose these are, the signet and the cord and the staff'" (Gen. 38:25). Judah realizes they are his and says, "She has been more righteous than I, inasmuch as I did not give her to my son Shelah" (Gen. 38:26).

The reason we remember Tamara is because no woman in history touched God's heart as deeply as she did. Tamara fulfilled God's long-awaited wish. Remember the stories of Jacob and Esau and Cain and Abel? They are repeated through Tamara's womb!

Tamara was pregnant with twins. Tamara's sons, Zerah and Perez, began to fight while inside the womb over who would be the first to come out. Zerah sticks his hand out first and a red cord is tied around his wrist to signify he was first. Zerah was the firstborn, and is, therefore, in the Cain-Esau position. Then something unprecedented happens: the two brothers changed positions inside the womb and Perez emerged ahead of Zerah! Exactly 40 generations later, Mary received the blessing of the Holy Spirit and Jesus was conceived inside her womb. Mary's faith and circumstance mirrored that of Tamara.

Other Women in the Bible

Before we begin Mary's story, let us take a quick look at the stories of other important women in the Bible. Remember, Tamara had an incestuous relationship with Judah, her father-in-law, while promised to Shelah.

Rahab: According to the Book of Joshua, Rahab was a prostitute in Jericho. The king of Jericho told Rahab to watch for any Hebrew spies who might be wandering through the city. Instead, Rahab hid them from the king's soldiers. Later, when Jericho is destroyed, only Rahab and her family survived. She eventually becomes the wife of Salmon, who is of the tribe of Judah.

Ruth: Ruth has her own book in the Old Testament. Ruth is the mother of Obed, who was the father of Jesse, and Jesse was the father of King David. Ruth's husband was the late Mahlon. According to the same tradition that had Tamara marry Onan, the closest kinsman of her deceased husband should take his property and his widow. In Ruth, Chapter 2, Ruth takes a liking to Boaz, who is a relative of her deceased husband, but not his closest kinsman. She waits until he is asleep and then lies down with him in bed naked. When he wakes up, he is surprised to find a woman in bed with him. She says to him, "Spread your skirt over your maidservant, for you are next of kin" (Ruth 3:9). She was making an offer most men wouldn't refuse! However, Boaz rejected her offer. He said he wasn't her closest kinsman-redeemer because there "is a kinsman nearer than I" (Ruth 3:12). Eventually, Boaz meets with this kinsman, they come to an agreement and Boaz marries Ruth. They become the great-great-grandparents of King David.

Bathsheba: Bathsheba is the wife of Uriah, one of King David's generals. One day, the king was on a rooftop and spotted Bathsheba taking an outdoor bath. She was naked in a deliberate attempt to tempt the king. David took great interest in Bathsheba and decided to seduce her. The following is an excerpt from Moon's 1970 speech, "The Change of Blood Lineage: The Real Experience of Salvation by the Messiah."

> "Actually, the mother of King Solomon was Bathsheba, who was originally the wife of Uriah before King David stole her. Then, how could the child from that union become King Solomon? Bathsheba was in the providential position of Eve in the Garden of Eden before the fall. King David was Adam, and Uriah was in the position of the archangel. The archangel distracted the spouse of Adam with love and stole her away, making her fall. A reversal is needed then to indemnify that a person in the position of the archangel's wife had to be restored to the position of Eve. Therefore, the child who was born on the foundation of that reversal could be born as a child of heavenly love, a child of glory. Solomon was such a child of glory" (Moon 1970).

Mary

Mary's story is very close to the story of Tamara. Mary conceived a child while she was engaged to Joseph. All her relatives and neighbors were suspicious as to how she conceived. They all knew Mary was a virgin and not yet married. They surely didn't believe her when she told them she conceived by the Holy Spirit. Even Joseph, her fiancé, had a hard time accepting it until an angel appeared to him in a dream.

Mary, like Tamara, is believed to be guilty of illicit sexual activity and the penalty for adultery is death. And, just like Tamara, Mary is steadfast and faithful to the will of God. Just like Tamara, Mary risks her life to produce God's true lineage and give birth to His son, Jesus.

Conception of Jesus

The following topic is rather controversial because it offers a totally different view than what Christians believe about the conception of Christ. Was Mary impregnated by the Holy Spirit as she claimed, or did she have a sexual encounter with someone in her town who would be the biological father of Jesus? The new revelation by Moon revealed Jesus had a biological father and not a divine one.

Christians, who for 2,000 years believed and taught Mary was impregnated by the Holy Spirit, will, no doubt, be extremely shocked by this statement! We just read about four women in the Bible whose stories showed how their sexual relationships caused them to conceive. Mary was no different than those women before her. Just as God guided those women to their men, there was also a holy man in Mary's time who held God's seed. That man is believed to be Zechariah, a priest, and father of John the Baptist.

There were many unanswered questions about Mary's pregnancy. Joseph, Mary's fiancé, had difficulty accepting it. We read in Matt. 1:19, that Joseph decided to divorce Mary "quietly." However, that evening, an angel appeared to Joseph in a dream and said, "Joseph, son of David, do not be fear to take Mary your wife, for that which is conceived in her is of the Holy Spirit" (Matt. 1:20).

Another point to consider. Why did Zechariah's question to the Archangel Gabriel get him in trouble, but Mary's question did not? In Luke 1:20, the Bible tells us Gabriel told Zechariah his wife would bear him a son, and Zechariah had a question. When Gabriel told Mary she would give birth to Jesus, she had a question as well. But, here's the issue: When Zechariah asked a question, why was he struck dumb for nine months, but Mary was blessed? Was it really a question of faith? What really happened in the temple between Gabriel and Zechariah? Should Zechariah have known better, being older and a learned religious leader? The scripture says, to whom much is given, much is required. Could there be other reasons besides those traditionally held beliefs? Was he struck dumb because he didn't believe his very old wife, Elizabeth, could conceive and bear him a son or was he struck dumb because he didn't believe what the angel ordered him to do—that is, to sleep with Mary! I think the difference between Zechariah's response and Mary's response is in the way they both responded. Zechariah asked how this could be. I am a religious man, I cannot do this. It's against God's commandment. Mary asked how it will be done. I am willing to do anything for my Lord. I believe Gabriel's instruction to Zechariah was a faith-breaking instruction that was too much to bear.

It is remarkable how Zechariah and Mary's stories resembled Abraham's story with his wives, Sarah and Hagar. Here's another question: Could there be a reason for the similarities? And, another: Why was Zechariah murdered at the altar? Was he murdered for adultery? Although no one knows all the details. I believe Mary and Zechariah were driven to each other by a force beyond them. Those forces were none other than God willing to fulfill his purpose. Knowing how delicate and fragile this situation might be, God appeared to Joseph and told him Mary was impregnated "by the Holy Spirit." This was done solely to protect Mary's life from being taken by the law and to protect Jesus.

Although there were quite a few books written about Mary's conception, the first person who revealed this secret was Moon. Although the Divine Principle contained no mention of Zechariah's sexual encounter with Mary, Moon talked about this secret in private meetings with his church leaders in the early 1980s, and, later, this information was released to church members. I, personally, had heard of this in 1984 from the Rev. Reiner Vincenz, state church leader at the time. But, the book that stood out for me was Mark Gibbs' *The Virgin and the Priest* (2008). I first read a review of this book on the Internet. Later, I bought it and read it from cover to cover.

Purity of Bloodline

According to Gibbs, the Jews rejection of Jesus was because he was linked to the Pharisees. The sect had its origins in the temple. Many priests were Pharisees, and their main task was to spread the practice of the purity law among the public and priesthood. According to Gibbs:

> "If Mary were in her period of betrothal, then she would not have been recognized as a concubine, so by definition, Jesus was born a mamzer [someone who was either born of an adulterous affair, born of incest or someone who has a mamzer as a parent]. As the illegitimate son of a priest, he would have been barred from holding priestly office" (Gibbs, 86).

The Pharisees were strong advocates for keeping records, and had, in the past, demanded high priests resign if there was any question of illegitimacy. A family register kept in Jerusalem recorded the details of all births, and it is certain that illegitimate births were registered for the sake of the purity of the community. Gibbs noted the genealogy of the priesthood was the most important, and relevant documentation could be accessed by anyone with the appropriate credentials. If any family had such a blemish, the members would have tried to keep it secret whenever possible. The genealogies of Jesus that we see in Matthew and Luke were created with this in mind.

Gibbs included a verse from the Bible that testifies to this. In John 8:41, Jesus accused the Pharisees of trying to kill him; and their response was: "We were not born of fornication; we have one Father, even God." Interesting! This could only be interpreted as an accusation that Jesus was illegitimate, and if so, the Pharisees must have known the details of his parentage to make that charge.

Also, while researching this subject, I came across a surah in the Qur'an that supports this idea (Qur'an 19:17-21). In this Surah, Mary's primary fear of returning to her home, supposedly from Egypt, was not because of the fear that Herod might kill her baby son, but because she was concerned how her relatives would judge her for committing adultery. The miracle in this surah was, that as a baby, he (Jesus) knew his mom's fear and spoke to her, encouraging her to return home and assuring her he will speak to her relatives. When Mary and Joseph arrived in the village, the relatives met them on the road and began to chastise Mary for the shame she has brought them.

> "Then she carried him and brought him to her people. They said, "O Mary, indeed you have done a great evil."

> "O sister of Aaron, your father was not an evil man, and your mother was not a fornicator." So, she pointed to him (baby Jesus). They said, "How can we speak to a child in the cradle?" (Jesus) said, "Indeed, I am a slave of God. He has given me the scripture and made me a prophet. And peace be upon me the day I was born, and the day I will die, and the day I will be raised alive" (Qur'an 19:22-33).

"This was marked by Muslims as one of Jesus' greatest miracles. Gibbs continued:

> As the family background of public figures was subject to a great deal of scrutiny, chances are that many could not accept lessons from Jesus because they considered him a mamzer, and worthy only of disdain. The charging of illegitimacy was the most damning of all because it summarily disqualified Jesus from the leadership of the Israelite community. This apparently was a source of deep frustration" (Gibbs 2008, 87).

Christians, on the other hand, took this meaning differently and put more emphasis on the Immaculate Conception as proof Jesus was not like any other ordinary human. Jesus was different because he was conceived by the Holy Spirit. Therefore, He is sinless, holy and "pure." In the Christian view, a pure messiah must be untouched by human sexuality.

As McCarthy commented, when we look deeper into what elevated Jesus to the "sinless" and "pure" status, we can conclude it was not the nature of his conception. There were many elements and conditions involved. We learned an amazing new truth about God. He turned what could have seemed to be a sinful and unforgiving act into a good, pure and well-fulfilled act. Even the Jews confused this concept. They expected the Messiah to come from pureblood lineage despite the stories recorded in the Old Testament about the five women.

CHAPTER 22

The Dead Sea Scrolls

Jesus and John the Baptist's Connection to the Essenes

Since the discovery of the Dead Sea Scrolls between 1946 and 1956 at Khirbet Qumran in the West Bank, there has been new speculation surfacing that suggests both Jesus and John the Baptist, were, at one time in their lives, members of the Qumran Jewish separatist sect known as the Essenes. More shockingly, the scrolls revealed concepts that threaten the established traditional Christian models of thought and interpretation.

Coincidently, it is fascinating how things were accomplished in mystifying ways but appeared to happen for a reason. As I was writing about John the Baptist and the return of Elijah, I was struggling with how I could make a breakthrough. Someone in the church community told me about Mark Gibbs' book. So, out of curiosity, I visited a New Age bookstore near my workplace. I was looking for books on spirituality and dreams when I stumbled upon another book whose captivating title caught my attention. It was called *The Secret Initiation of Jesus at Qumran: The Essene Mysteries of John the Baptist,* written by Robert Feather (2005). These two books, as well as a few other important books I have read while writing this book, were like presents from heaven. I believe this was God providing me with His support as I worked on this book. These two books were brilliantly written and highly inspiring. They focus on the Qumran Essenes and the possibility that Jesus and John the Baptist were a part of this secluded Jewish community.

Although both authors strongly expressed the same views on this topic, they both presented their own research. In *The Virgin and the Priest,* which is considered one of the most controversial books ever written, Gibbs focuses his attention on Jesus' lineage and birth and the bitter conflict between Jesus and John the Baptist. (Gibb's book, *The Virgin and the Priest* was derived from Moon's revelation). This, I believe, was supporting Moon's revelation about Jesus' true story and John the Baptist's split from Jesus' ministry.

Drawing from 30 years of research of the history of religions, Hebrew texts and Jewish tradition, heretical art and the Dead Sea Scrolls, Gibb's presents a challenging and highly controversial take on the validity of the Christian doctrine of the virgin birth, claiming that Zechariah, the father of John the Baptist, was Jesus' biological father. Gibbs traces the history of Christ and John the Baptist, challenging the traditional Christmas story, which the author believes to be a controlling and pervasive conspiracy of silence by scholars and theologians.

On the other hand, Feather, in his book, not only provides his insight on the Jesus and John the Baptist connection to the Essenes, but he also devoted his attention to the origin, rituals and history of this devout, but reclusive, sect. Although Feather traces the origin of the Essenes back to the Pharaonic period in Egypt, he gives a fascinating, yet brief, history, of the sequence of events from the time the Romans arrived in 63 B.C. to the destruction of the Second Temple in 70 A.D., and the massacre and expulsion of the Jews by the Romans in 72 A.D.

In one of his earlier chapters, Feather spoke about the chaotic atmosphere in which Jesus was raised. There were divisions and struggles between dominant Jewish sects. Besides the Zealots, those who were prepared to fight the Romans, there were a few other competing Jewish factions. The Pharisees were the most prominent of all the Jewish sects, and they emphasized the need to return to the teaching of the scripture, instead of getting involved in political agitation. The Sadducees, who, as Feather noted, represented the wealthier class, supported the high priests of the temple and cooperated with the Romans so they could live an easier life. There were also the Samaritans, who followed their own brand of Judaism, and the Essenes, a minority group of Jews who lived and operated at Qumran. All had cast their influence on the life of Jesus and Christianity, in general.

Feather introduces noble insights from his many years of research of various ancient Scriptures, forcing religious scholars to look more closely at the Dead Sea Scrolls and the Qumran community, which produced and preserved documents relevant to Jesus' time. Through the eyes of scholars, such as the Rev. Jozef Milik (1922-2006), a Polish biblical scholar and Catholic priest who was the first to decipher and analyze the Dead Sea Scrolls, Feather proffers the argument that not only were Jesus and John the Baptist members of Essenes, but there is also strong evidence for connections between the roots of Christianity in the Qumran community because Jesus was raised, educated in the scriptures and influenced by the Essenes. This ideology became part of his ministry, and, thus, the origin of Christianity.

The Missing 30 Years of John and Jesus' Ministries

There is a lot of evidence supporting the influence the Essenes' had on Jesus and John the Baptist. But, to keep the story interesting, I will present a few examples from Feather's book.

(1) The first example is related to Jesus and John the Baptist's membership in the Essene community. Here, Feather quotes Luke 1:80, which indicates John the Baptist has been a member of the Essenes since his childhood. "And the child grew and became strong in spirit, and he was in the wilderness till the day of his manifestation to Israel" (Luke 1:80).

To support this statement, Feather quotes from the Roman historian, Flavius Josephus. He wrote in his book, *The War of the Jews: The History of The Destruction of Jerusalem* (2009), that it was customary for the Qumran community to adopt "children from others, at an age when their spirit is still malleable enough to easily accept instruction." John Allegro, a member of the original Dead Sea Scrolls translation team, also pointed out John the Baptist's parents were elderly, and when his father died, he may have been adopted by the community.

(2) Missing years: People who study the scriptures know very well there was no mention of Jesus or John's whereabouts from the time they were born until they were in their 30s. John the Baptist, too, was not mentioned in the Bible for approximately 30 years, until we read about him baptizing Jesus in the Jordan River.

In *The Virgin and the Priest,* Gibbs mentions Zechariah's death. He was murdered by Jewish mobs because he had an affair with Mary. He, too, pointed out Jesus was given by his mother to the

Essenes community from childhood to be raised and schooled in a strict, religious way.

(3) Jesus was taught the scriptures by the Essenes. As noted in Luke, Jesus amazed the people with his knowledge of the scriptures at such a young age, when they exclaimed, "How is it that this man has learning, when he has never studied?" (John 7:15). Jesus was only 12 years old when he surprised the Jewish elders by his knowledge of the scriptures without ever having been schooled. These two books are inspiring and very educational, and I highly recommend them.

I am deeply sorry if I offended anyone with this story on Jesus' conception. I had no intention of disrespect toward any religion., particularly toward Jesus himself. In fact, I deeply believe Jesus Christ is the Messiah and Savior, and God sent Him to the Israelite 2,000 years ago. Having said that, this book is about telling the truth as I received it. Another reason for talking about this subject is the false concept held by the Jews, Christians and Muslims on what exactly the Messiah supposed to be. Fundamentalists, whether they are Jews, Christians or Muslims, believed the Messiah is a supernatural being that is endowed with supernatural powers. Bible's stories, such as Elijah being lifted up to heaven on a chariot of fire (2 Kings 2:11); Moses splitting the Red Sea in half (Exod. 14:21); the transfiguration where Jesus' face is shining as the sun and his raiment was white as the light (Matt. 17:1-8); and the story of the prophet Mohammed face's shining like the brightest light, were embedded in their beliefs. But, as the biblical history tell us, prophets from Noah to Abraham, Elijah to Abraham and Moses to Jesus, to Mohammed, all born in the flesh, had their own families, wife, siblings, aunts and uncles and so forth, and lived a regular human life. The only difference is they were chosen by God and had a divine nature about them and were chosen for their tasks as mediators between humans and the divine. There is too much antihuman in religions, yet God can't keep away from them. This alone tells a lot about God and His love for human beings. More on this subject in later pages.

My mom, holding sister Habara, and Gram-ma Hana and uncle Mohammed, upon a visit to our home.

My mom (l to r), sister Habara, and Gram-ma Hana. Behind them is a camel my father had just bought for me for farming use.

My father Mansour and my mother
Yemna Bashia, in front of our home.
My father is holding his new radio.

My father holding sister Habara, sitting in front of our house. He has a tea kit in front of him, and his new radio hangs on a nail on the wall above him.

This image of the man behind the camel is not me, but it describes 90% of how I was in my teen years working on the farm.

My brother Mohammed, who died in a car crash in Italy; and who I believe, he is one of my guardian angels.

Uncle Taib, my other guardian angel who came to me in the dream of the "funeral Procession" and who later God used him to appear to me in the dream that I called "Hologram" and he is also in the spiritual world.

This is Reverend Moon's first church in 1952—
built with cardboard paper.

Courtesy of Family Federation for World Peace and Unification

This great work has been started by one man. But it has reached millions and each of you (Unificationists) has become that one man. Thirty years ago, in a small hut in Korea, in miserable condition, I preached the same message that I am preaching today: world unification, Love of God, Kingdom of God here on earth. Everyone laughed at me and called me a really crazy man, sitting there in that cubby hole, such a dirty, smelly place talking about the Kingdom of God, just like your parents are now, so my own relatives were then. Some of my relatives were saying: "Rev. Moon, he's crazy! He just has something wrong in his head." Now, however, when the people hear me say, "I will bring the Kingdom of God here on Earth! I will make an impact that will shake the world!", then instead of saying, "Are you crazy?" everybody begins to tremble.

—Rev. Sun Myung Moon
May 30, 1976

Reverend Moon at anti communism rally on June 7, 1975 in Seoul, South Korea.

Courtesy of Family Federation for World Peace and Unification

Reverend Moon's anti communism rally on June 7, 1975 in Seoul, South Korea drew an overwhelming crowd of over 1.2 million people!

Courtesy of Family Federation for World Peace and Unification

Reverend Moon's Bicentennial God Bless America Rally at Yankee Stadium on June 1, 1976, in spite of bad of weather, drew over 40,000.

Courtesy of Family Federation for World Peace and Unification

Reverend Moon's Bicentennial God Bless America, Washington Monument rally on September 18, 1976; Reverend Moon set a new record when over 300,000 people attended this rally!

Courtesy of Family Federation for World Peace and Unification

A welcoming poster—that I had handwritten—to welcome Reverend and Mrs. Moon on their arrival at Moscow Airport.

©*Copyright* ***Providential Partners*** *Mahjoub Family Archive*

Security badges attendees wore at the Moscow conference.

Reverend Moon is being welcomed by Soviet officials and interviewed by the Moscow press.

Reverend and Mrs. Moon walking in Moscow airport to the VIP Lounge, with a crowd of press following them.

Reverend and Mrs. Moon greet their guests in the receiving line during an evening reception.

Reverend and Mrs. Moon greet their guests in the receiving line during an evening reception.

During the Opening Plenary Session, Larry Moffitt of the World Media Association introduces World Media's founder, the Reverend Sun Myung Moon.

Reverend and Mrs. Moon with President Gorbachev.

Courtesy of Family Federation for World Peace and Unification

HRH Princess Eva Marie, my wife Cynthia Mahjoub, HRH Andrej Karageorgievich, Prince of Yugoslavia and the first Romanoff prince to set foot on Russian soil since the Bolshevik Revolution of 1917.

Myself and Mr. Hugh Spurgin, M.P.A., M.Div., Ph.D., now an educator at Bridgeport International Academy, Connecticut.

My wife Cynthia and I, taking a walk in Red Square.

Myself talking with young Soviet soldiers from Azerbaijan, who we met that day in Red Square.

Reverend Moon talking to me during the matching session a few minutes before he matched me with my perfect "providential partner."

Our first picture together, a few minutes after we have been matched to each other.

The Holy Wine ceremony in Korea. This picture was taken during the moments I was receiving the profound vision I share in the Holy Wine section in Chapter 33.

My wife and I posing for a photo after our Holy Blessing Ceremony.

A mass-wedding of 5,837 couples in 1982 at the Jamsil Gymnasium in Seoul, Korea… Mass weddings grew ever larger; most recent mass wedding was for 40,000 couples in October of 2009.

Courtesy of Family Federation for World Peace and Unification

The Reverend and Mrs. Sun Myung Moon in North Korea to meet with its former President Kim Il Sung II in 1990.

Courtesy of Family Federation for World Peace and Unification

President Reagan holds a copy of Rev. Moon's News World predicting his landslide victory.

CHAPTER 23

Schisms in Religions

Judaism

Why does schism exist in religion? It is simply because there is no complete truth in all the established religions? At most, some religions might have half-truths, and some may have quarter-truths. Therefore, religions keep splitting into different sects. The Bible and the Qur'an are not the literal words of God but are historic documents of human expression of truths. As the Bible said in John 16:12-13 and John 16:25, there is more truth to come. I really do not have much to say about the Jewish people other than I feel both sympathy and disappointment for them. I am sympathetic because they have endured much bloodshed and suffering. They are a great, loving and hard-working people, as well as a successful and highly intelligent people. Their contributions to the world in the fields of business, science and education are unmatched. I have a great love and respect for them just as I have respect for all people of every religion or race, and love and respect them for their religion and prophets.

As a restaurant manager, many of my regular clients are Jewish. They love me, too, and even call me Ari. That is a Jewish name. At first, I thought they were mispronouncing my name. I later discovered they were calling me Ari because they thought I was Jewish! I never bothered to correct them.

That said, however, I am disappointed with the Jews because they missed the opportunity to receive God's everlasting blessing. They should have accepted Jesus' coming 2,000 years ago.

There seems to be a general misconception by the Jewish people that their suffering and persecution was because of the Christians and Muslims.

But, the truth of the matter is this: History tells us the original cause for their persecution and expulsion from their homeland was created by their own defiance against the commandments and breaking the covenant with God. God made an everlasting covenant with Abraham that was renewed with his son, Isaac.

Isaac's son, Jacob, had 12 sons, and these sons and their families grew in numbers and became known as the 12 tribes of Israel.

What people may not know is God also made a covenant with Abraham and his second wife, Hagar, that their son, Ishmael, would also be blessed. Through him will also come the 12 tribes/ princes (Gen. 17:20). More will be written about this subject in upcoming chapters.

God promised the Israelites they would be His covenant if they obeyed His commandments (Deut. 28:9-10). They would be a blessing to all nations of the world. Thus, they would keep their covenant with God, and He would keep His covenant with them.

As we will see, the blessing was a conditional blessing and not what the ancient Israelites understood it to be. Here is where the Israelites began to run into trouble. They felt the blessing was theirs and theirs alone and the blessing could only be passed on through blood lineage. It was not for anyone outside the tribes. The Israelites even defied God and worshipped other gods, married Gentiles and arrogantly saw themselves as superior to other nations.

Repeatedly, prophet after prophet warned the Israelites what would happen if they continued to disobey God's commandments. Moses prophesied, "And the Lord will scatter you among all peoples, from the one end of the earth to the other" (Deut. 28:64). Despite this warning, the Israelites constantly broke God's commandments. They fought among themselves and split into two kingdoms: The Northern Kingdom was called the Kingdom of Israel; and the Southern Kingdom was called the Kingdom of Judah.

Ten of the 12 tribes lived in the Northern Kingdom and the other two fled to the Southern Kingdom after the northern tribes were conquered by the Babylonians and forced into slavery. About a century later, the Southern Kingdom was conquered as well. Their capital city, Jerusalem, was destroyed in 586 B.C. Many Israelites fled to neighboring countries; some escaped to other, faraway countries.

A few centuries later, God showed mercy toward His people, and many of the tribes returned. They rebuilt their temple, and Jerusalem and prospered for many centuries. The Jews became renowned across the world for their achievements in philosophy, science, medicine and business. Jerusalem became the world's center of trade. God began to prepare them for the coming of the Messiah. Once again, God sent a prophet, Malachi, to remind the Israelites of their covenant with God and warned them of the coming of the Messiah.

> "Remember the law of my servant Moses, the statues and ordinances that I commanded him at Horeb for all Israel. Behold, I will send you Eli'jah the prophet before the great and terrible day of the Lord comes. And, he will turn the hearts of fathers to their children, and the hearts of children to their fathers, lest I come and smite the land with a curse" (Mal. 4:4-6).

But, again, the Israelites didn't listen. They rejected Jesus as their Messiah, and, ultimately, He was crucified. After the time of Jesus, Jerusalem was again destroyed. This time by the Romans. The Jews were scattered over much of the world. Today, there are Jews in every country. This is why the Jews endured horrible suffering.

God loved His people very much. He had compassion for them, forgave them and promised to send them a messiah! Their Bible speaks of this in Zech. 8:7-8, 20-23. Let us read:

> "Thus says the LORD of hosts: 'Behold, I will save my people from the east country and from the west country, and I will bring them to dwell in the midst of Jerusalem; and they shall be my people and I will be their God, in faithfulness and righteousness'" (Zech. 8:7-8).

This is what the LORD Almighty says further:

> "Peoples shall yet come, even the inhabitants of many cities; the inhabitants of one city shall go to another, saying, 'Let us go at once to entreat the favor of the LORD, and to seek the LORD of hosts; I am going.' Many peoples and

strong nations shall come to seek the LORD of hosts in Jerusalem, and to entreat the favor of the LORD" (Zech. 8: 20-23).

Now, many Jews, as well as Christians, will argue that the preceding Bible verses are meant for the coming of the Messiah or, as Christians believed it to be, the Second Coming of Christ. I say no, that is not true. Both are wrong because judging from Jesus' own words in Matt. 11:13, when he said, "For all the prophets and the law prophesied until John," Jesus' comment was to explain that John the Baptist was the last prophet and all prophecies mentioned in the Old Testament that pertain to the coming of the Messiah were, in fact, about him. Which came first, the Book of Zechariah or John the Baptist? On the other hand, since the first attempt during Jesus' time failed, these verses can be applied to the Second Coming of Christ.

Division in the Jewish Faith

In the Jewish faith, we also find divisions among Orthodox, Conservative and Reformed Jews. We don't hear much about their struggles like we do in Islam today or in The Reformation. The Jewish population is a small margin of no more than 13 million worldwide (www.simpletoremember.com/vitals/world-jewish-population.htm). Their new nation-state has not yet reached its first century, and it is still fighting for survival. But, it is known that the Jewish faith split into four or more denominations. In Jesus' time, for instance, as we've already mentioned: Sadducees, Pharisees, Samaritans and Essenes.

Before I move on to my next chapter, I want to mention a story I found in a book titled *The Secret Destiny of America: The Occult Significance of the United States* by Manly Hall, which fascinated me greatly and put me in total awe. It is about the world's first democrat, Akhenaten, a Pharaoh of Egypt. As the author noted "Born several thousand years too soon," Akhenaten was the first realist in democracy, the first humanitarian, and the first internationalist (Hall 2011, 22.) He believed the duty of the ruler is to protect his subjects' rights: the right to live well, think, dream, hope and aspire. For five years, Akhenaten devoted his life to creating the perfect doctrine in the city in which he built for the Ever-Living God. Here, he taught the mystery of the Divine Father and wrote simple and beautiful poems that have survived throughout time.

It is interesting how much his story reminds me of Jesus' story. To Akhenaten, God was not a mighty warrior ruling over Egypt, speaking through his priests, nor a Supreme Being flying in some war chariot leading armies of destruction. Aten/God was the gentle father who loved all his children despite their race and desired they should live together in peace and harmony.

Even more, God, or aten, created all the lesser creatures, whether they were birds nestled in the papyrus reeds along the banks of the Nile or dragonflies with colorful wings that hovered over quiet pools and the lotus blossoms. Aten was the father of all beasts, flowers and insects. He had fashioned them in his wisdom and preserved them with his love and tenderness.

Akhenaten, seated in the garden of his palace, spent many hours watching the flight of birds and listening to them. He said he found Aten in all of them, and his heart went out to them, and he gave thanks for the goodness in everything that lived.

This was a pharaoh who traveled alone through the countryside, met the peasants, conversed with slaves, and shared the simple food of the poor. He listened to everyone and respected them because, in his subjects, he sought and found the life of Aten. He saw the universal god shining through the eyes of little children, beheld the beauty of God in the men who worked in the fields. He could not understand why others did not see God in everything as he did.

When I read this story, I was astonished by the depth of love and understanding of God this pharaoh had. Somehow, it seemed to contradict the story of the Exodus, which gave the impression that the Egyptians and their pharaohs were evil. This story made me wonder why God sent the Jews to Egypt in the first place and allowed them to be held captive for 400 years. Could it be God wanted the Jews to learn something about God from Egypt's pharaoh and his love and understanding of God? I mean, this pharaoh even refused to kill his enemies because he saw God in them. This, unfortunately, led to his death!

Christianity

When we take a closer look at Christianity, it is shocking to discover there are approximately 2,700 different sects. Among this large number, there are 240 different denominations that claim to be from mainline Christianity (http://infomory.com/numbers/number-of-christian-denominations/)! Since the Protestant Reformation in the 16th century, Christianity has divided into many denominations, and their struggles and differences have increased. Although it is not that noticeable today, these differences may be felt in the pulpits and in the preaching of the ministers. Each denomination claims to have a better understanding of Christ's teaching than the other, as well as a better method of serving God. There are also racial divisions and hatred between churches of different races. When Christians are confronted about these divisions, they will say something like: "We are the body of one Christ made of many parts." Yes, it is true. But, Christ's body is perfectly united in one direction! There are no conflicts between His body parts. His feet, for instance, can't protest and tell His mind: 'No, I don't want to go that way.'"

If Jesus were to return today, to what denomination would He choose to appear first? Catholics? Presbyterians? United Methodists? Evangelicals? Pentecostals? No matter how much Christians may try to hide or defend the existing divisions in their denominations, they cannot do so because they are visible to everyone.

A church is a financial institution, and the more members a church has, the richer it becomes. If you are not a member of a denomination, that denomination believes you are not saved, and you must be baptized again. How many times must people be baptized to be saved?

Sometimes, I feel sympathy for those who want to return to God but can't decide which church to attend. It is a humongous problem! It is a problem that is extremely difficult for many. It is also difficult to unite one religion, never mind three. Perhaps with a new revelation from God, it would be possible to solve all religious differences and establish peace in our world.

Although these divisions are present in all three Abrahamic religions, they are only symptoms of much bigger and more complicated problems that lie deep within their theologies. These are the issues I want to address in detail, and Christianity, in particular, because it is the main religion that expects Christ to return. It might be interesting to note that Sunni Muslims, which is the largest branch of Islam, also strongly believe Jesus will return in the Last Days.

Islam

Schism in Islam and Problems of Extremism

Islam is no different than Christianity. It has its own schism, although it was not as large as the one Christianity faced. Because of the nature of Islam's Sharia law, many of its denominations were hidden for fear of persecution or death. The most notable schisms in Islam today are manifested in the struggles and wars between the two dominant branches of Islam: Sunni and Shiite. The Iran-Iraq War, which lasted from 1980 to 1988, and what is happening in Iraq and Syria today, are examples of this schism.

The thing I abhor about Muslim extremists is the way they combine their faith with politics and relate it to the Palestinian struggle. Islam, as a faith, is being highjacked by fanatical militant groups, such as al-Qaeda and ISIS, which are calling for a jihad, or holy war, against the West, particularly the United States. Extremists see the United States and Israel as their archenemies.

There are two issues that trouble me the most about my Arab brothers, who consider themselves moderates, that I feel I need to address. The first is about the double standards most Arab nations practice. They say it's OK for Muslims to go to foreign countries, such as France, Germany, Italy, the United States, and so forth, build mosques and witness freely and convert as many as they can without government interference. They can also get involved in politics and use these countries' constitutions to support their legitimacy. However, when foreigners come to their countries, and they discover these people are missionaries, the government would deport them immediately or throw them in jail. This is not right. The second issue that troubles me is the Arab moderates' silence and their lack of interference with and correction of their extremist brothers. In fact, I have a quote I thought would complement what I wanted to address on this issue. "The darkest places in Hell are reserved for those who maintain their neutrality in times of moral crisis." It was said by 13th-century Italian poet Dante Alighieri, best known for "The Divine Comedy."

Arab moderates watched in silence as their extremist brothers wreaked havoc all over the world, terrorizing and killing innocent people in public places, such as restaurants, bus stops, train stations and even schools. Since 9/11, militant Islamists have held the world hostage, carrying out their evil acts in the name of Islam and Allah. No country was brave enough to stand up to them and speak out against these atrocities. No one confronted these terrorists and asked them why they were doing what they were doing. These extremists were left alone to do what they wanted, distort the Qur'an to suit their radical views and brainwash innocent and uneducated people into believing that what they were doing was just.

To camouflage their identities, they gave themselves religious names and dressed in black and green uniforms, the same colors of the Kaaba, or Sacred House, in Mecca. They use symbols, such as the sword and crescent, so anyone who sees them would automatically assume they are the good defenders of Islam!

To be honest, when I hear the words "Allah hu Akbar" (God is Great), I am terrified because, usually when Muslims, particularly extremists, say these words, either something tragic has happened or is about to happen! This holy phrase has either been misused or its meaning has been distorted. Therefore, I am deeply concerned about the moderate Muslims' silence and the fast-growing and frightening influence these extremists have over Muslims. In fact, in my book, *Honor Thy God,* I talked about this problem and predicted if the Arab nations remained silent and do not do anything about these extremist factions, there will come a day when they will find themselves wrapped up in the extremists' distorted and brutal interpretation of Islam. And this, of course, is what happened!

The Arab uprising of 2011, which was called "Arab Spring," began in Tunisia and spread like wildfire across the Arab world, from Tunisia to Egypt, then Libya and Jordan, and then to Bahrain, Algeria and Syria. What started out as a call for freedom and democracy became a call for new authoritarian Islamist governments to implement the Sharia law.

The following is from *Reconciliation: Islam, Democracy, and the West (2008)*, written by the late Benazir Bhutto, former prime minister of Pakistan, and published about two months after her assassination in December 2007. Personally, I believe she was a saint sent by God. He used her to open the Muslim world's eyes and see that the faithful were being led astray. She is a martyr. I discovered her book in an unusual way! I was talking about the problems of Islam and desperately searching for words to describe how I felt. Then, my wife gave me this book as a birthday gift. Bhutto's book is a must-read for Muslims and non-Muslims who seek to learn the truth about Islam.

In my view, there is no person who understood the true and false interpretations of the faith of Islam better than Bhutto. She was a prominent and respected world leader, serving nonconsecutive terms as prime minister. Pakistan, during that time, became the hotbed and stronghold for extremist movements, such as the Taliban in Afghanistan and al Qaeda in Iraq. She was well-versed in Islam as well.

When I read her book, I was amazed at how she managed to escape from the first assassination attempt on Oct. 19, 2007. This attempt, called the Karachi bombing, killed at least 180 people and injured at least 500. She survived, however, and it occurred to me the reason she wasn't killed was she had not finished her book. Bhutto talked about her manuscript, which she had in her possession at the time of the attack, and how her aides collected the pages that had blown away and were covered in blood!

On International Terrorism

I really learned a valuable lesson from Bhutto about the Muslim extremist problem. The international terrorist movement has two goals. The first is to unite the Muslim population into a one-world Islamic political party like that of the Civil Rights Movement in the United States. Although it sounds like a religious movement it is, in large part, a radical, political movement!

The second goal is to provoke a confrontation between the

West and the Muslim world, which would be guided by its own extremist interpretation of the Qur'an.

The 9/11 attacks, the 2004 train attack in Madrid, Spain, the 2005 attack at a London subway station, the 2003 attack on a commercial compound in Riyadh, Saudi Arabia, and other attacks in Malaysia are all examples of how the radical extremists try to inspire bloody confrontation with the West: By killing the innocent.

Those who pervert Islam by committing these crimes are described in the Qur'an as "going astray from the right path." That could mean:

1) Murdering another human being.

2) Spreading mischief (fasad) in the land (Qur'an 2:191-193, 2:217, 4:88-91).

They claim to speak for Islam, denigrating democracy and human rights, and argue those values are Western values and conflict with Islam. They also deny girls a basic education, blatantly discriminate against women and minorities, ridicule other cultures and religions, rant against science and technology and endorse brutal totalitarianism to enforce their medieval views, according to Bhutto.

There is a lot of hypocrisy in the Muslim world, Bhutto said. Muslim leaders and even intellectuals are quite comfortable criticizing outsiders for the harm that has been inflicted on fellow Muslims. However, nothing is said when the violence is Muslim on Muslim. The Iran-Iraq War and what is happening now between the Shiites and the Sunnis in Iraq are two such examples. To address these events would be considered politically incorrect!

On Jihad

There are two meanings for Jihad, and, to be honest, until I read Bhutto's book, I never thought of the word in that way. The first one is a "greater jihad"; this is an internal jihad. It means to fight within oneself to become a better person. This is a struggle centered on eradicating selfishness, hate, wickedness, etc., to develop a good and godly character.

The second is centered on personal conduct during a time of war or conflict. The prophet Mohammed is said to have remarked when he came home from a battle: "We return from the lesser jihad to the greater jihad." This shows how important it is for us to struggle to be our best. It is a nonviolent struggle to make us better people. The greater, internal jihad is more important.

Suicide-Murders/Bombers

Bhutto said extremists who allege that the Qur'an supports terrorist actions do not have the support from the Qur'an. Suicide and/or murder are specifically and unambiguously prohibited in the Holy Book.

> "For this reason did we prescribe to the children of Israel, that whoever slays a soul, unless it be for manslaughter or for mischief in the land, is as though he slew all men; and whoever keeps it alive, is as though he kept alive all men; and certainly our messenger came to them with clear argument, but even after that, many of them certainly act extravagantly in the land" (Qur'an 5:32).

Allah is One and the Same God

I believe Westerners misunderstand who Allah is. Most believe Allah is only the God of Islam, but this is incorrect. The word "Allah" in Arabic means God, and Allah is the one and only God, the same God of Judaism and Christianity. This is why the Qur'an calls all believers of three faiths "People of the Books," not of the book. The three holy books, the Torah, Bible and Qur'an, are all viewed as texts that were revealed to mankind by God.

Commonalities in the Three Religions

If a Jew or Christian were to read the Qur'an, the person would recognize his or her own religious teachings in certain passages. The Qur'an, in a sense, is like the Christian Gospels. This is why both the New Testament of the Bible and the Qur'an revere all the Jewish prophets and carried many of the Old Testament stories forward. These extraordinary commonalities should promote tolerance between them. The following are readings from the Qur'an.

> "Say we believe in Allah and what has been revealed to us, and what was revealed to Ibrahim [Abraham] and Ismail [Ishmael] and Ishaq [Isaac] and Yaqoub [Jacob] and the tribes, and what was given to Musa [Moses] and Isa [Jesus] and to the prophets from their Lord; we do not make any distinction between any of them, and to Him do we submit" (Qur'an 3:65).
>
> "Surely, we revealed the Taurat [Torah] in which was guidance and light; with it the prophets who submitted themselves (to God) judged (matters) for those who were Jews, and the masters of divine knowledge and the doctors, because they were required to guard (part) of the Book of God, and they were witness therefore; therefore fear not the people and fear me, and do not take a small price for my communications; and whoever was not judged by what God revealed, those are they that are the unbelievers" (Qur'an 5:44).
>
> "Surely, we revealed to you as we revealed to Nuh [Noah] and the prophets after him, and we revealed to Ibrahim [Abrahim], Ismail [Ishmael], and Ishaq [Isaac] and Yaqoub [Jacob], and the tribes and Isa [Jesus] and Ayub [Job] and Yunus [Jonah] and Haroun [Aaron] and Sulaiman [Solomon] and we gave to Dawoud [David]" (Qur'an 4:163).
>
> "And we sent after their footsteps Isa [Jesus], son of Marium [Mary], verifying what was before him of the Taurat [Torah] and We gave him the Injeel [Gospel], which was guidance and light, and verifying what was before it of Taurat [Torah] and a guidance and an admonition for those who guard (against evil)" (Qur'an 4:46).

Astonishingly, although the Qur'an instructs the faithful to believe in the three Holy books and names them, we find in most Islamic countries, these are among the most forbidden books. Quite remarkably, the Qur'an acknowledges that other religions can lead to salvation. It says:

> "Surely those who believe, and those who are Jews, and Christians, and the Sabians, whoever believes in Allah and the Last Days and does good, they shall have their reward from their Lord, and there is no fear for them nor shall they grieve" (Qur'an 2:62).

When Muslims are confronted with these verses in the Qur'an, they give many excuses why people shouldn't read the Bible because Christians changed many words and cite the different versions. They would ask, "Which one do you want us to believe?"

Even though there are different translations, its main content remains unchanged. There is no excuse for not allowing people to read it.

Another thing I learned about Islam from *The Virgin and the Priest* is the idea that the author connected Mohammed and Islam to the role of the firstborn son and tied them together with Elijah and John the Baptist.

How is Elijah significant to both Judaism and Islam, and how does he relate to Mohammed? Just like Elijah, Mohammed received the Qur'an in a cave. Author Gibbs traces Islamic roots back to the Qumran sect. Much of Islamic law and ritual is centered on practices advocated by John the Baptist, according to Essene rituals.

The Essenes believed in strict adherence to the laws, especially fasting, animal sacrifice, circumcision and daily ablution. Muslims practice all these. They say prayers five times a day, wash before prayer, and fast for 30 days during Ramadan.

Gibbs also mentioned a significant revelation that Muslims held toward Jesus' crucifixion: Jesus was not crucified but lifted to Heaven alive and God put another person on the cross to be crucified in His place!

To support this, let me share this:

> "I did not succumb to them as they had planned. But I was not afflicted at all … I did not die in reality, but in appearance, lest I be put to shame by them. It was another, they their father, who drunk the gall and vinegar; it not I they struck me with the reed; it another, Simon, who bore the cross on his shoulder. It was another upon whom they

> placed the crown of thorns … and I was laughing at their ignorance" (Bullard and Gibbons 1990).

After discovering this truth, I couldn't understand the Muslims' logic. How can they believe in Jesus' virgin birth, but refuse to accept Jesus' death on the cross and his resurrection? There is good news on the horizon, however. A window of hope had come, foreshadowing Muslims recognition of Jesus's death on the cross. Just as recently as Nov. 15, 2017, I watched a video of Professor Ravi Zacharias International Ministries, stating that after hours of talk with a high-ranking Syrian cleric on the subject of Jesus' death on the cross, he mentioned an interesting statement made by the Syrian cleric. The imam said, "The time has come for the Islamic world to stop asking if Jesus Christ died and start asking why?" (Zacharias, 2012).

Let's think about the imam's statement. It dawned on me that Muslim scholars-theologians must have believed in the Jewish scriptures, particularly the story of Elijah, which is found in 2 Kings 2:11. It talks about how God lifted the prophet Elijah to Heaven alive on a chariot of fire and promised the Israelites He -- God --would send him back at the Last Day before the appearance of the Messiah (Mal. 4:4-5). If we examine the Qur'an, it clearly shows Muslims believed and revered the Old and the New Testaments of the Bible. In my humble opinion, Muslim scholars must have borrowed the idea from the Jewish scriptures (Jesus didn't die but God lifted him up to heaven alive, so he could send him back in the Last Days). Also, another point, Muslims were disgusted by the idea of portraying God as a weak and helpless God and allowing Himself to be humiliated and killed by men. To Muslims, the crucifixion of Jesus is very shameful and dishonorable.

It is interesting to note it is this idea of a literal returning of the prophet Elijah from the clouds of heaven that was the cause of the Jews disbelief in Jesus and, I believe, would be the same stumbling block for Christians at the Second Coming of Christ.

CHAPTER 24

Reformation in Islam

Although I believe all Abrahamic religions need to be reformed again, Islam is in a greater need to be reformed to the new truth that the Rev. Moon is teaching. We have witnessed how radical Islamists apply the teachings of the Qur'an to their political and justice systems. This is very much like the time of the prophet Mohammed. It is becoming crystal clear that if Islam is to remain a religion of peace, it must undergo a reformation just like Judaism and Christianity did.

Islamic extremism has been on the rise since it began in 1979 in Iran by Ayatollah Khomeini. There were the wars in Afghanistan and Iraq after 9/11 and the rise of Islamic extremist radical groups, such as ISIS in Syria and Iraq, Boko Haram in Nigeria, and other splinter groups operating in North Africa. It is apparent, after what has been discussed and debated in the media and on the Internet, that Islam is in its early stages of reformation.

A decade of war and terror has produced, what I would call, a list of alarming "theses" in Islam that needed to be reformed like those Martin Luther nailed to the door of the church in Wittenberg, Germany, in 1517. Although not as many, these "theses" will give us a closer look at several issues in Islam that have caused concerns in recent years over the use of the Qur'an and Sharia law.

We will look at Islam as a faith, the Qur'an, the prophet Mohammed, and Sharia, which is the source of much of the disturbing and harsh use of punishment in the judicial systems of many Islamic countries. This alarming system of public execution, such as public beheading, stoning, dismemberment and flogging, is not only used by radical extremists, but it is also applied in most fundamentalist nations, such as Saudi Arabia, Iran, Yemen, Qatar and other Middle Eastern countries that adopted Sharia law into their constitutions. Let's begin with the Sharia law and it uses.

Sharia and the Qur'an

The Qur'an, which is sometimes spelled as Koran, is the holy book of the Muslims. Every word in the Qur'an is seen by the Muslims to be the infallible words of Allah, God. They were spoken by God and given directly to the prophet Mohammed.

Fundamentalist Muslims, particularly extremists, use the Qur'an as a manual to guide and instruct them. They also use it to issue "fatwas," or edicts. I don't doubt the Qur'an is the word of truth. However, upon closer examination, we see that just as in the Bible, the Qur'an is inundated with contradictions, written in metaphors and symbols. Therefore, just like the Bible, the Qur'an cannot be taken literally. The Qur'an, at times, favors peace and plurality, and, at other times, it favors wars, terror and separatism. I might be repeating myself.

After 9/11 and the wars in Afghanistan and Iraq, the whole world was held captive and debated Islam. There were thousands of documentaries, talk shows and articles that didn't favor Islam or Mohammed.

Sharia Law and Caliphate

Sharia law

Sharia law is an Islamic strict moral code derived from the Qur'an and the teachings of Mohammed.

Sharia law influences the legal code in most Muslim countries. It is a set of regulations that pertain to marriage, divorce and inheritance. There are so many varying interpretations of what Sharia means that, in some countries, it is incorporated into their political systems, particularly in criminal law, which is highly controversial. Some interpretations of Sharia law are used to justify cruel punishment, such as public flogging, amputation, stoning and beheadings. Islamic radical extremist militants, such as ISIS in Syria and Iraq and Boko Haram in Nigeria, are perfect examples of this disturbing application of Sharia law.

Caliphate

A caliphate is a form of Islamic government that is led by a caliph, someone who is accepted to be a political and religious successor to the prophet Mohammed and a leader of the entire Muslim community (Kadi and Shahin 2013, pp. 81-86).

The radical Islamic extremist group, ISIS, fighting in Syria and Iraq, announced the establishment of a caliphate in June 2014. In an audio recording that was distributed online, the Islamic State of Iraq and Syria (ISIS) declared its chief, Abu Bakr al-Baghdadi, "the caliph" and "leader for Muslims everywhere." Baghdadi accepted this allegiance. So, from ISIS' point of view, he is the sole leader of the Muslim world.

Ever since Mohammed's death, a caliph was named "the prince" or "emir" of the believers until the caliphate was abolished by the Ottoman Empire in 1924.

The problem with the ISIS caliphate is it will never be accepted by Muslims. There are two reasons for this. The first is ISIS cannot force its caliphate system upon a modern-day society, especially with its corrupted version of the Qur'an and the inhuman use of Sharia law. Second, ISIS is an illegitimate terrorist organization made up of rebels fighting the Syrian government. It has no authority over any nation and is not recognized nor welcomed by the Muslim world. There is more on this in Bhutto's book, "*Reconciliation: Islam, Democracy and the West* (2008).

Islamists' Distorted Use of Sharia

Since the rise of ISIS, the war in Syria has spread like wildfire and spilled into Iraq. What disturbs me greatly about these extremists are the inhumane and gruesome public executions of innocents. They use quotes from the Qur'an to support their distorted views. In every country they have occupied, whether it's Syria or Iraq, they have ravaged cities and villages, killed men by hideously dismembering their bodies and hanging them on lampposts for everyone to see, so no one will dare to fight back. They take women and young girls as sex slaves and force boys into military training, so they can die for their cause. Then, to threaten the world, they send videos of these killings to countries all over the world. I have never seen such barbaric and horrific killings except in the movies.

The Prophet

An article for *USA Today* said:

> "Muslims consider the honor of the Prophet Muhammad to be dearer to them than that of their parents or even themselves. To defend it is considered to be an obligation upon them. The strict punishment if found guilty of this crime under sharia (Islamic law) is capital punishment implementable by an Islamic State. This is because the Messenger Muhammad said, "Whoever insults a Prophet kill him" (Choudary 2014).

The perfect example of extremists using the Qur'an to legitimatize their barbaric actions is the Jan. 7, 2015, massacre of staff members at the satirical weekly newspaper *Charlie Hebdo* in Paris. Extremists affiliated with al-Qaeda, or ISIS, initiated the attack simply because the newspaper printed a cartoon of the prophet Mohammed. The newspaper is known for its satirical mockery and ridicule of religions and politics. However, whatever made *Charlie Hebdo* persist in its work on the Prophet Mohammed may have also created enough anger among Islamic radicals. It caught worldwide media attention and may be the catalyst for Islamic reform. Being respectful of all religions is a very important component of peace and reconciliation. No other religion or political individual has ever reacted with such disdain and outcry as the Islamic fundamentalist states, and Islamic radical extremists, in particular.

Islam hasn't always banned the depiction of Mohammed. In fact, it has a rich heritage of images and icons that date back to the 13th century.

The Observer, a part of *The Guardian*, published an article about Muslim art on Jan. 10, 2015, that focused on the prohibition of depictions of the prophet.

Educated readers will benefit greatly from the knowledge in the article, particularly in the wake of the *Charlie Hebdo* tragedy.

> "To many Muslims, any image of the prophet Muhammad is sacrilegious, but the ban has not always been absolute

> and there is a small but rich tradition of devotional Islamic art going back more than seven centuries that does depict God's messenger. It began with exquisite miniatures from the 13th century, scholars say. Commissioned from Muslim artists by the rich and powerful of their day, they show almost every episode of Muhammad's life as recounted in the Qur'an and other texts, from birth to death and ascension into heaven" (Graham-Harrison 2015).

Even I remember as a young boy seeing artistic images of the prophet riding on a flying horse that was half-man and half-beast in my village marketplace, depicting Mohammed's night journey to the Temple Mount before he ascended to heaven.

To have honor and love for the prophet is beautiful and fine. But, you cannot force your belief on other people who are not Muslims or who have issues with your notion of the prophet. We are not living in the 6th century. We are living in the 21st century where all faiths are challenged. With the advent of technological achievement, higher learning and social media, what had been kept in the dark, particularly religious teachings, is now on the rise. Religious truths, which were once pushed under the rug for thousands of years, are now bursting out of control.

Mohammed's standard of morality has become the focal point of everyday debate in recent years.

Let's take a closer look at the prophet.

Muslims take Mohammed's morality as the standard for Islam. This view was accepted by the people of Mohammed's days because it was the norm; that's how wars were fought then. The Romans, Jews and Christians did the same. However, when examined by today's standards, we find Muslims' claims on Prophet Mohammed are being challenged.

I have no doubt Mohammed was a true and legitimate prophet sent by God for a specific providential mission. However, having said that, judging by today's standard, many people doubted him. By today's standards, some people believed Mohammed was not perfect. He had nine wives, one of which was only 9 years old. Because of this, many men in the fundamental Muslim countries, marry preteen girls and have more than one wife. This was a normal practice in the ancient times and done for political reasons. It was practiced not only by the prophet Mohammed but even in other cultures. King Henry VIII of England (reign: 1509-1547) had six wives. Two of them – to Catherine of Aragon and Anne of Cleves – could be considered political alliances. During wars, neighboring monarchies made allies with each other. Kings married their children or preteen siblings to the children or siblings of other kings. So, in truth, Mohammed is not to blame here.

Having said that, although this problem no longer exists in Christianity today, in today's standard, anyone, whether he is a prophet, president or ordinary person, if he had sex with a preteen girl, he would be named a pedophile and would be arrested and jailed. Warren Jeffs, the former fundamentalist Mormon leader, was convicted of child abuse and sentenced to life in prison without parole for this serious offense.

Islam Does Not Mean Peace

Another misconception held by Western countries is the word Islam means peace. This is incorrect! The true meaning of "Islam" means "surrender." As understood by extremist and fundamentalist Muslims, Islam means submission to the divine commands of the one and only supreme Allah/God. This is where the trick is. To Muslims, the Western concept of freedom of expression conflicts with their Islamic beliefs. They argue that speech and action are determined solely by Allah. Yet, they (Muslims) take freedom of action and issue fatwas, judge, kill and terrorize their subjects any way they like in the name of Islam and Allah as if Allah (God) Himself is judging and doing the killing!

So, where is Allah in all this? In an increasingly unstable and insecure world, the fear of potential consequences of insulting Muhammad or doubting the Qur'an is known and felt by Muslims and non-Muslims alike. But, should this be held as eternal truth?

Respect and Tolerance Are Keys for Peace and Reconciliation

But, again, viewing Islam and the prophet Mohammed with a negative misunderstanding does not encourage peace and reconciliation. Instead, it could lead to more retaliation and war by Muslims. We must keep in mind that whatever we discuss about the prophet's life, even if it doesn't conform to the standards or laws of our modern world, it was the custom and culture of his time. We must be careful. We are dealing with a 1,400-year-old religion that is practiced by 1.6 billion people all over the world. The opposition, particularly evangelical Christians, want to generalize, stereotype and smear them so they can win the debate/argument.

To be fair, although some Westerners look at Mohammed and Islam with disdain, I want to remind them there were leaders in Judaism, Christianity and Buddhism who were considered "holy," but were, in truth, worse than Mohammed. In Jewish history, we read from 1 Kings 11:1-3 that King Solomon had 700 wives and 300 concubines! Who knows how many he killed? In other Bible stories, we read that some countries were laid waste and all the inhabitants—men, women, children and even their animals—were all killed in the name of God and religion. In Christian history, we read about many horrific events that were committed in the name of Jesus Christ. During the Crusades, the Catholic Church barbarically slaughtered millions of Muslims and Jews. But, the Protestant Reformation in the 16th century changed that. Christianity changed.

Luther's "Ninety-Five Theses" started the disputes and protests against clerical abuses, especially nepotism, simony, usury, pluralism, etc. My hope is Islam is going through its own reformation right now because when you look at what extremists are doing to the Islamic faith, there is a lot that it needs to reform and change.

Part Three

Preparation for the Second Coming

CHAPTER 25

Signs To Be Observed

Having shared my story on how God miraculously lead me to meet the Unification movement in the most dramatic way, and having shared the new revelation of truth I learned from the Rev. Moon's teaching, a few questions remain. Is our time the Last Days? And, if so, when will the return of the Messiah take place? Were there signs given in the 20th century that support this claim? One thing we must keep in mind is the Last Days' theme is the Second Coming of Christ.

Why is it important to know about the Last Days and the Second Coming of Christ? It is because, if we are religious people and believe in God and His words, we know we are obligated by our faith to believe what was promised and commanded to come. How did God say He will reveal the signs on the Last Days? He didn't say He will reveal signs of the Last Days through the news media, such as CNN, MSNBC, FOX News, newspapers, such as The New York Times or The Washington Post, or social media. As mentioned in the Bible, God said He would reveal the news of the Last Days in dreams (Acts 2:17) and (Joel 2:28-29).

Another question you might ask: How do we know we are in the Last Days? More than 80 percent of Christians and Muslims believe our time is the Last Days. Why? Because many of the biblical prophecies have come to pass! As mentioned earlier, there have been more prophecies fulfilled in the 20th century than during any other time in Christian history. One of the greatest biblical prophecies was made by Jesus in Matt. 24:32-34. It was fulfilled in 1948 when the Jewish people returned to their Holy Land. In Matt. 24:32-34, Jesus gave a clear prophecy on Israel Rebirth and the time of His return. Let's read:

> "From the fig tree learn its lesson: as soon as its branch becomes tender and puts forth its leaves, you know that summer is near. So also, when you see all these things, you

> know that he is near, at the very gates. Truly, I say to you, this generation will not pass away till all these things take place" (Matt. 24:32-34).

This is phenomenal! Israel, a nation that had not really existed for nearly 2,000 years since it was destroyed by the Roman Empire in 72 AD was declared a sovereign state by an act of the United Nations on May 14, 1948. The nation was born in a day. The miracle of Israel's rebirth was prophesied exactly in Isa. 66:8:

> "Who has heard such a thing? Who has seen such things? Shall a land be born in one day? Shall a nation be brought forth in one moment? For as soon as Zion was in labor she brought forth her sons."

> Let us read a few more Bible prophesies on Israel's rebirth. In the Last Days:

> "I will bring you out from the peoples and gather you out of the countries where you are scattered" (Ezek. 20: 34).

> "For the children of Israel shall dwell many days without king or prince, without sacrifice or pillar … Afterward the children of Israel shall return and seek the Lord their God, and David their king; and they shall come in fear to the Lord and to his goodness in the latter days" (Hos. 3: 4-5).

> "In that day the Lord will extend his hand yet a second time to recover the remnant which is left of his people … He will raise an ensign for the nations, and will assemble the outcasts of Israel, and gather the dispersed of Judah from the four corners of the earth" (Isa. 11: 11-12).

It is interesting to note that even the Qur'an has a similar prophecy on Israel's rebirth as a sign of the Last Days. Let's read …

> "And We said Pharaoh to the Children of Israel: 'Dwell in the land, and when there comes the promise of the Hereafter, We will bring you forth in [one] gathering" (Qur'an 17:104)

Now, you might wonder if I am right that the present day is in the Last Days era, where is the Messiah? Hold on! As I mentioned earlier, Jesus gave us a clue, which was stated in Matt. 24:32-34. Let's read that Bible verse again:

> "From the fig tree learn its lesson: as soon as its branch becomes tender and puts forth its leaves, you know that summer is near. So also, when you see all these things, you know that he is near, at the very gates. Truly, I say to you, this generation will not pass away till all these things take place."

What generation was Jesus talking about? Was he talking about a generation in his time? No! The generation Jesus was talking about is none other than the generation that witnessed Israel reinstated as a sovereign independent state! To be specific, the generations that will witness the Second Coming of Christ are the generations born before World War II and the "Baby Boomers," who were born after World War II. The Messiah was born in 1920, and the generation that was born in the same decade as him was the prepared generation. However, because of World War II, the Messiah needed time to mature. The generation that is really prepared are the Baby Boomers. We are truly living in the Last Days. Another way we can tell our present time is part of the Last Days are the significant signs that our world is in a Messianic age that has never been seen before. Just think about it. Out of the chaos and distraction of the world wars came a great change. There have been the phenomena of rapid technological and scientific change in our time, including space travel and exploration, television, the Internet and social media. This has transformed our world into a global village. Only 50 years ago, we didn't have any of these things! Add to this the spiritual movements that were occurring in the 20th century. Movements, such as the Pentecostal Movement, New Age and Interfaith movements, all mushroomed during this period.

The New Age Movement: On the spiritual level in America, we have also witnessed significant signs. The rise of three Spiritual Movements happened to sprout around the same time: New Age, Pentecostal and Interfaith. The New Age is, in fact, a free-flowing, decentralized, spiritual movement. It is a network of believers and practitioners who share similar beliefs. In the first decade of the 21st century, the movement gained a very wide following. The New Age movement became popular during the 1970s as a reaction to the failure of Christianity and the failure of secular humanism to provide spiritual and ethical guidance for the future.

The Pentecostal Movement (Joel 2:28-29): The Pentecostal Revival Movement is a renewal movement within Protestant Christianity that places special emphasis on a direct personal experience with God through the baptism of the Holy Spirit. For those who don't know or have forgotten, the Pentecostal Movement was ignited and spread like wildfire throughout the United States and to all parts of the world after the Azusa Street Miracle in the early 20th century that fascinated church historians for decades and has yet to be fully understood and explained. What is the Azusa Miracle? For more than three years, the Azusa Street "Apostolic Faith Mission" conducted three services a day, seven days a week, and hundreds of thousands attended, hoping to receive the Holy Spirit. From Azusa Street, the revival spread throughout the United States. The Azusa Street Revival became a historic Pentecostal revival meeting, which took place in Los Angeles in 1906; it is the origin of the Pentecostal Movement. It was led by an African-American preacher named William Joseph Seymour. The Pentecostal Movement is, by far, the largest and most important religious movement of the 20th century. In 2000, there were an estimated 560 million Pentecostals in the world.

The Interfaith Movement: The Interfaith Movement also began in America roughly at the same time as the Pentecostal Movement. Its first meeting occurred in Chicago. In 1893, The World's Congress of Religions hosted its largest international gathering of 5,000 religious leaders for a formal interfaith dialogue with the iconic words, "Sisters and brothers of America!" The question to ponder is "Why did these movements happen to occur at the same?" There is no reason for this phenomenon other than to prepare the people of the world for the Second Coming of Christ! One perfect example of this and the fruit of this preparation is Billy Graham. There were no mentioned signs in the Bible of a returning Elijah preceding the return of the Messiah, such as the one found in Mal. 4:4-6. However, when you read Graham's story, you will be amazed. Graham was a sure sign of the Messiah is on the Earth, speaking at mass rallies and on speaking tours. At the same time, Graham was preaching to thousands in the 1970s and '80s.

The Occult Movement: The turn of the 20th century was a period of intense spiritual searching in America, Asia and Russia. It is the period that produced great psychologists, such as Vladimir Bekhterev, a Russian psychologist-hypnotist; Russia's Rasputin, Austrian Sigmund Freud and Switzerland's Carl Jung, as well as Edgar Casey, Harry Houdini and fortune tellers in America. From roughly 1890 to 1914, these countries' educated classes exhibited a fascination for mysticism and the occult and all manner of the supernatural, from table turning and hypnotism to telepathy, fortune-telling and mediumship. Toward the turn of the 20th century, the fascination for the occult became widespread. It went beyond America's artists and intellectuals and reached deep into the middle class. Let's not forget to mention the tense spiritual environment that was engulfing the world like wildfire, particularly in Korea and the United States. The spiritual revival movements produced great religious evangelical leaders, such as America's Billy Graham and Korea's Sun Myung Moon.

CHAPTER 26

Billy Graham: America's John the Baptist/Elijah

As I mentioned earlier in the John the Baptist chapter, the mission of the Rev. Billy Graham, as part of the Older Brother/ Younger Brother pattern, was crucial. Graham was the Elijah/ John whom God had prepared.

On Bible.org, Robert L. Deffinbaugh, pastor of Community Bible Chapel in Richardson, Texas, wrote about the significance of Graham's mission and compared it with that of John the Baptist.

> "A few days ago, my wife and I watched a special televised broadcast of Billy Graham's evangelistic campaign in Dallas, Texas, last fall. There was some great music by Michael W. Smith and the Gaither Vocal Band. Then, when it came time for Billy Graham to speak, he was introduced by former President George Bush. What a wonderful compliment to Mr. Graham and to his faithfulness in preaching the gospel to many presidents and their families over the years. If Jesus were to preach at a football stadium in Dallas, Texas, who would you expect to introduce Him? I can assure you that John the Baptist would not be at the top of the list. Indeed, I doubt that John would have been on the list at all. In a sense, one could say that John's mission in life was to introduce Jesus as God's promised Messiah, the hope of all the ages" (https://bible.org/seriespage/john-baptist-and-jesus-matthew-31-17).

In the world today, there has never been a John the Baptist figure on the global scale greater than Billy Graham! As *Time* magazine (Gibbs and Duffy, 2007) put it:

> "From Truman to Bush II, he's had a job no one has ever had—a spiritual guide to the most powerful men in the

> world. However, the Scriptures never foretold the return of the John the Baptist or Elijah in our time. But, truly, if we tune our innermost spiritual senses and study the life of Graham and how he was chosen, prepared and raised by God to occupy such a high calling, we would be amazed by the similarities between him and John the Baptist."

Just like John the Baptist, Graham was a wanderer. He is "a preacher who had no church, and who spent his life preaching to football stadiums full of people whom he never saw again" (Gibbs and Duffy, 2007). Graham was an inspired and charismatic minister who touched the hearts and souls of millions of people around the globe. He awakened them and rekindled their spiritual fire to receive the returning Christ. This, in a sense, is like John the Baptist, who went before the Lord to prepare the people for His return.

Graham recounted his early life in his book *Just As I Am: The Autobiography of Billy Graham* (2007). In the chapter "180-Degree Turn," he spoke about his hometown, Charlotte, N.C. He said, in 1934, Charlotte was considered to be one of the leading churchgoing cities in the United States. In a way, this city could be considered the "New Jerusalem," which was being prepared by God to raise a modern-day John the Baptist figure, just as Pyongyang, North Korea, could be considered the New Jerusalem of the East, which was being prepared by God to raise a messiah-like figure.

Graham spoke about his father's dramatic spiritual experience. One night, during a church meeting, the preacher called his father to the platform and threw his arms over his father's shoulders and announced to the crowd: "Here is a young man whom God has called to preach, I'm sure" (Graham 2007, 23). After that experience, he was sick for days. He could neither eat nor sleep and didn't know what had happened to him. Deep in his heart, though, he knew the Lord had something planned for him. He believed he would know when the time was right.

Years later, his father remembered a prayer his preacher, the Rev. Vernon Patterson, had prayed: "Out of Charlotte the Lord would raise up someone to preach the Gospel to the ends of the Earth." Graham, who believed his father sincerely, wanted to fulfill the preacher's call but had no way to do it. As Graham explained: "In fact, he privately hoped and prayed that his firstborn son might someday fulfill the old Methodist evangelist's prophecy by becoming a preacher in his stead" (Graham 2007, 24).

At that time, the young Graham had no idea he would be the person delegated to preach the Gospel to the world.

Graham's appointment with destiny was sparked the night he heard the Rev. Mordecai Ham, a Southern Baptist minister from Oklahoma, speak. Ham had been invited by a few Charlotte ministers and the Christian Men's Club to preach at their scheduled revival meetings in Charlotte's largest tabernacle, which could seat 5,000. The preacher was well-known for his "stern and fiery" preaching on sin and Hell and judgment by fire in The Last Days. His sermons often got published in newspapers and thousands of people would flock to his revival meetings. The news he was attending the revival meeting reached every house in Charlotte. The entire city prepared for his arrival, including the Graham family.

It is interesting how God uses certain people to forward his predestined plan through them and their prophecies. And, in this case, we are referring to Patterson, who foresaw a man from Charlotte, who would preach the Gospel to the whole world. He also prophesied the Graham family would fulfill that prophecy.

Later, in a parallel way, God used Ham as an instrument on the night Billy attended the revival meeting. And, Graham had a spiritual experience that was similar to the one his father had.

Apparently, Graham's parents attended a few revival meetings and heard Ham's lively sermons. They were inspired and believed the preacher brought good hope and inspiration to the city more than any other revival meeting had in the past. His parents tried to get him to attend, but the younger Graham wasn't interested. As he said in his book:

> "Despite my parent's enthusiasm, I did not want anything to do with anyone called an 'evangelist' – and, particularly, with such a colorful character as Dr. Ham. Having just turned sixteen, I told my parents that I would not go to hear him" (Graham 2007, 24).

What attracted Graham to this preacher was that he was a mighty fighter! Ham came to the city to deal with a scandal that had occurred on a local school campus, and rumors were spreading some angry students were planning a surprise demonstration against him in front of the stage. It was this event that stirred Graham's curiosity, and he decided to see what would happen. A few minutes after the evangelist began his sermon, Graham found himself "spellbound." In some mystifying way, the preacher was getting through to him, and he was hearing another voice: "The voice of the Holy Spirit." From that night on, the young Graham became a faithful attendant and never missed a revival meeting.

There was something so powerful about this preacher that Graham was eager to hear more from him. And, then it happened, sometime around his 16th birthday. (Interestingly, the Rev. Moon was 16 years old when he also had a spiritual experience, in which Jesus appeared and asked him to take on his mission!) That night, Ham finished preaching and extended an invitation to Graham to accept Christ. Graham responded and walked to the platform and accepted Christ, and, when he did, his life changed forever. As Graham said, "There were signs, though, that my thinking and direction had changed, that I had truly been converted. To my own surprise, church activities that had bored me before seemed interesting all of a sudden" (Graham 2007, 31).

From then on, God began to train Graham for his ministry. Graham recounted his training period in the "Called to Preach" chapter of his book, where he mentioned how he practiced his sermons by preaching to nature. As he said: "I would paddle a canoe across the Hillsborough to a little island where I could address all creatures, great and small, from alligators to birds" (Graham 2007, 49).

I can truly relate to his story because it reminded me of my early years in the Unification Church and the spiritual experience I had in a park (See the "An Hour with God" section in Chapter 34).

Graham was truly God's special messenger who was chosen to prepare the world for the return of Christ. As spiritually attuned as he was an educated in pastoral theology and hermeneutics, the theory of text interpretation, which includes the interpretation of biblical texts, Graham should have sensed that, perhaps, the Messiah might possibly appear in his time, and might even have come from Pyongyang, which Graham, in his book, referred to as the New Jerusalem of the East in the chapter, "Through Unexpected Doors in the 1930s."

Sincerely, I don't wish to accuse or offend a great man of God, such as Graham, but the truth of the matter is, when I read Rev. 2: 17, I question whether he understood the Book of Revelation and the prophecies contained in it that refer to Christ's Second Coming:

> "He who has an ear, let him hear what the Spirit says to the churches. To him who conquers I will give some of the hidden manna, and I will give him a white stone, with a new name written on the stone which no one knows except him who receives it" (Rev. 2:17).

Had Graham put these two prophecies together and prayed about them, God might have revealed to him something about Moon. But, on the other hand, I understand, it is not so easy. Unfortunately, Graham fell into the same ditch as John the Baptist. Like John the Baptist, he did not know his visitation. God had done miraculous works, pulled him out of the farm, led him to the highest mountaintop, connected him with the world's greatest leaders during five of the most crucial decades, and served every U.S. president during that time. As the *Time* cover story said: "From Truman to Bush II, he's had a job no one else has ever had a spiritual guide to the most powerful men in the world" (Gibbs and Duffy 2007).

God loved and supported Graham's evangelical revival mission, which reached hundreds of millions of people worldwide. Why? It was not only because he was preaching the Gospel to the world, but, most importantly, it was because he was preparing the world for the return of Christ. Like John the Baptist, Graham worked with millions of people and brought them to Christ, but he did not connect them to the Lord of the Second Coming. According to Jesus' words, John was the greatest prophet of all. But, because he failed his primary mission, he became the least among prophets, and, likewise, Graham did as well.

Unfortunately, all these great men, who God had raised and prepared, did not realize the specifics of their missions and ended up missing their appointed hour. And, in a sense, this is an answer to Graham's yearning question, which one can find on the back cover of his book:

> "I have often said that the first thing I am going to do when I get to heaven is to ask, "Why me, Lord? Why did you choose a farm boy from North Carolina to preach to so many people, to have such a wonderful team of associates, and to have a part in what You were doing in the latter half of the 20th century? I have thought about that question a great deal, but I know also that only God knows the answer" (Graham 2007).

Could it also explain why all the presidents for whom Graham served as a spiritual guide, confessed to him they felt something was lacking in their presidencies? He said: "Every president I think I have known, except Truman, has thought they didn't quite get done what they wanted to be done. And, towards the end of their administration, they were disappointed and wished they had done some things differently" (Gibbs and Duffy 2007).

After reading this quote, I could not help but think of President Ronald Reagan. As great a president as he was, Reagan made a big mistake when he allowed the government to sentence Moon to jail during his presidency. It was not enough that Moon served his sentence. And, even though Moon was innocent, Reagan did not pardon him and clear his name. Neither did any other president after him. Moon really loved America, truly loved Reagan and supported his election campaign. Moon believed Reagan was the anointed man of God to lead this country and the world to peace and safety. Reagan was the country's 40th president, and Moon recognized the number 40 is God's providential number! We could find the number 40 repeated in all major providential events in the Bible. Had Graham understood his mission, God would have used him to create miraculous achievements.

As we have read in earlier chapters, God prepared these early spiritual groups in Korea to receive the young Moon as their Messiah on the local and national level. In the Western Hemisphere,

God had also prepared Graham to take on John the Baptist's mission. Graham's life story was similar to Moon's life. Spiritually, they were like distant cousins. It is really amazing how these two men appeared to resemble each other in the way they have evangelized the world. Looking at photographs and reading through Graham's book, I cannot help but marvel at the similarity in the size of the mass rallies or conventions these two men managed to gather, drawing together hundreds of thousands of people at a time. Like Graham, Moon drew one of the largest crowds in history. More than 1.2 million people attended Moon's "World Rally for Korean Freedom" in 1975 (Quebedeaux 1982, 176). In the United States, Moon drew the largest crowd at the Washington Monument, with more than 300,000 in attendance! (Buckingham 2010, 74)

Interestingly, there is another important question to consider. Could it be a coincidence that Graham's wife, Ruth, spent her teenage years in Pyongyang during the Korean War? I wonder what school and church she attended while she was there (The Washington Post 2007). Could she have heard the rumors about this young man from Korea proclaiming to be the Messiah? Could she have talked about her years in Pyongyang to her husband or children? It would be very interesting to know. Therefore, in closing my chapter on Graham, I would like to pose a question similar to the one Deffinbaugh asked at the beginning of this chapter: If Christ, at His Second Coming, was to speak at RFK Memorial Stadium in Washington, D.C., or at the Washington Monument, who would you expect to introduce Him and support Christ's mission better than Billy Graham, the man God had prepared? It is interesting to note Moon stirred up mainstream media with major speaking tours in every state. He spoke in many places, including Madison Square Garden and RFK Memorial Stadium in Washington, D.C. Where was Billy Graham then? Had it crossed his mind that Moon could possibly be the returning Christ? Or did he deny Moon like John the Baptist denied Jesus Christ? After all, in a 1952 speech titled "Second Coming," Graham gave an extensive list of 32 signs of The Last Days that were fulfilled in our time. He strongly believed the Second Coming of Christ could happen at any time. Unfortunately, Graham fell into the same hole as John the Baptist. He believed Christ would return on a literal cloud (https://www.youtube.com/watch?v=SFZXJmAljl4&feature=share).

With all this in mind, I leave this subject to the readers to pray, meditate and discover the truth for themselves. As I have said, I have great respect and appreciation for Graham, and there is no question in my mind he was the greatest man of God of the 20th century. But, I still think about the Unificationists' claims regarding him and his relationship with the John the Baptist mission. Graham had been visited by numerous Unification Church leaders on several different occasions, but he didn't accept what they told him, and he waved each one off.

Now, let's deal with the prophecy on the Second Coming in greater detail.

CHAPTER 27

Second Coming of Christ

When Will Christ Return?

The chosen generations prepared to receive Christ at The Second Coming are the generations born between World War II and the "Baby Boomers."

> "From the fig tree learn its lesson: as soon as its branch becomes tender and puts forth its leaves, you know that summer is near. So also, when you see all these things, you know that he is near, at the very gates. Truly, I say to you, this generation will not pass away till all these things take place" (Matt. 24:32-34).

Although, in Matt. 24:36, Jesus said: "But of that day and hour no one knows …," which indicates to me it would be fruitless to speculate as to when He will return. However, in that same verse, He says the father knows, and Amos 3:7 says, "Surely the Lord God does nothing, without revealing his secret to his servants the prophets."

Jesus' prophecy, which was stated above and mentioned in John Price's book, *The End Of America,* was His answer to his disciples' initial question of "When shall these things be?" The phrase, "until all these things," was in reference to events He said would happen in The End Times, including prophecies about the antichrist, the tribulation and the Lord's return to Earth. So, what did he mean when he said the generation that sees the fig tree bloom would not pass away until all those things have happened? What does a fig tree have to do with The End Times prophecy?

Before we examine this issue, let us first understand something about the fig tree. The following is an explanation of the fig tree noted in Price's book: "Hosea [9:10] described Israel in this way: 'When I found Israel … it was like seeing the early fruit on the fig tree" (Price 2013, 4-5).

Over time, the clear consensus has been that the fig tree is an allegorical identification of Israel and its rebirth in the land as prophesied in both the Old and New Testament (Deuteronomy 30 and Matthew 24). Journalist Mike Evans, in his book, *The Return* (1996), wrote: "The fig tree has always been a symbol of the nation of Israel. The leaves of fig tree are common ornaments on government buildings in Israel" (Evans, 1996).

Therefore, it's important to understand that when Jesus told his disciples about the rebirth of Israel and used a future budding fig tree to describe it, His words were a symbolic prophecy. Price provided a Bible verse that illustrated how Israel rejected Jesus. Mark 11:13 says as Jesus was on his way to Jerusalem in the days before he was to be crucified, he left Bethany, just east of Jerusalem. On the way, he saw a fig tree. Alas, the fig tree, although covered with leaves, had no figs on its branches. Jesus spoke to the tree and admonished it for not bearing fruit. He then pronounced this particular fig tree would never bear fruit, a malediction that was confirmed the next day when Jesus and His disciples passed by the same fig tree, which had "withered away to its roots" (Mark 11:20).

Obviously, as Price noted, this was more than just talking to a tree. One of the stated signs of God's blessings on the Israelites was "every man will sit under his own vine and under his own fig tree" (I Kings 4:25; Isa. 36:16, Mic. 4:4). Fig trees bear fruit and are blessings to their owners. This particular tree was no blessing because it had literally no figs, and, thus, symbolically, no spiritual fruit. So, as Jesus ended his earthly ministry, he gave a symbolic assessment of Israel's rejection of him. According to Price, He found no fruit on the fig tree that represented Israel and declared the tree would not bear fruit. His statement, of course, was accurate because, at that time, Israel did not bear spiritual fruit. It withered away and was dispersed a few short years after the rejection of its Messiah.

Now, let's return to Jesus' prophecy that another fig tree would bloom and signal The End Times. As Price noted, there has been some significant dispute as to what Jesus meant when He said, "the generation" would see the fig tree rebud (Israel return) and would not pass away or die until "all these things (The End

Times prophecies He gave us) have all happened" (Price 2013, 6). What, then, did Jesus mean when He said, "the generation?" In this verse (Matt. 24:32), Jesus is speaking of the generation that was in existence at the time or witnessed the budding of the fig tree. It would not pass away, or die out before all the prophesied events happened. So, this brings us to the timing. The prophecies about the Jews returning to their homeland were fulfilled in 1948 when Israel became a sovereign nation. In other words, the generations that were born between 1920 and 1948 and saw the rebirth of the fig tree/Israel on May 14, 1948, are the generations that witnessed the Second Coming of Christ!

So, according to many spiritual leaders' observations of biblical indicators of "the End of Times," when all these signs occur, the last generation of people before the Second Coming of Christ will face many challenges, such as wars and catastrophic natural calamities. In a sense, these signs have already happened (World War I and World War II). Recently, many signs have come to pass. Israel has been re-established. There have been several natural calamities, such as earthquakes, hurricanes and tsunamis. Then came 9/11 and the wars in Afghanistan and Iraq. Most recently, the stock market collapsed to an unprecedented low level of a providential number, 777 points, in 2008 (www.marketoracle.co.uk/Article6528.html). The Emergency Economic Stabilization Act of 2008 was enacted to fix the subprime mortgage crisis. The $700 billion the U.S. Treasury used to solve the problem panicked Americans and affected the World Bank and economies of other countries. It was a worldwide catastrophe!

According to Price's interpretation of Matt. 24:32-34, the second advent of the Messiah occurred sometime after the World War I (Price 2013, 5). Again, one would ask, if the Messiah has already come, why haven't we witnessed the final judgment and glory of The Second Coming? As I explained earlier, the Lord will not literally come on a cloud. The Second Coming will occur by the Messiah's birth on Earth and not as Christians expect Him to appear: on a cloud. The purpose of the cloud was for saints and purehearted and faithful believers to rise spiritually to the level of the Messiah.

Biblical prophecies on the Last Days, or End Times, and the

coming of a "New Age" have been predicted by other religions as well. If biblical prophecies, such as Matthew 24, aren't enough to convince readers about this, there are others told by numerous spiritual sages and prophets to whom God had revealed his secrets. Among them, I would like to mention four: Nostradamus, Edgar Cayce, Arthur Ford and the Korean Book of Prophecies.

Would Christ Come on the Cloud?

Christians have traditionally believed Christ will return on a cloud. However, in Luke 17:24-25, we read that Jesus, anticipating what will happen at the Second Coming, said, "For as the lightning, flashes and lights up the sky from one side to the other, so will the Son of man be in his day. But, first, he must suffer many things and be rejected by this generation." So, if the Lord should come again amid power and glory, with the trumpet call, who would dare deny and persecute him? However, if he does not come on a literal cloud, and instead be born of flesh, as in the First Coming, then it becomes apparent why Jesus said he would first suffer before finally being recognized.

Before I start this chapter, I must explain an important point concerning the "Messiah." Christians and Muslims adopted the Judaic theological views on the Advent of the Messiah, Last Days and Second Coming of Christ, which lay heavily on the views held by the Essenes.

According to the *New World Encyclopedia*, the word Messiah was developed during the Babylonian exile of the Jewish people. One of the earliest prophecies was written in the 8th century BCE by the prophet Isaiah, who wished for a more powerful, righteous, political and militaristic ruler than who was occupying the throne at the time. It refers to the coming of a new Davidic king who would unite Israel (Southern Kingdom) and Judah (Northern Kingdom), conquer the surrounding nations and enable the return of the Israelites, who were taken into captivity by the Assyrians (Isa. 11:10-14). Approximately a century after Isaiah, the prophet Jeremiah reiterated Isaiah's prophecy:

> "Behold, the days are coming, says the Lord, when I will raise up for David a righteous Branch, and he shall reign

> as king and deal wisely, and shall execute justice and righteousness in the land. In his days Judah will be saved, and Israel will dwell securely. And this is the name by which he will be called: The Lord is our righteousness" (Jer. 23: 5-6).

The Hebrew term "Mashiach" literally means "the anointed one," and refers to the ancient Jewish practice of anointing kings with oil when they took the throne (www.jewfaq.org/mashiach.htm). This is very similar to the ceremonial inauguration of U.S. presidents, but instead of being anointed by oil, they swear on the Bible. However, it should be noted that to the Jews, the word "Mashiach" does not mean "savior." The notion of an innocent, divine being who will sacrifice himself to save sinners is a purely Christian concept with no basis in Jewish belief (www.jewfaq.org/mashiach.htm).

By the 1st century BCE, the Jews interpreted their scriptures to refer specifically to someone appointed by God to deliver them from oppression under the Roman Empire. However, the Israelites' concept of "Mashiach" had two opposing ideas of what the Messiah was expected to be. This complicated matters even further when Jesus began his public ministry and proclaimed himself to be the Son of God. The ideals based on the Book of Isaiah, emphasizing the Messiah as a Prince of Peace and deliverer of Israel from oppression represented one trend of thought. The apocalyptic promises of supernatural intervention by prophets, such as Zechariah, Joel and others, represented a more otherworldly trend.

In the 1st century BCE, the Essenes reacted against the corruption of both priestly and political authorities and foresaw the imminent coming of the Day of the Lord, in which both a divine and a Davidic messiah would arise to lead the "children of light" in a battle against the Romans, Gentiles and other "children of darkness." In the period when Jesus was born, there was much confusion and political and religious upheaval abounded. Among the emerging sects were the Pharisees, who saw the Messiah as a deliverer, just as Isaiah had predicted. Others expected cataclysmic events, such as described in the Book of Daniel:

> "I saw in the night visions, and behold, with the clouds of heaven there came one like a son of man, and he can to the Ancient of Days and was presented before him. And to him was given dominion and glory and kingdom, that all peoples, nations, and languages should serve him; his dominion is an everlasting dominion, which shall not pass away, and his kingdom one that shall not be destroyed" (Dan. 7:13-14).

Such were the messianic hopes and expectations that flourished a few decades before Jesus' birth, approximately 37-34 BCE. Tragically, the much-prepared chosen people failed to recognize Jesus as their messiah. He was never understood, branded a blasphemer and, ultimately, crucified! After Jesus' death, the Jews rebelled against the Romans, which led to the destruction of the Second Temple and the expulsion of the Jews from Jerusalem in 70 AD.

Christianity emerged in the 1st century AD as a movement among Jews who believed Jesus was the Messiah. However, the Christian concept of the Messiah remained unsolved, and the conflicting trends of thought continue to haunt Christianity today! Evidently, the Christian concept of the Second Coming of Christ is modeled after Daniel's supernatural concept that a divine messiah would appear in the clouds of heaven. This, of course, has caused much debate in the latter part of the 20th century.

As the new millennium drew closer, there had been much talk and anticipation about the "End of Time," the Mayan calendar and the Second Coming of Christ. TV documentaries and church sermons still continue to talk about it. So, the question remains: Would the returning Christ come on the literal clouds or would He be born in the flesh just like He did the first time?

Could Moon Be the Returning Christ?

Personally, in my humble opinion, I believe he is. Based on what we have read so far from Jesus's story and why he wasn't recognized by the Israelites of his day, it is clear the Israelites had a different view of what kind of a being the Messiah is and the manner in which he would return. And, so do the Christians.

Contrary to their expectations, the Messiah was born of the flesh like the first time. Just like John the Baptist, the returning of Elijah came in the spirit and mission. Elijah's spirit was born in John's body. Therefore, it will also be with the return of Christ as well. Christ's spirit and mission will return and be birthed in the flesh into a different person. That person, I believe was the Rev. Moon. Let's add to this is my own personal story that you have read—the unending chain of prophetic dreams, visions and coincidences that guided me throughout the course of my life, down to the last minute. The way God delivered me to Moon is a pure miracle. There are no coincidences. I reiterate: How many in this world would do just as I did? I received two powerful dreams instructing me to do urgent things, one informing me of a not-so-distant great promise awaiting me somewhere unknown and ordering me to "go out" and look for that promise, and the other giving me a numerical date when I would find that promise. How many would leave everything behind—job, family and community you lived in—and travel from state to state randomly searching for that promise? I did! And, I met that dream promise on Oct. 6, 1981, just as the dream told me (See the "Outdoor Concert" dream in Chapter 9). Or, what about the dream I had the night before that? When my uncle urgently begged me to accept and believe in what God had appointed me to do? (See "Funeral Possession" dream in Chapter 9) Let's not forget the dream I called "Submarine Invasion" (Chapter 11), which confirmed Moon's status as the Messiah.

There are many unbelievable spiritual encounters told in stories by Unificationists about how they were guided to the movement that were published in books, blogs and other social media. These books include *Messiah-My Testimony to Rev. Sun Myung Moon,* by Dr. Bo Hi Pak, one of Moon's early disciples and translators. Another book called "*I am in This Place: Testimonies About Jesus and Sun Myung Moon,* is a collection of testimonies of Unificationists, compiled by Clark Eberly, who tell their stories of what brought them to the movement. You can download the .pdf files for free. There are as many profound stories reported by Unification church members that could fill thousands of books. Negative Christians and communists, with the help of the media, have spread lies and made a mockery of Moon and his movement, which is very similar to what the Jews did to Jesus Christ.

It is time now that you heard the truth from Unification church members themselves and learn what led them to join the Unification movement despite the false accusations and propaganda against Moon and his church by the mainstream media and others who have persecuted Moon and his followers for decades. They called him a heretic and his movement "a cult" and called his followers brainwashed Moonies. Remember, Jesus Christ and the early Christians were also persecuted and seen as members of a cult and a heretical religious movement.

We marvel at Bible stories about dreams, of the dreams of Jacob and Joseph, but we have never considered God can still communicate with us, people of the modern time, through dreams just as He did then. These dreams alone explain why I joined the Unification movement. After all, the Bible tells us that in the Last Days, He "will pour out my Spirit upon all flesh, and your sons and your daughters shall prophesy, and your young men shall see visions, and your old men shall dream dreams (Acts 2:17).

In the 25 years I lived in Europe, Middle East, Asia and the United States, no one had ever approached me and tried to witness to me about God, Jesus Christ or any other faiths. God seemed to have an intense interest in guiding me to the Unification movement in such dramatic and miraculous ways. All the dreams, coincidences and passions that shaped my destiny were pointing in one direction: to the Rev. Moon. Based on how God delivered me to the Unification movement, the world was ready and prepared to receive the returning Messiah. The turn of the 20th century was like a mother in labor waiting to give birth to her child.

The Messiah was born Jan. 6, 1920, in the midst of the most turbulent period in modern history, between World War I and World War II. How greatly important, yet frightening, this period was.

Throughout the past 2,000 years of Christian history, there have been a few people who claimed to be the Messiah. No greater messianic claimant had arisen than the late Rev. Moon, who passed away Sept.3, 2012. Although the Unification Church proclaims its founder to be the Second Coming of Christ, I personally believe he is the Messiah for many reasons. One reason, in particular, is the way I was delivered to his movement. Also, I believe it is because of his teachings and the new revelation on Jesus and the crucifixion, as well as his take on John the Baptist and the miracle of his works, including the mass weddings where millions of couples worldwide are married at one time. No president or pope could match this. Therefore, it is obviously a sign Moon was the expected Messiah.

The church's messianic teachings affirm traditional Christian doctrine that Jesus' death on the cross brought atonement for the sins of mankind. However, it also maintains the traditional Jewish position that the original messianic mission was to go much further and establish God's reign on Earth. Moon taught that Jesus' death was a tragic mistake. He should have lived longer, gotten married (possibly to Mary Magdalene) and had a "true family" with children free of the original sin. Therefore, at the Second Coming, the spirit and mission of Jesus Christ will return in the body of a new person, just as the spirit and mission of the prophet Elijah returned and worked through John the Baptist (Mal. 4:4-5 and Matt. 11:14;17:13) to complete the messianic task.

The formal title given to the messianic couple (Moon and his wife, Han Hak Ja) in the Unification Church is "True Parents." It is believed the Messiah's mission is carried out, not by one man, but by a couple, a restored Adam and Eve, who, as true parents, founded a new lineage free from original sin. Together, they would establish all mankind as the true sons and daughters of God. The process of engrafting is conducted through the "Blessing of Marriage" offered by the Rev. and Mrs. Moon.

The question of whether Moon is the Second Coming of the Messiah depends heavily on faith and prayers. Just as in Jesus' time, the Messiah God sent was rejected by the very people He was trying to help. "He came to his own home, and his own people received him not" (John 1:11). The Apostle Paul testified that "none of the rulers of this age understood this; for if they had, they would not have crucified the Lord of glory" (1 Cor. 2:8). But, on the other hand, we find there were a few "prepared" believers who followed him. So, why did some people believe in the Messiah and others did not? The answer is, first, the Bible tells us God had already prepared the people for the Lord, and, second, as I noted earlier, it depended upon an individual's sincere prayers to find out whether he or she is one of those who God had prepared and whether he or she thirsts for God's love and truth. The following chapter focuses on Nostradamus' eight clues to identify the "New Teacher" or Messiah for the New Age.

CHAPTER 28

Nostradamus Prophecies

A Teacher from the East

Of the many people who wrote books on Nostradamus' prophecies, no one intrigued me more than John Hogue. I felt something special about this man, especially about the way he came to know this medieval prophet.

Hogue's deep interest and passion in interpreting Nostradamus' prophecies fascinated me from the minute I read his book, *Nostradamus and The Millennium* (1987). Hogue said he first learned about Nostradamus in 1967 when his sixth-grade social studies class was watching a documentary on the takeover of Nazi Germany called "The Crooked Cross." As he commented: "Over four centuries ago, (declared the narrator), a Frenchman named Nostradamus predicted a day when the German child would know "no law" and follow the banner of the crooked cross" (Hogue 1987, 1).

It is interesting how Hogue expressed his experience when he was a sixth-grader and how the prediction Nostradamus made about Hitler was, as he said, "engraved and filed away in my mind, which would secretly germinate in my subconscious mind for seven years" (Hogue 1987, 1).

I especially was fascinated by the way Hogue put it. His comment made me think about the man I met in London's Hyde Park almost 40 years ago. His statement, "You think you are alive, but you are dead," had always stuck in my mind. But, in many ways, we are like a fertile ground where God plants His "seeds" that will germinate in our subconscious for future plans. I am quite certain many people today carry these same seeds.

In Chapter 12, "A New Awakening," Hogue interprets Nostradamus' eight clues to identify the "New Teacher" or Messiah for the New Age, the present. In his book, *Nostradamus: The Complete Prophesies,* Hoge listed 12 possible candidates, most of whom were spiritual and religious leaders who had come to America from India and the Far East in the mid-1960s and early '70s. Hogue wrote about this unprecedented period and cited the quatrain that indexes the date: Q75=1975. This is also the year Helena Blavatsky, a 19th-century Russian occultist, predicted a messenger would come to the West (Hogue 1997, 803).

Hogue includes photos and introductions of the 12 candidates, one of which was Moon. In the photo, Moon and his wife were wearing crowns on their heads with white gowns, officiating at a mass wedding ceremony.

The eight clues identifying the true Messiah, or, as he said, The New Teacher, are:

(1) The teacher will come from the East.
(2) He will fly through the sky.
(3) He is a controversial figure.
(4) His name is Moon.
(5) He travels far and wide.
(6) He had been imprisoned.
(7) He is outlawed.
(8) He has the color red.

Hogue's book clearly identified the significant prediction made by Nostradamus. Most of his predictions shockingly came true! He even foretold the outbreak of World War II and Hitler, the downfall of the shah of Iran, Khomeini's rise to power and the return of the Jews to their homeland. Let us look at Nostradamus' prophecy on the Second Coming based on the eight clues mentioned above:

(1) From the East—Teacher Flowers in the West.
The long-awaited will never return.
He will appear in Asia (and be) at home in Europe.
His teaching "flowers" in the West (Hogue 1997).

As Hogue understood from this quatrain, the long-awaited Jesus Christ will never return. The new world teacher (Messiah) will come from the East (Asia). This quatrain reflects the prophecy given in the Book of Revelation in the Bible (Rev. 3:11-12). Jesus said of his return He would come with a new name. Jesus, in fact, referred to the coming of another person as a "conqueror" to whom Jesus will give his own "new" name and give him the morning star and power over the nations and shall rule them with the rod of iron (Rev. 2:17, 26-29).

(2) He will fly through the sky.

He will fly through the sky, the rains,

and the snow and strike everyone with his Rod.

He will appear in Asia and be at home in Europe (Hogue 1997).

Note: This quatrain says this teacher will fly over the land (on a plane), shock the world with the rod of his mouth (truth), his controversial teaching. He will come from the East (Korea) but will live in the West (America).

This quatrain is also about Moon. Personally speaking, there is no one on Earth who had traveled or had given as many speeches as he did. To me, the rod does not mean stick; rather it means a powerful and controversial message of truth.

(3) His Name Is Moon.

Second of the last of the Prophet's name will take Diana's day (the moon's day).

The young sage, alone, with his mind, has seen it.

His disciples invite him to become immortal (Hogue 1997).

Note: Moon proclaimed to the world he was the Second Coming of Christ and all his followers believed he was the returning Messiah. "The young sage alone with his mind has seen it." This can only refer to the time when the 16-year-old Moon was praying on a mountain and Jesus appeared to him asking him to take up His mission. Moon talked about how he entered the spiritual world and met with Jesus and other religious leaders, including Moses, Abraham, Buddha and Mohammed.

(4) The Teacher travels and creates controversy.

(5) He will travel far and wide in his drive to infuriate.

(6) Delivering a great people from subjection (Hogue 1997).

If you consider (4), (5) and (6) together, Moon ignited the world with his speeches, most of them about God's providence and where America and Christianity stand in relation to God's providential plan for the 20th century leading to the New Millennium, especially in the sixth clue, which says, "delivering a great people from subjection" (Hogue 1997), which could only mean the liberation of the world from communism.

(7) The Teacher is outlawed.

"A man will be charged with destroying the temples and religions will be altered by fantasy, ears filled with ornate speeches" (Hogue 1997).

Note: Moon was prohibited from re-entering England, Germany, Japan and France because of false accusations and controversial charges against him. He was blamed for breaking up families and making his followers live strict lives. The largest bulk of this controversy came during Moon's busiest period, the decade between 1974 to 1984 when he held rallies and had speaking engagements.

(8) The Color Red

"Against the red ones religions will unite" (Hogue 1997).

Moon's symbol is the Red Sun rising from the East. In his book, Hogue concluded his discussion of Moon by saying He fits more of Nostradamus' clues than any other teacher at which Hogue had looked. Moon antagonized the world with his claims that he was the Second Coming of Christ. None of the other candidates claimed this. He was an anti-communist, who delivered a great people from subjection (Eph. 104-105). He was a controversial figure, imprisoned six times for his beliefs and banned from entering some countries. He had the name "Moon" and the color red; and he came from Korea, the East, or Asia, as the Bible and Nostradamus referred to it.

Thus, Moon matched all of Nostradamus' clues. Hogue did a great job in understanding and interpreting Nostradamus' words because, as he noted, Nostradamus had to cloak his revelations, so he wouldn't be considered a heretic.

But, as great as he is, I believe Hogue is still learning new things about Nostradamus and his prophecies. He even said so in his book. I did notice one error, however. When Hogue was speaking about Moon, he said: "there was no connection with Hermes or the color red" (Hogue 1994, 181). But, in his book, *Nostradamus: The Complete Prophecies*, Hogue said, "Reverend Moon's symbol is a red rising sun in the East" (Hogue 1997, 806). I am sure if Hogue looked deeper into Moon's teachings, he would probably have discovered something about Hermes Trismegistus, Greek for the Egyptian god Thoth, god of wisdom, learning and literature.

This was no surprise to me because God was the prime motivator for me to write this book, and, as I noted before, God has always provided me with great writing material. As they say, "God works in mysterious ways." Here is what God led me to discover about Hermes.

We must understand Nostradamus was deeply interested in alchemy and Hermetic wisdom of the 16th century, which greatly influenced intellectual and scientific pursuits at the time. As described in *The Ultimate Illustrated Guide to Dreams, Signs and Symbols: Identification and Analysis of the Visual Vocabulary and Secret Language that Shapes our … and Dictates our Reactions to the World* by Mark O'Connell, Raje Airey and Richard Craze (2012), alchemy is directly linked with the teachings of Hermes. Hermes' philosophy was based on the relationship of the microcosmic and macrocosmic worlds. Applied to alchemy, this means the human microcosm, where the body, soul and spirit meet, is directly related to the elements, the stars, planets, moon and sun. The most fascinating writing on the philosophy of alchemy, that, in my opinion, reflects the teachings of Moon, is the chapter "Alchemical Transmutation/Sacred Marriage (O'Connell, Airey and Craze, 2012). It is described as follows:

> "The main symbol of alchemy is the uniting of the king and queen within the fire of love. The union is symbolized by the marriage of sulphur (masculine) and mercury (feminine) or of the sun (spirit) and moon (soul). Alchemy presupposes that humans are in a state of chaos and discord, having lost their connection with "Eden", the primordial state of contentedness. The image of the sacred marriage refers to the renewal of this integral nature through the coming together of the central forces within us" (O'Connell, Airey and Craze 2012, 155).

The above description on the "image of sacred marriage" is very similar to Moon's perspective on salvation through the Holy Wedding. Good men and women of faith who received the Holy Marriage Blessing enter the "New Eden." Guided by the new truth (covenant), the couples would give birth to children free from original sin and build God's New Kingdom. This chapter sums up everything about the teachings and practices of Moon!

Hogue mentioned Moon moving away from the Nostradamus' "Teacher Is Outlawed": "Reverend Moon is moving in with the mainstream evangelical Christians and by being involved in politics in which he and his church were major supporters of President Reagan and President George H. W. Bush" (Hogue 1987, 806).

Hogue needs to understand, first, as Nostradamus predicted, Moon was banned by a few countries. And, second, in Moon's viewpoint, the Messiah came to restore "all things" on the foundation that God had established by Jesus. The New Teacher came to unite Christianity and all religions into "One World Family, Under One Parent God." He was to restore politics into one God-centered ideology. He was to unite sciences and religions. Moon did all this. In his lifetime, Moon established and founded many religious, political, scientific, business and artistic organizations. All testify to Jesus' word when he said: "You will know them by their fruits" (Matt. 7:16). In my book, *Jerusalem Appointment with Destiny*, you will find all the good works Moon had done.

CHAPTER 29

The Legendary Spiritual Medium: Arthur Augustus Ford

Arthur Augustus Ford was one of America's greatest spiritual mediums of the early 20th century. During World War I, while serving in the Army, he realized he had psychic abilities. He would "hear" the names of the people who were serving with him, and, a few days later, they would appear on the casualty list. After he returned from the war, he discovered he had an unusual, but powerful, gift: He could communicate with the dead. He joined the spiritualist movement, and, in 1921, he became a trance medium.

By 1929, Ford had become popular as "Houdini's medium" when, through his helper, Fletcher, he revealed the secret code Houdini and his wife, Bess, had arranged to reveal if he could return.

Later in 1967, Ford, on national television, claimed he contacted the deceased son of a prominent Episcopalian bishop.

Let us now look at what Ford said about Moon. It is better to read Ford's book, *Unknown, But Known: My Adventure into the Meditative* (1968), in its entirety, in which he wrote about Moon. There were many very interesting things discussed in this segment, including truth, New Age and spiritual matters. Here are a few things that were said (Ford 1968, 113):

Setting—1

Sitting, Arthur Ford, November 2, 1964: As Ford fell into a trance and contacted his spiritual friend, "Fletcher," Ford was asked by a group of Moon's close associates if he could tell them something about their teacher, who happened to be present at the moment.

Ford answered them and said Moon's mission was to be a "teacher," a revealer for a new age. Fletcher continued to explain that, at the end of the age, there must be one who will become the voice of God. He spoke about his relationship with God and the rest of the world, as well as prophets from the past: Abraham spoke and became the voice of God for the tribe. Moses spoke and became the voice of God for nations. And, Jesus spoke and became the voice of God for the whole world.

But, the anointed one cannot die. God cannot die. The effort that is now necessary and the divine purpose for which Moon was brought into your consciousness is simply stated in this way: "He is the voice of inspiration, the guide to restore mankind, and understanding of his full nature and relationship to God."

Setting—2

Sitting with Arthur Ford, March 18, 1965: This time Colonel Pak, Moon's aide and interpreter, asked Ford: "Could you ask him in connection with the New Age, more specifically, the mission of our leader (Rev. Moon) here today?"

Fletcher said Moon was one of those who would be the human instrument through whom the world teacher will be able to speak. And, he was chosen because the New Age can only be ushered in through the eastern gate of the City of God—and that gate had been sealed since Jesus' crucifixion. It could not be opened until the New Age, into which you are now. When the teacher comes, people will be ready to receive him.

"Jesus of Galilee will not return"—it is not necessary. The Christ who manifested through him is eternal—he will manifest again; he is Moon about whom I have been talking" (Ford 1968, 126).

CHAPTER 30

The Korean Books of Prophecy

God had promised He would reveal His secrets to His servants, the prophets. As we have read, in Jesus' time, God revealed His secrets to the prophet, Malachi. Malachi gave a clear sign of how and when the Messiah would appear.

In Jesus' time, God revealed His secrets through the Archangel Gabriel, who told Zechariah, the high priest, that he would have a son and he shall call him John, and he would prepare people for the coming of the Lord (Luke 1:68-79). God also appeared to the shepherds, the Three Wise Men and Mary and Joseph.

Two thousand years later, God once again revealed His secrets to prepare the world for the Second Coming of Christ. As we have read above, God revealed His secrets to Nostradamus about 500 years ago. In a way, Nostradamus could be considered a prophet. Four hundred years later, God revealed His truth to highly spiritually gifted people, such as Cayce and Ford, in the United States and a few other very spiritually prepared Christian leaders in South Korea, such as Kim Baek Moon, pastor and founder of the Israel Jesus Church, and Huh Ho-Bin, founder of the Inside the Belly Church, which I will introduce in the next chapter.

Because God revealed His secrets to Nostradamus, Ford and Cayce, does that mean He could have also revealed them to Eastern sages and prophets? The answer is "yes!" You will be amazed by what you will discover in the Korean Books of Prophecy (Kyuk-am yu-rok). God revealed His secrets to numerous Eastern prophets over thousands of years.

Kyuk-Am-Yu-Rok: Korean Books of Prophecy

The following compilation in The Korean Books of Prophecy is based on my studies of the work by Mo Koo Sung from his book, *Who Is He?* (1998).

According to Sung's book, Nam Sa Go, author of the Kyuk-am Yu-rok:

> "… was born in the fourth year of King Joon-Jong of the Chosen dynasty (1509) and died in the fourth year of King Sun-Jo (1571). He was extremely knowledgeable about astrology, geography and feng shui. Under the reign of King Myung-jong he served as a magistrate responsible for ceremonial offerings and gravesites" (Sung 1998, 684).

In his book, Nam wrote about both past and present events. The most accurate accounts predict the events that have occurred in Korea and the world for the past 100 years. These predictions have been supported, and are 100 percent accurate (Sung 1998, 684). The book also contains prophecies about The Last Days, the Second Coming of the Messiah, and how and where the Messiah would appear.

To appreciate how accurate this prophet was, and before I introduce his prophecies, let us first examine his prophecies concerning the events that occurred in Korea and how he saw them unfold, approximately 450 years ago. In a way, Nam was the Nostradamus of the East.

The Historical Validity of Korean Prophecies

What follows are the recorded prophecies about Korea's general fortune, its change in political power, its 36-year subjugation under Japanese rule and then liberation, the division of the peninsula and its reunification and prophecies of the Last Days.

Prophecies on Japan's Annexation of Korea

1. In September of the 4th year of Yung Hee, the Yi dynasty will come to an end. "Destroying the existing sound moral customs of Korea, Japan will degrade morality and ethics, will abolish old studies and systems and will establish a new educational system."

Note: This prophecy was proven to be accurate when Japan annexed Korea in 1910.

2. For 36 years following the Japanese annexation of Korea, Koreans will be a people without a king and will become sons

of Buddhist monks, where they (the Korean people) do not even know Buddha.

Note: The Japanese authority issued a decree that said all young men had to cut their hair short and serve as Buddhist monks.

3. Japan will first rise as the Sun rises in the East, and when the time comes, it will set beyond the western mountain. When will this time be? It will be when the war between Japan and China becomes a part of World War II.

Note: This was amazingly accurate!

4. Beginning in the years 1894 and 1895, and ending in the years 1944 and 1945, Japan will rise and shine like the sun and then set like the sun at dusk. In the year 1945, Japan will fall, and its people will return to their country in great despair.

Note: This is exactly what had happened to Korea when Japan annexed it and took total dominion over its people for 36 years. Even the dates of occupation and defeat of Japan was 100 percent correct!

5. The Korean people will be divided into two and they will yearn for each other in tears, with a bridge between them.

Note: Panmunjom's Bridge of No Return and the Freedom Bridge in Imjingak, a park in Paju, are the crossings at the Demilitarized Zone (DMZ) between North and South Korea.

6. At this time, if one wants to live, one must pass the 38th parallel without delay. Three years, starting from the year 1950 will be years of turmoil, and Busan will be the only area remaining in which one can avoid this trouble.

Note: This prophecy was also 100 percent correct. The Korea War started in 1950 and lasted three years. The area around Busan was one area that wasn't invaded by North Korea because of a defensive perimeter surrounding it.

Chung Gam Nok Book of Prophecy

The writings of Chung Gam Nok, Collection of Prophecies, date back approximately 1,000 years. His prophecies about the fate of the Korean nation, the world wars and division of the Korean peninsula were all proven to be accurate. This great Asian prophet even predicted Gen. Douglas MacArthur's successful Incheon landing operation! The following are some of his predictions.

Korea's Division of North and South

1. There will be an effort to continue a dynasty for the second generation in North Korea, but, to no avail; it will end. Negative winds will blow at a tree from all four directions; thus, it will be hard to endure. Six multiplied by six equals 36. After 36 years of Japanese colonial occupation transpire, Korea will enjoy good years. A beautiful country in the East will be divided into two: one white, the other red, (democratic and communist) but, eventually, it will be united again.

The Condition of North Korea

2. North and South are confronting each other militarily. It is a very dangerous state of imminent warfare. Concerning this division of one race and one nation into two, by the time of reunification and return to the original division state, there will be many people starving and stricken ill. How many will survive? Famine and starvation will occur repeatedly.

Note: This is what has happened to North Koreans since the country was formed in 1950 under the rule of Kim Il-Sung, and run by his son, Kim Jong-Il and, now, grandson, Kim Jung-un.

Gen. Douglas MacArthur

3. Oriental people (white clothes) and Western people (blue clothes) will mix together and endure a life of meaningless worms. The countryside and cities to the West and South will be engulfed in the misery of war.

Translation: the Korean War.

4. At this time, there will be a general (MacArthur) who commands soldiers in the sea and on the island to protect the country from danger. When these soldiers cross the Geum River and save the people throughout the land, a great heavenly fortune will arrive. However, at that time, soldiers of the Chinese army will suddenly intervene in the war and fight against the soldiers of the general who came across the sea from the island.

5. The general who came across the sea to fight the war of defense is the one who defeated Japan. He is the commander of the Allied forces of the Southeast. This general, who is helping

the white forces (South Korea), tries to expel the Chinese forces. However, the Red Army calls itself righteous and tries to take the entire peninsula and even Cheju (Jeju) Island.

Yet, the Red Army will be forced up to the northern boundary of Korea, and, thus, the war will end in three years' time, leaving the land of Korea devastated.

It is really amazing how accurate this sage was. His predictions were as clear as pure water!

Korean Prophecies on The Last Days and The Second Coming of Christ

As we have read from the above predictions, revealed to Asian prophets, they were all accurate! Isn't this amazing?! What then, do these same prophets tell us about The Last Days and The Second Coming of Christ?

Signs of the Last Days

Mo Koo Sung, in his book, gave 12 signs about who, where and how The Second Coming would happen. Just as we read about Hogue's eight clues with Nostradamus, I chose to introduce eight clear clues the new messiah must match. They are:

(1) His Name is Moon.

(2) He will be born in North Korea.

(3) He will be ridiculed and unjustly imprisoned many times.

(4) He is the one who pursues the unity of religions.

(5) He comes from the combined religions of East and West.

(6) He is the one who will match and marry many good religious people.

(7) He is well-known in the East and in the West.

(8) He will marry a second time.

Let us now examine what the Korean prophecies said how the Second Coming of the Messiah would happen.

1. His name is Moon.

Two holy men appear. The first one is not the real one, but the one who comes the second time is the savior. When heaven sends him to the Earth secretly, his family name is "Moon."

Note: In the above prophecy, the two holy men are Jesus, the first one, who because of his crucifixion could not complete his mission, and the second was Moon as The Second Coming of Christ. "The first one is not the real one" could also be in reference to Kim Baek Moon, pastor of the Israel Jesus Church. Moon attended this church in his younger years after his family converted to Christianity.

2. He will be born in North Korea.

The holy man is born north of the 38th parallel and comes with God's great mission. He is like a man, but he is not a man. He is the one prophesied to come to the nation, but no one in this world discerns the holy man. Alas! Everyone must awaken. The center of the capital of Korea is the command post.

3. He will be ridiculed and unjustly imprisoned many times.

He must have the experience of prison. He must endure a difficult life of entrapment and walk a path through the land of death for the sake of being truthful and receive ridicule and unjust blame. He will suffer and shed tears and blood and reach out to the four corners of the world. Who will realize this man is the holy man? This man is the most troubled man in the world. This one is none other than the holy man (Messiah).

Note: This prophecy clearly speaks about Moon's agonizing six prison sentences and indignation. The sixth time was in 1986 in Danbury, Connecticut. In Hang Nam prison in North Korea, Moon endured severe torture under the communist regime and almost died.

4. He is the one who pursues the unity of religions.

He will unite Confucianism, Buddhism and Christianity, and he will come as the true man (holy man) with great benevolence. He comes to this world of the Buddha and he comes as master of the religions of Confucianism, Buddhism and Christianity and to bring all other religions into oneness. He is the one who comes to this world for the second time.

Note: Moon's church is known as "Unification Church" for short, but its real name is HSA-UWC (The Holy Spirit Association for the Unification of World Christianity). Although his teaching is based on the Judeo/Christian Bible, Moon's religious background is Buddhism and Confucianism. His mission is centered on uniting all religions. For this, he founded the Assembly of

World Religions, where leaders of every religion have met every year since 1970.

5. He comes from the combined religions of East and West.

It is God's dispensation that, in The Last Days, one man will be born and represent the entirety of Confucianism, Buddhism and Christianity, as well as other religions. He is the master of both the East and the West. He is the holy man coming from the olive tree and he appears to be a man, but he is not. He comes as three in one body, those of Chung-Do-Ryung, Buddha and Jesus Christ.

Note: Moon's family members were Buddhists and Confucianists until he was 10 when they converted to Christianity.

6. He is the one who will match and marry many good religious people.

He is the one who would match and marry many good men and women who believe in God. Matching good men and women, the holy man will live comfortably. Those good men and women who receive his matching and returned gratitude to God in prayer will receive precious children.

Note: As the world knows, Moon is famous for his "Mass Wedding/Blessing" ceremonies. In the Unification Church, children who are born of blessed couples are called "blessed children." This explains the meaning of "Precious Children."

7. He is well-known in the East and in the West.

Note: Again, who doesn't know about Moon? With so much media exposure, whether it is positive or negative, religious or political, he is well-known all over the world.

8. He marries a second time.

The one who is to come will establish a foundation in the early part of his life. In his middle years, he will meet a prearranged spouse and remarry.

Note: It is true Moon married a second time because his first wife was from a fundamentalist Christian background and didn't approve of his ministry. She left him. As he was reaching middle age, around 40, he married Han Hak Ja. Their marriage in 1961 was marked as the first "Holy Marriage Blessing."

So, again, as we have seen, it is amazing how they were proven correct and came to pass.

There is no one on Earth who could match the above descriptions except Moon! He came from the East (Korea) in the role of savior and Second Coming of the Messiah to save mankind, and he met all the above qualifications.

I learned about these great prophecies seven or eight years after I joined Moon's church. So, I didn't join the Unification Church because of them. I joined because I really believed God had predestined that I would meet the Lord of the Second Coming! To me, there are three main reasons why I believe Moon is the Messiah.

First, my life story is a testament to how God planted and sowed the seeds in my mind and moved me to meet Moon in a preplanned, synchronized time and place, just as He sent me dreams and mysterious coincidences to guide me toward the Unification Church missionaries. This, to me, was a great sign, as well as a miracle! As mentioned earlier, this event occurred after I had had two dreams in Salt Lake City—"The Funeral Procession" and "The Outdoor Concert."

Second, my conversion experience was also profound. I had heard about the controversies surrounding Moon and his church, so I was a bit worried about my involvement. On the other hand, I was so deeply touched by the truth and the love of God that the movement was teaching, all I needed was a little help to tell me I was in the right place. God came to my rescue! When God spoke to me, he approved my involvement with the church, saying it was His plan for me.

The third was the truth Moon taught in the Divine Principle, which we call the "Completed Testament." It is a compilation of stories and lessons, such as the "Principle of Creation," the "Fall of Man," the "Mission of the Messiah," "Jesus' Sad Story and His Crucifixion" and the "Last Days and the Second Coming of Christ." These chapters were the most powerful revelations of truth I had ever heard! Once one understands these chapters, everything else that is presented in the Divine Principle becomes very clear. More importantly, the hidden mysteries of the Bible become excitingly and enthusiastically clear and enjoyable and inspiring to read.

So, after I learned these truths, things became so obvious. I thought to myself: "If God truly exists, and if all the Holy Books, the Bible and the Koran are His words of truth, then the Divine Principle is the highest and clearest of them all!"

Having read all the prophecies, I cannot help but be amazed at how they acted out what Jesus said about his return! In fact, two chapters in Revelation mention the returning Messiah will have a new name.

In Rev. 3:11-12, Jesus said when He returns He would come under "my own new name." In fact, in Rev. 2:26-28, Jesus referred to another person – "he who conquers"—who would come in his place and have power over the nations and shall rule them with a rod of iron and will give him the Morning Star. He also said he will "come like a thief" at night (Rev. 3:3). From Jesus' own perspective, the Christians view of the "rapture" has no place to stand above Jesus' own words!

Having shared thus far what I have learned from Moon's profound teachings, it gives me the greatest pleasure to introduce to you this enigmatic holy man of God, the Rev. Sun Myung Moon.

CHAPTER 31

Sun Myung Moon

A Command Must Be Obeyed

Having arrived at my chapter on the Rev. Sun Myung Moon, it is important, therefore, we understand a little bit about this enigmatic man's background and early years, from his childhood to the age of 16 when he received the calling from Jesus Christ. It is also important to understand the pitiful condition of his war-torn country, Korea, which has endured ruthless Japanese occupation and a brutal communist regime. Also, we should understand the spiritual phenomenon that was engulfing the country during this time, as well as the condition of his family and village in which he was born and lived.

We need to understand Korea was very much like Israel in Jesus' time. The Israelites suffered untold persecution at the hands of the Romans. Likewise, the Korean people also suffered under Japan's occupation. The Eulsa Treaty, or Japan-Korea Treaty of 1905, which was signed by Prince Ito Hirohumi and five Korean ministers, deprived Korea of its diplomatic sovereignty and made it a Japanese protectorate. Ye Wang-yong, who served as minister of education, became prime minister under the treaty. He was a figurehead, much like King Herod Antipas or Caiaphas. And, just like Pilate, a governor-general was installed, and military officials were appointed in every district to control Korea's domestic affairs.

Like Rome, Japan had forced its will upon the Koreans, dictating what its politics, diplomacy and economic affairs would be. Japan's atrocities against the Korean people were very much like the Romans in Jesus' time. People who dared to challenge Japan's authority were imprisoned and executed and some were deprived of their freedom. And, just as Pontius Pilate decorated the holy city with graven images (Exod. 20:4-5) of a divine emperor, Japanese militarists, during World War II, forced every church in Korea to install a kamidana, an altar for the Japanese Shinto gods. Korean Christians were compelled to worship at Shinto shrines.

The Christians, on the other hand, were much like the Pharisees and Sadducees. They collaborated with Japan authorities to persecute and imprison Moon for no reason other than preaching God's word. The forced annexation of Korea by Japan in 1910 had caused much suffering and loss of lives. When a movement for independence started on March 1, 1919, the Japanese killed thousands of civilians in every part of the peninsula. It was similar to how the Romans dealt with revolting Israelites 2,000 years ago. The Japanese military searched every village for these loyal Koreans. They gathered young and old into a building and set it on fire. Everyone inside was burned alive. The Koreans, who were killed in the March 1 Movement, were predominantly Christians (Bae 2007). Toward the end of its colonial rule, Japan imposed a strict policy. Its aim was to stamp out Christianity, thus forcing Christians to worship at Shinto shrines. Those who didn't comply were imprisoned or killed. The Korean people suffered for 40 years until the end of World War II.

Five years after Korea gained its independence from Japan, the country was once again in great chaos. The Korean War, which raged across the 38th parallel, was not just a civil war. It was, in fact, a conflict between democracy and communism. This is the condition in which the young Moon grew up. As we will later examine, his life and ministry reflect Jesus' life and ministry.

Many stories were written about Moon. Most writers often gloss over some of the details. They don't pay much attention to these highly important early years of his life, which paved the way for him to receive his calling. It would not serve Moon justice if we did not speak about his early life and how God worked through him.

Although there were volumes of stories written about Moon's early life and public ministry, in my view, those stories were great, but short and without depth. That is, except for Michael Breen's book, *Sun Myung Moon: The Early Years 1920-53* (1997). Breen was one of the first British members of the Unification Church and a highly educated journalist. This empowered him with a great ambition to make several trips to Korea, interview people and collect stories from Moon's early members so he could write his captivating story. The following are footnotes taken from Breen's book. I would recommend reading the entire book. Moon's autobiography, *As a Peace-Loving Global Citizen,* was released in Korea in August 2009 and became a best seller for a few years in Korea. It was later translated into English and many other languages and is available now in the United States. For those who seek to know the truth, I can't stress enough how crucial it is to read these two inspiring books.

> "Born Jan. 6, 1920, Sun Myung Moon was a strong, but wild child. He was stubborn and difficult to control. Once he made up his mind, he wouldn't back down. He had the nickname "day crier," because once he started to cry, he wouldn't quit. He would throw a tantrum, jumping up and down and running around the house screaming and injuring himself until he bled" (Breen 1997).
>
> "He would cry so loudly that the whole neighborhood could hear him. In fact, his parents felt that he controlled them. Years later, his mother told one of his followers that she was never able to discipline him. Villagers said they recognized that from the age of 5. He had an unusual character. Once, his uncle, who was considered the village elder, came into the house after watching Moon playing. He said, "that boy will either become a king or a terrible traitor" (Breen 1997) As noted by Breen, as a child he was just like the stereotypical Pyong-an Province character, who is said to be "a tiger coming out of the woods" (Breen 1997, 23).
>
> "He was also very intuitive as a child. As he noted in his biography: "From when I was a child, I have a certain peculiarity; I could know things that others didn't, as if I had some natural paranormal ability. From the time I was eight, I was well known as a champion matchmaker, I only had to see photographs of a prospective bride and groom and I could tell everything" (Moon 2010, 35).

Until the age of 10, Moon was mischievous and wrestled a lot with other boys. They didn't want to fight with him because he was strong, and they were afraid he would beat them. Later, however, Moon stopped fighting and became more thoughtful of his words and actions.

Moon's early schooling was the traditional instruction in Chinese characters, which Koreans had been using for reading and writing up until the 16th century when Hangul, or the Korean alphabet, was created by Emperor Sojong. Students were taught with Confucian texts. By the time he was 13, Moon knew the essential Chinese characters by heart and received recognition for being the best student. Later, however, he demanded his father enroll him in a formal public school. He told his father: "I don't want to continue with the traditional informal school, where students only learn calligraphy. I want to go to a formal public school, where students learn how to build and fly airplanes" (Moon 2010).

Not surprising, at 14, after he convinced his parents to transfer him to elementary school, and after he passed the preparatory school studies exam, he was transferred to third grade at The Osan School.

The Osan School was a nationalist school established by Yi Sung Hun, an active member of Korean's independence movement during Japan's occupation. Not only was the Japanese language not taught, but students were actually forbidden to speak Japanese. The young Moon had a different opinion about this, however. He felt, "we had to know our enemy if we are to defeat them" (Moon 2010, 42). So, by the time he graduated from grammar school, he was fluent in Japanese. On his graduation day, he shocked everyone with his rather critical speech, which he gave entirely in Japanese, that said: "Japanese people should pack their bags as soon as possible and go back to Japan!" (Moon 2010). The audience was shocked, but he wasn't afraid. He said these things in front of the chief of police, county chief and town mayor. He said he took after the spirit of his great-uncle Yun Guk Moon, one of the great leaders of the Korean independence movement. He said things no one else dared to say. Nothing happened to him that day, but the Japanese authorities marked him as a person to be watched. Later, when he tried to go to Japan to continue his studies, the chief police refused to approve his application. And, later, that caused him problems.

In 1942, Moon finally managed to get his papers approved and went to Japan to continue his studies. As he was on the Busan-to-Shimonoseki ferry, however, he became upset over the miserable condition his country was in because of Japanese rule. Moon wept uncontrollably for hours that he was leaving his beloved homeland behind. He pledged he would return and bring the liberation of his country with him. It is interesting to note that most children his age would be crying because they would miss their families, not because they miss their country. This only demonstrates how patriotic Moon was.

In Tokyo, he entered Waseda Koutou Kougakko, a technical engineering school affiliated with Waseda University, and began to study electrical engineering. As we will later see, after his encounter with Jesus at 16, his burning passion to know God's will, and his love for his country, never kept him at ease. Despite the Japanese ban against Christianity, Moon spent much of his free time studying the Bible. On his desk in his room, he had three Bibles open side by side to the same verse, one in Korean, one in Japanese, and one in English. The desire to know God's word consumed him. He would read the same verse in the three languages over and over, underline the verses and write notes in the margins. His Bibles were covered with so many highlights and notes that, at times, they were hard to read. Only he was able to understand them.

He joined the Korean student underground independence movement and was elected to a major position. The secret police knew about his activities. The police not only kept a close eye on him but arrested him many times, beat and almost tortured him to death because he refused to name the students who were involved in the movement.

After studying in Japan for a year, he returned to Korea to find nothing had changed. Japan's tyrannical rule was still dominating the Korean people and worsening by the day. He returned to Heukseokdong, a neighborhood of Dongjak-gu in Seoul, and attended Myungsudae Church and continued his quest to know

God's truth. He read the Bible and prayed constantly. He kept detailed diaries of all the new realizations he received, which were answers to many of the questions he had struggled with over the years. As he noted in his biography, on days when he had a great number of realizations, he would fill an entire diary. It all happened so fast. He said, during this intense period, he realized "The relationship between God and mankind is that of a father and his children, and God is deeply saddened to see their suffering" (Moon 2010, 77).

> "The kingdom of heaven that God desires to build is not someplace we go to after death, he said, God wants this world, where we live now, to be the completely peaceful and happy world that He created in the beginning. God certainly did not send Adam and Eve into the world for them to suffer, he said. I had to let the world know this incredible truth" (Moon 2010, 79).

Moon's Family Conversion to Christianity

The conversion of the Moon family to Christianity was precipitated by a spate of disasters, which struck the family about 1931. When Moon was 16, five of his young siblings died in a year! No words could describe the heartbreak his parents felt at losing five of 13 children in such a short amount of time. The mystery of sudden deaths seemed to spread to other clan members and neighbors in the village. Many homes lost their livestock in one night! On the advice of his uncle, Kyung-chu, Moon's family and his two other uncles and their families joined the village church in Sangsa-ri.

As Breen stated:

> "The bereavement took the family beyond the original motive for conversion, which had been to seek the backing of the powerful Christian God and end the run of bad fortune, and deeper into their new faith. His own grief, and the pain of seeing his parents grieve for their children, underscored for the young Moon what was later to become his core teaching: that of God as the grieving parent of a

lost mankind. God, too, had lost his sons and daughters" (Breen 1997, 30).

The suffering of his family seemed also to parallel with the suffering of his country and the world. There seemed there would be no end to war or suffering around the world! Overwhelmed by these tragedies, Moon couldn't comprehend this series of tragic events. He asked, "Why do these tragedies happen to good people?" He thought the words of God he was hearing in the church were not sufficient enough to give him the answers he was seeking.

To relieve his frustration, as well as his aching heart, he immersed himself in deep prayer and Bible study. He began to ask: What is the purpose of life? Does God exist? Is God really all-powerful? If He is, why does God stay there and watch a world full of sorrows? If God created the world, did He also create the suffering that is in the world? As a teen, Moon's heart was overwhelmed with these questions, and, therefore, he chose to take his burning questions to God in his prayers.

In his prayers, whenever he expressed his anguishing questions and problems to God, he felt his suffering and sorrow were eased and his heart and mind were at peace. From then on, Moon began spending more and more time praying. This soon developed into an everyday vigil. He prayed throughout the night, all the time. It was during this intense prayer period on the night before Easter and the year he turned 16 that he prayed all night on a nearby hill. He begged God to tell him why He created the world with so much suffering and sorrow? Why was the all-knowing, all-powerful God leaving the world in such pain? Then, the next morning, which was Easter Sunday, Jesus appeared to him in an instant, like a "gust of wind," and said, "God is in sorrow because of the pain of humankind. You must take on a special mission on Earth, having to do with Heaven's work" (Moon 2010). As He said, he clearly saw the sorrowful face of Jesus and heard His voice. Jesus told him about the work he would have to do to save humanity.

Moon's first response was, "I can't do this. Why me? I am only a boy?" He was really afraid and in despair over what to do. No matter how much he tried, Moon couldn't forget the moment he met Jesus. The encounter changed his life forever. Soon after, though, his mission became clear, and he began a series of rigid Bible study and prayers. The stubbornness and tenacity he had in his childhood returned, and he used these God-given characteristics to follow His will. Once he immersed himself in prayer, he would weep for hours over words he had received from God. As he once said, "God's words were like 'coded messages.' God had placed in my hands the key to unlock the door to secrets" (Moon 2010, 63).

With this covenant, Moon's life was changed forever. To find a standard for his faith, he studied and prayed about the biblical figures and Christian saints. In his prayers and meditations, he met spiritually with Jesus and the disciples, analyzing their revelations of truth. It was during this period of analysis he came to know a truth about Jesus that no one had known before. "I have studied science. I am a very scientific person and I do not want any blind faith. I do not want the God of concept. I want the God of life, and God is life, itself. That God I seek" (Breen 1997, 32).

He realized no system of thought, no religion, not even Christianity with its promise of salvation, had provided mankind with a complete way out of Hell. No Christian had reached perfection after Christ. He wanted to know why not. If we fell away from God and no one has climbed back, then something is missing. What is it that blocks us from God? In his prayer, Moon battled with evil forces, and, at times, he was overwhelmed by the fear that billowed through his soul.

As reported by Breen, Moon once tried to explain those dark forces he encountered in his prayers. He said, "If you knew what it was like, your heart would stop" (Breen 1997). He said faith kept him going. "I knew that God was living. I knew that God had chosen me for this mission" (Breen 1997).

Over the years, the inner search kept pointing him again and again to the origin of the fall of Adam and Eve. Whenever he came to the fall of Adam and Eve, he felt as if it were his own business. He felt the sadness of God to see Adam's fall. He also felt Adam's sorrow in himself. In each event, Moon put himself in the position of those involved and felt their pain with them and with God. As he said, "it is not someone else's history, but my own life" (Breen 1997).

In his journey into human history, he saw the life of God's people is one of suffering and sorrow. God has also been experiencing grief and sharing the suffering of His children throughout history. He, too, felt pain and loss. In explaining the biblical story of the Garden of Eden and man's fall from God, he asked: "What happened? Did it really all begin with eating fruit?" He felt the idea was too ridiculous. In churches, preachers sermonized about Adam and Eve's disobedience. But, surely God, as a loving father, could forgive disobedience over something as trivial as eating food. He felt the story had to be figurative. For it to be so devastating and final, the Fall of Man had to involve love, the heart of God's creation. He thought God created Adam and Eve and placed them on Earth to multiply and fill the world with children of goodness.

He realized a kingdom on Earth where they could live and experience a life full of joy, peace and happiness. But, Adam and Eve couldn't wait for God's time and started their marriage life prematurely. The children who were born from the fall did not trust each other and brought about an incident where one brother murdered the other.

> "The peace of this world was shattered, sin covered the world, and God's sorrow began. Humanity committed another terrible sin by killing Jesus, the Messiah. So, the suffering that humanity experiences today is a process of atonement that it must pass through as God's sorrow continues" (Moon 2010, 78).

As Moon read and reread the Bible, praying and meditating on its contents, it seemed to him the central events after Adam kept coming back to this story of Adam's family. The lives of Noah, Abraham and Jesus seemed to be an echo of Adam. Why? As the first family, Adam's family was to be a model for God's purpose for creating man. Instead, it became a model for failure. When his praying and meditation were over, Moon said he confronted Lucifer, who he believed had caused the fall of Adam and Eve. He believed the fall was caused by illicit love.

As noted earlier, in his biography, Moon said, on days when he was receiving answers to many of the questions with which he had struggled over the years, he would fill an entire diary. It was as if his years of prayers and search for truth were answered. It happened in a short time. It was as if a ball of fire were passing through him. During this period, he discovered the relationship between God and mankind is like that of a father and his children, and God is deeply saddened to see mankind suffering.

At the end of his spiritual struggle, when he was sure of the truth he had discovered, Moon sought confirmation before he started his public mission. He began a 40-day fast. He said that, during this period, he met Confucius, Buddha, Mohammed, Jesus and other religious leaders in the spiritual world. Although he came from a Protestant background, Moon recognized all major faiths contained truth. In his spiritual communication, he said, he was given their approval of his discoveries. Moon's search for the principle, he said, lasted nine years.

The part of Breen's book that fascinated me was as God was preparing the young Moon for his mission, God was also preparing a people for him. A new set of Christian spiritual movements was forming all across North and South Korea at the time. In his first year away from home, he attended church services at the Jesus Church, a Pentecostal church in the Heukseok-dong neighborhood of Seoul. The Jesus Church was one of six churches established in 1928 by Mary C. Ramsey, the first American missionary in Korea. Within the church, there was a lot of spiritual activity. For example, one of the church members received a revelation the church should join with another spiritual group led by a notorious spiritual woman on Korea's west coast. One such spiritual woman was Kim Bom-joon. She prophesied Korea was the new Israel and, one day, missionaries would leave Korea and travel the world and the Messiah would come to Korea. She also prophesied the Messiah had already been born in Pyongyang.

Korea's John the Baptist Figure, Kim Baek-Moon

Kim Baek-Moon was a Korean religious figure very much like Billy Graham but on a smaller scale. Kim preached on the national level, but Graham's mission was a worldwide one. Both men were representative of the prophet Elijah and prepared people for the returning Christ. They were to work with and support the Messiah, Sun Myung Moon. In November 1943, Sun Myung Moon married his first wife, Choi Sun-kil. It was an arranged marriage between the couples' parents. Choi, like Moon, had unique characteristics. She was a beautiful and intelligent girl, but also stubborn and headstrong. Her relatives were well-to-do and were members of a fundamentalist Presbyterian Church in Cholsan County in North Pyong, a province that had no tolerance for other denominations, particularly for the church Moon attended. Meanwhile, Moon took a job as an electrical engineer at a construction company. The newlyweds settled in Heukseok-dong.

Around the end of 1945, Moon and his wife moved from Heuksok-dong to the neighborhood of Songdo-dong. They started to attend a church in Sangdo-dong, Seoul, which was also attended by a few members of the Jesus Church. The small church was led by a 35-year-old charismatic minister whose name was Kim Baek-Moon, He, in turn, was a highly respected charismatic and scholarly preacher.

Kim's conversion to Christianity in the 1930s coincided with a period of widespread spiritual activity in Korean Christian groups. As Breen noted, thousands had begun speaking in tongues and having revelations they could not understand (Breen 1997). During revival meetings, many participants became ecstatic, as if they were drunk in the spirit. Kim questioned why the spirit of God came in this way. What was the purpose? After much prayer, he received an answer: the spirit came to prepare the way for the Lord, to cleanse the souls of those it came to, but not to excite their senses. But, above all, it came because God wanted to find one man. To bring His kingdom, God needed to start with one person, someone who would be a new Adam. The purpose behind the spirit's coming was to make one perfect man. Kim said Korea was the Israel of the modern era, and it is where the Second Coming of Christ would occur. Most of his congregation were members of the Jesus Church.

In 1945, he formally established the Israel Jesus Church in Sangdo-dong and a small prayer center in Supcho-ri, near Paju. Kim also established a retreat near Paju. Two men and 10 women joined him at this location, and, here, they lived celibate and faithful lives. As Breen noted, the church Kim started in Seoul was a small congregation, comprised of many intellectuals and other influential figures. If Kim ran into opposition from the Christian establishment for his heretical views, he would be able to call on powerful allies. One of the deacons was the wife of the owner of *The Chosun Ilbo*, Korea's main daily newspaper, and her daughter was one of the members who lived at Kim's retreat. Another woman among the faithful was the wife of Lee Bom-sok, who, in 1948, was to become South Korea's first prime minister (Breen 1997, 68).

Among Kim's faithful and devoted church members was Moon. He was deeply involved in biblical studies, prayers and volunteering with the church. Church members began to notice his deep spirituality. Kim Yong-jin, who was one of two men at the retreat, recalled:

> "Moon studied the Bible in Kim's church, as I did. The special thing about him was that he had not received a formal theological education; he asked Reverend Kim many detailed questions, unlike the ordinary questions which the others asked this is like Jesus when he was a boy, teaching the elders in the temple" (Breen 1997).

Hong Yi-sun, one of the female celibates, remembered: "Sun Myung Moon prayed very much" (Breen 1997). Kim told his followers that Moon had profound spiritual wisdom. Several months after Moon joined the group, Kim placed his hand on Moon's head and said the Wisdom of Solomon was within him. This was like John the Baptist testifying to Jesus.

In early 1946, a spiritual phenomenon occurred. The Holy Spirit came, and Jesus is said to have appeared to Kim and told him Korea is the new chosen nation. He also received the revelation, "You are Israel." Kim prayed day and night asking God what this revelation meant. He received the answer that he would have the mission in the future to spread the new teaching throughout the world (Breen 1997, 69).

As Breen noted, from the perspective of the Unification Church, Kim's recognition of Moon was the providential event and precondition for the group to receive the Holy Spirit. Kim should have recognized Moon was the Second Coming of Christ and should have led his followers to understand Moon is the Christ they had been waiting for.

Unfortunately, Kim's failure to recognize Christ in Sun Myung Moon mirrored John the Baptist's failure to recognize Jesus as the Messiah! Kim's simple acknowledgment of Moon's wisdom was similar to John the Baptist testifying to Jesus after he saw the Holy Spirit descend on Jesus in the form of a dove. The question is how serious was Kim's acknowledgment of Moon's wisdom? As noted by Breen, the revelation, "you are Israel," must have created confusion in Kim's head (Breen 1997). Did he see Christ in Moon, or simply thought of him as a gifted student—clever but inferior to himself? Or, perhaps, was Kim consumed by his own spiritual search to recognize the spirituality in Moon, which had impressed other members of the group? Or did he indeed recognize it, but felt threatened by it? (Breen 1997, 70).

However, Moon's impression on other members of the group began to create competition, and the situation between the two men gradually began to worsen. Not soon after, the two inspired men decided to separate. Kim's followers recalled he asked Moon to leave his church. Moon also concluded he would not be able to work with Kim's group and decided to leave. He stayed close to Kim and his group, however. They were like a family to him.

Sometime in June 1946, while Moon was on his way to buy rice from a nearby town, he received an urgent revelation that told him he had to go to Pyongyang immediately. God had prepared a special devout group for him there. He couldn't help but follow the will of God. So, he took the train to Pyongyang. He carried nothing but his Bible, which was filled with highlighted notes. He arrived in Pyongyang on June 6, 1946. As he commented in his autobiography, "God's commands are very serious, and they must be followed without reservation or hesitation" (Moon 2010, 86).

Pyongyang: Jerusalem of the East

Pyongyang in 1946, after the liberation from Japan, was still a dynamic center for Korean Christianity. Denominations that were banned by the Japanese had re-established themselves. There were churches and spiritual revivals everywhere. Christians called the city the "Jerusalem of the East." Even Billy Graham commented on it in his autobiography.

After Moon arrived in Pyongyang, he was unsure of how he would begin to find this group of people God told him about. When he arrived in the city, he stayed at the home of Seob Choi Rah, who lived in the Kyongchang-ri neighborhood near Pyongyang's West Gate. The young preacher began to hold revival meetings in Rah's home. Rah was the mother of one of the female celibates in Kim's special prayer team. It was there where he met his first devoted disciple, Won Pil Kim (Breen 1997).

For service, everyone dressed in clean white clothes. Moon would be up at the crack of dawn, praying for hours to prepare to preach God's word to all who attended the 10 a.m. Sunday service. This was the routine the 26-year-old Moon had established in his first storefront-like church. He continued this routine until he passed away in September 2012 at the age of 93. Moon prayed and meditated for hours before he delivered his sermons.

To prepare for the Sunday services, members would sing the same hymns for hours, which made it a very passionate service. They become so moved and inspired, they would cry. The general public called the church "the weeping church." Many people had very moving spiritual experiences. Some would go into trances, others would prophesy, and still others would speak in tongues. Early members, such as Grandmother Sung Do Ji and Grandmother Se Hyun Ok, came to the church because they each had a dream in which they were told. "A young spiritual teacher has come from the South and is now across from Mansudae" (Moon 2010). No one else told them. When the Holy Spirit did its work, people were cured of long-existing illness, as if they were never sick.

Another testimony reported in Breen's book comes from Kim Chong-hwa, who lived near the house where Moon was preaching. Kim Chong-hwa was the women's group leader at the Somunae-pak Church, one of the largest Presbyterian churches in Pyongyang. It is really fascinating to see how God willed His destiny to be carried out by His prepared people and groups. This lady began to spread the news to her church friends and relatives, telling her husband's cousin, Kim In-ju, also a Presbyterian, "A great preacher has come from Seoul. Why don't you come and hear him?" (Breen 1997). Shortly after, they went to a worship service where Moon was preaching.

There, they were met with a few surprises. First, they noticed the room was divided with men on one side and women on the other. Here, men and women sat separately from each other. As the service began, they were further puzzled by the unorthodox style of service. Instead of the one-hour service they were used to attending, with a few hymns and a short sermon, this small church group seemed to have no format. Even the hymns they sang were unfamiliar. Some songs were sung repeatedly over and over again. As the small congregation sang, the two women noticed the young preacher was weeping, with tears visibly pouring down his face.

Another thing that deeply moved them was Moon's praying was so different from any praying they had ever heard. There was such great intensity and feeling. "I had never been so deeply struck by anyone's prayer in my whole life," commented Kim In-ju to her friends (Breen 1997).

Next, the two ladies were blown away by Moon's unforgettable sermon. Kim In-ju recalled Moon reading a passage from the Bible and then preaching. His sermon was about how Jesus' death on the cross was not God's original plan. Jesus should have lived much longer so he could fulfill God's plan of salvation. As he preached, he wept. The women were jolted by the idea that Jesus' death was not destined. They had understood salvation was possible only by the virtue of Jesus' death on the cross. They had never considered anything else. It had never occurred to them that Jesus should not have died that young. Kim In-ju found herself crying.

That night, she dreamed she was traveling through a dark tunnel. At the end of it, she met Moon. A funeral procession was passing. Fluid from the decomposing body was leaking from the coffin and onto her clothes. She was afraid. Moon wiped her clothes clean and told her to go to a garden. There, amid beautiful flowers, she met Jesus, who took her hand and guided her as she walked.

From that day, Kim In-ju became a frequent visitor to and a member of Moon's prayer group. She began to feel so close to God and have dreams about Jesus. In another sermon, Moon taught that Korea was the second Israel and the return of Jesus would occur in Korea. But, he said, the return would not happen in either the spiritual or supernatural way that Christians expected. He said, just as the mission of the Old Testament prophet Elijah passed in the time of Jesus to John the Baptist, so the mission of Jesus would pass to another.

After this sermon, Kim In-ju prayed to God, asking Him from where in Korea the Lord would come. In her prayer, she had a vision. Jesus appeared, walked into the room, bowed His head and began to pray. "This daughter of yours has to go a very long and difficult way. Let her complete this journey without going astray." The voice was that of Moon.

As she finished praying and said, "Amen," she looked up and saw, not Jesus but Moon. She felt she had received the answer to her prayer. Moon was the Christ. God had given to Kim In-ju many intimate spiritual experiences to connect her with Moon. One time, she felt directed by God to read the prophecies in Isaiah, Chapter 60, and heard a voice within her say, "this is the chapter that Teacher Moon is to fulfill." The next morning, she went to see Moon. But, before she could say anything, he asked, "Didn't God tell you last night to read Isaiah 60, and didn't He say this was the chapter to be fulfilled now?" Kim In-ju had many such encounters with Moon. Such spiritual experiences—far from being unusual—were common among Moon's early followers (Breen 1997, 73-74).

In his first few weeks in Pyongyang, Moon attracted a new group of followers. Most of them were middle-aged Christian women, such as Kim Chong-hwa and Kim In-ju, who had come from bigger churches. They were so moved by the depth of Moon's knowledge of God and sincere devotion, that they joined his women's prayer group. Preparation for Sunday service started on Saturday night. Some of the spiritual women would pray overnight, and others would arrive in church early on Sunday morning and continue the prayer to support the preacher and be a channel for God and spiritual world to deliver God's message.

From this small, highly inspired group of people at Rah's house, God worked his next plan to lead the young Moon to the well-prepared spiritual group God had been preparing him for since 1924. God's arrangement for Moon to meet this group was not an ordinary one. He had to go through much suffering and agony to meet this spiritual group in prison!

I don't understand why? God seems to work His providence of salvation through tragedies and sorrowful events. As we have read, when the time was right, God called on the teenage Moon by having his parents lose five of their children in one year. In a way, this is what pushed Moon to begin his spiritual journey. He began to seek answers to fundamental questions about God and the meaning of life until he had his personal encounter with Jesus at 16. Now that Moon was 26 and had a good foundation in Pyongyang, God was ready to move on with His plan and connect His anointed man to a specially prepared spiritual group. Once again, this was to be fulfilled through tragic events and difficulties. This time, Satan tried to destroy Moon, by smearing his name with false rumors, and turning Christian churches against his teachings, which resulted in his imprisonments!

Persecution Begins

Every successful work of God must have opposition.

If man's work for God doesn't have opposition, there is something wrong with it. Everywhere Moon went, he stirred up the opposition. Trouble came, and trouble always follows the preaching of the Gospel of Christ, because Satan doesn't like it.

The forces of evil do not like the searchlight pointed in their direction because "men loved darkness ... because their deeds were evil" (John 3:19).

The trouble for Moon and his small congregation was twofold (Mahjoub 2010). First, there were the false rumors out of jealousy and envy from some of the spouses of congregation members. At prayer services, people became so inspired, they would stand up and dance and, sometimes, the service lasted for hours. Rah's house faced the road, and noise from the group began to attract attention. Those who attended this church without their husbands or wives began to experience problems at home. After hearing Moon's explanation that the Fall of Man had been sexual and how God's heart was broken by the loss of his children, many believers felt impure and stopped having sexual relations with their spouses. Suspicious husbands and wives came to find out what was going on and would see men and women in the same room, singing and talking together for hours, which was unusual in Korea at that time! In an attempt to destroy Moon's image, Satan started rumors about orgies, which spread all over the town. An angry husband was convinced the young, handsome preacher was having an affair with his wife and reported him to the communist authorities.

Second, other Christian ministers were jealous and envious. As the congregation gained more and more members, people from other churches joined the congregation. At one time, 15 core members of a very prominent church in Pyongyang came to Moon's church as a group, causing members of the church's board to lodge a strong protest against Moon. As more people began attending Moon's services, the ministers of these established churches complained to the police.

On Aug. 11, 1946, in response to the complaints, agents of the police came and took the young preacher into custody again. He was charged by North Korea's communist government with spying for Syngman Rhee and with disturbing the social order. Moon was in prison for almost six weeks. During his interrogation, he was accused of being a spy for the U.S. government, which was backing the South Korean president at the time. They wanted to know why he had come from the south and lived in Pyongyang without an identity card. He explained he had come to preach the word of God, but they didn't believe him. After his interrogation, he was savagely beaten, declared innocent and, near death, released from prison. The authorities notified his followers they could come and collect him. When his followers came to get him, they were shocked. He had been thrown out into the yard, half-dead from the beating. He was vomiting so much blood, they thought he would die.

Although this might seem like an unjust and unethical way to have a good man walk the difficult and thorny path, for reasons only God knew, this was His way of restoring mankind. Founders of all religions had to endure persecution and rejection and walked the path of bitter suffering. Interesting! Moon's prison story reminds me of Joseph's story and how he met the pharaoh's former head butler and chief baker in prison, and where Joseph ended up being not only released from prison but becoming the pharaoh's second-in-command.

This is how God planned to connect Moon with His prepared spiritual group in Daedong Prison. When Moon walked into his prison cell late at night, other prisoners in the crowded cell were sleeping. As Breen commented:

> "His experience behind bars in Seoul made him mindful of the social code among prisoners. The first rule was that, whatever his job or crime, the new arrival is at the bottom of the ladder. He accordingly took a space by the toilet" (Breen 1997, 75).

The next morning, the cell chief, the prisoner who had been there the longest, was shocked to see Moon in his cell. He called Moon over and to everyone's surprise, when Moon sat down beside him, the man bowed respectfully and said, "Now I have met the man I wanted to meet." He introduced himself as Mr. Hwang and explained to Moon that he was a member of a spiritual group that had received revelations they would meet the Lord in prison. The man continued to explain that their group leader, a lady by the name of Heo Ho-bin, and other group leaders were also in the same prison with him. "Last night, I saw her bowing to someone in a dream, and when I woke up this morning, I saw the man was here in this cell. It was you" (Breen 1997, 75).

The story began in Cholsan County, in North Pyongsan, North Korea, with a village woman called Kim Song-do. She converted to Christianity after being cured of a mental illness by a faith healer. Later, the woman found she had the gift of healing. As her faith deepened, she began to receive revelations on the Second Coming.

> "Jesus appeared to her and told her that the Fall of Adam and Eve was caused by adultery, that his crucifixion has been the result of the mistrust of his own people, that the Second Advent of Christ would occur through another

man and that he would appear in Korea. Jesus then instructed Mrs. Kim to write these revelations down and teach them to the people. Kim began holding services at home, teaching that believers should repent for the death of Jesus as if they had killed him themselves. She taught that men and women should prepare themselves for the coming of the Lord, that single people should not marry, and married men and women should refrain from sexual relations. People came to see her from all over Korea, and she told them to prepare for the coming Messiah. Her followers expanded to nearby towns and to Jeongjiu, Anju, Sukcheon, Pyongyang, Haeju and Seoul" (Breen 1997).

As recounted in Breen's book, Mr. Hwang, the chief prisoner, continued with his story about his spiritual group leader: In 1943, one of Kim Song-do's young followers told a person to whom he was witnessing that Japan would decline and Korea would become an advanced power in the future. He didn't know he was talking to a policeman! Kim and her two sons were arrested and tortured severely. They were freed three months later without charge. Unfortunately, weakened by torture, Kim Song-do died shortly after being released from prison at the age of 62.

Her mission, Moon's cellmate explained, passed to another lady, Huh Ho-bin, who was the leader of the Holy Lord Church in Pyongyang. Huh had a spiritual gift of her own. Jesus had appeared to her many times, revealing the astonishing new truth about his youth; even telling her "the new Lord is 26 years and you must serve him well, as you have served me" (Breen 1997). Every time Huh received a revelation, her stomach would move as if she were pregnant. This unusual phenomenon was cited by her followers as further evidence of the truth of Kim's teaching. Huh's group became informally known as "Bokjung-Kyo, which literally meant the "In-the-Belly" Church.

Huh received a revelation that Japan would surrender on July 7, 1945, by the lunar calendar (Aug. 16 by solar calendar). She was so sure about her revelation and wasn't afraid to speak about it publicly. That is what led to her arrest by the Japanese colonial authorities. At her trial, she was asked, "Who is higher, God or the emperor?" "God," she shouted! She was sentenced to death, but Japan was defeated a few days before the sentence was to be carried out.

In prison, she had received another revelation that the emperor, whose voice had never been heard, would broadcast to the people. Her followers believed her, and the prophecy came true not long after that. Then, she told her followers that God had said she would meet the new Lord when Japan falls. After she was released for the first time, she received another revelation that she would meet the Messiah in prison.

In 1946, leading members of the In-the-Belly Church gathered in a place where they thought they would meet the Lord. Instead, they were arrested by the Communist authorities and imprisoned. Because the group lived on donations and many members had sold their properties and donated money, the authorities accused the church leader of fraud. However, during the interrogations, the police were unable to find any evidence to corroborate the charge. They decided on a face-saving pretext to release them—the leaders would deny Huh's belly moved every time she had a revelation. They refused, despite the threat of torture. Mr. Hwang told Moon that Huh's brother had already died from beatings. "Your group is specially prepared by God," Moon said to his cellmate. "I will take all responsibility if you deny your experiences to the authorities. Just deny the facts and you will be released. Please tell Mrs. Huh to do the same" (Breen 1997). Shortly afterward, Huh's husband was transferred to the same cell as Moon. Moon gave him the same advice as he had given Hwang, but Huh's husband said he would follow his wife. Moon smuggled a note to her that said, "The writer of this note has a mission from heaven. Pray to find out who he is. If you deny everything you have received, you will be released." After Huh read it, the note was discovered by a guard. Moon was exposed as the culprit and severely tortured for it (Breen 1997, 79).

Unfortunately, like the Israelites in Jesus time, the group failed in its mission and did not follow Moon's instructions when he told them to deny Huh's belly moved. As noted by Breen, had this incident had a happier outcome, Moon may have taken his new followers to South Korea. Instead, he stayed in Pyongyang and was arrested a second time (Breen 1997, 81).

Once again, God had prepared a special group to receive the Messiah, but, like Kim Baek-Moon, leader of the Israel Church, and his congregation, the members did not understand what God had hoped to fulfill: that is to receive and have complete trust in the new Lord and follow His way. Had Huh simply prayed when Moon had sent her the note, his older followers argued, God would have shown her, and she would have denied her revelations to the interrogators simply to obtain a release.

The interesting thing about these two spiritual groups is they were somehow connected. They even shared a church building and worshipped together at some point. Each of the spiritual leaders had his or her own special skills and spiritual gifts. For example, although they both carried a similar message, that the Messiah would appear in Korea in the flesh, and not as traditionally expected, both leaders, Kim and Huh, focused on their own specific spiritual work. Kim was a highly educated and organized individual who could have formulated Moon's doctrine and provided influence. Huh and her followers, on the other hand, could have brought disciplined spirituality to a new movement that could have been led by Moon had these two spiritual groups united. In fact, Huh was so sure about her revelations she bought a beautiful house in Pyongyang for the Lord and assigned 12 disciples and 70 apostles to serve the Second Coming of Christ (Breen 1997, 78).

As Breen noted, "As a prescript to this encounter, however, it should be noted that, when Moon's wife (first wife) left him and he remarried, his bride was the daughter of the only known survivor of Huh's group" (Breen 1997).

Had they trusted God, united and accepted Moon as their Lord, things would have been great, and God would have rejoiced! Unfortunately, the two groups split from one another because of theological differences, and all the preparations that were done by these two highly prepared spiritual groups ended in failure! Just like the situation between John the Baptist and Jesus, even though God had revealed to him who Jesus was, John continued to baptize people on one side of the river, while Jesus did the same on the other. It never occurred to him he should drop his ministry, bring his followers and serve as Jesus' chief disciple. The same is true for Kim and Huh.

After Moon was released from prison and recovered, he resumed his evangelical work. Within two years, his church grew larger. Established churches, however, wouldn't leave him alone. More and more members of their congregations joined his church. Finally, about 80 Christian ministers acted against him. They wrote a letter to the communist authorities. On Feb. 22, 1948, in response to the complaints, agents for the police came and took the young preacher into custody again and charged him with being a spy.

As Moon expressed in his autobiography, many of the most prominent ministers in North Korea came to the courtroom during his trial and accused him of many crimes. The communists also scorned him, saying religion was the opiate of the people. In prison, the authorities beat him constantly, almost to the point of death. But, he endured. As he noted, even as he was vomiting blood and seemed to be on the verge of death, he prayed:

> "God don't worry about me. Sun Myung Moon is not dead yet. I wouldn't let myself die. There was a mountain of tasks before me that I had to accomplish. I had a mission. I was not someone so weak as to be beaten into submission by something as trivial as torture" (Moon 2010, 92).

Each time he collapsed from the torture, he would endure by telling himself, "I am being beaten for the sake of the Korean people. I am shedding tears as a way of shouldering the pain of our people" (Moon, 2010).

Heungnam Concentration Camp

On May 20, 1948, after three months in prison, he was unjustly sentenced to five years in prison and transferred to Heungnam Prison, known as the world severest prison. The day he was transferred, he felt indignation and was full of shame. Moon was chained and tied to a thief, so he could not escape, and driven 17 hours across rough roads to the prison. The prison was a concentration camp that had a nitrogen fertilizer factory. Moon underwent two and a half years of indescribable suffering in the harshest of compulsory labor. Compulsory labor was a practice North Koreans learned from the Soviets. The Soviet government created this severe system of compulsory forced labor as punishment for its rival political and criminal prisoners. People who were sent to prison concentration camps were forced to undergo compulsory labor until they died.

Heungnam was on the coast, and, in winter, it was so unbearably cold. As Moon commented, the wind was so painfully cold, it cut into the prisoners' half-naked bodies. Day in and day out, from dawn until dusk, prisoners, with hands held and four abreast, were marched 2.5 miles to the fertilizer factory. They were surrounded by guards armed with machine guns. Anyone who caused his row to fall behind or failed to hold onto the hand of the prisoner next to him was beaten severely for trying to escape. At the factory, the prisoners were to dig the fertilizer out of a 60-foot-high mound. Prisoners were organized in teams of 10, and they were carried on the prisoners' backs and loaded on trucks to be shipped to Russia. In exchange, North Korea would receive outdated military equipment. If a team failed to meet its quota, its meal ration was cut in half. Moon commented, "Everyone worked as if his life depended on making the quota" (Moon 2010, 97). Prisoners were also exposed to sulfuric acid, which was used in the manufacturing of ammonia sulfate. Sulfuric acid was so harmful, it would cause hair loss and sores that oozed liquid would appear on the skin. Many prisoners would begin vomiting blood and die after six months.

On Oct. 13, 1950, U.S.-led forces landed in Incheon, pushed forward north to Pyongyang and attacked Heungnam with full force and boarded the prison. One bomb exploded about 12 feet away from where Moon and a few other prisoners stood. They were lucky; Moon and the other prisoners escaped unharmed. Everyone else around them was killed.

After being in prison for two years and eight months, Moon was in a terrible shape. He was dressed in tattered clothes. But, instead of going home like prisoners would usually do, Moon headed back to Pyongyang to look for the members of his group. After about 40 days, he only found a few. One was Won Pil Kim,

Moon's first disciple. Moon traveled south on foot with two other members, along with refugees in a long line that stretched about 7 miles. Moon even took with him a follower he met while in Heungnam, Mr. Pak, who has been released earlier.

Badly injured and unable to walk, Pak's family left him behind when they fled for their lives. Moon insisted he must save this man even if it meant he could face danger. To Moon, saving this one man was like saving the world. Moon carried this man on his back and, at times, on a bicycle. At this time, food was very scarce and hundreds of thousands of refugees had to eat. Moon and Kim made it through the gate, surviving on boiled rice, barley and potatoes and whatever they could find. They arrived in Busan on Jan. 27, 1951.

Busan was filled with refugees from the North. As Moon commented, "it felt like the whole country had gathered there. Any accommodation fit to live in was filled already" (Moon 2010, 112). There was no work and he didn't have any money. He was dressed in torn and filthy clothes and had one worn shoes. Moon felt as if he were the lowest of the low, a beggar among beggars. The only way he and his disciple could eat was to beg. After two months of wandering the city like a homeless person, Moon and Kim settled in Beomnetgol on the outskirts of Busan. They built their first home/church near a cemetery. The home was a tiny shack built with mud and discarded Army ration boxes that couldn't fit three people. This was where Moon started his ministry again and wrote the Divine Principle.

As he noted in his biography, nine years after his encounter with Jesus, his eyes had finally been opened to the true love of God. It was as if someone had turned on a movie projector, and everything that had happened since humankind broke God's commandment played out clearly before his eyes. All the secrets of the universe were resolved in his mind. The Divine Principle, as I noted earlier, reveals the most fundamental principles of God, humanity and the universe. It explains the entire providential process, beginning with God's creation of humanity, its fall and God's providence to restore them. It became the official Bible for the Unification Church and it is believed to be the Completed Testament of the Bible.

Mission in Busan

In Busan, Moon started his ministry with the same zeal and passion he had when he was in Pyongyang. As soon as he built his mud-hut church, he began to preach again. While he was writing the Divine Principle, he told his disciples its message would be spread all over the world one day. He prophesied that people from all over the world would venerate that hillside. Moon's prophecy sounded unbelievable then. Yet, it came true. Hundreds of thousands of people, including 10,000 Christian ministers from the United States, have made a pilgrimage to the spot since the 1980s.

What amazes me about the early years of Moon's ministry is that God and the spirit world were involved in his work and how quickly Moon's church grew. As in Pyongyang, when Moon started preaching in his mud-hut church, there were only three people listening. He was not preaching to just those three people, however. He felt even if they cannot be seen, he was preaching to thousands, even tens of thousands. As he preached, he envisioned all of humanity was in attendance. As I read this, I couldn't help but think of a similar experience Billy Graham had when he was training to preach in his ministry's early years. I also thought of what I had that I will share in the "An Hour with God" section of this book.

In the front, close to where the mud house was built, there was a well that was used by locals to gather some water. Not long after Moon started his sessions, people who came to the well, most of them women, would hear this man preaching at the top of his voice to no one. Soon, rumors began to spread that there was a crazy man living in the mud house. There were also rumors that this man was young and very handsome. Women, who came to fetch water from the well, peered into the ramshackle mud house and were shocked to see a man in wretched clothing shouting to the whole world. It is only natural that people began to whisper and spread rumors. Perhaps these rumors were the way for God to bring people to Moon. Among the curious were students from a nearby seminary, as well as a group of professors from the prestigious Ewha Women's University in Seoul.

One day, after he finished writing the Divine Principle, he put his pencil down and prayed. "The moment has come for me to evangelize. Please send me the saints to whom I may give witness" (Moon 2010, 118). That day, he felt the urge to go to the well, and, as he approached it, he met Hyun Shil Kang. She was startled when he said to her, "God has been giving you tremendous love for the past seven years." She jumped backward in surprise and replied, "It has been seven years since I decided to dedicate my life to God. How did you …?" She added, "I am an evangelist at the Beom Cheon Church, which sits in the neighborhood at the bottom of the hill. I am here because I heard there is a crazy man living in that mud house, so I have come here to witness to him."

The Holy Spirit did its work, and many students and members of prestigious churches joined his ministry. Among those who converted to Moon's church was Professor Young Oon Kim. She was a theologian at Ewha Women University and highly respected because she studied theology in Canada. Kim developed a system of critiques on Moon's theology specifically to challenge him and used her system to stop an influx of students going to Moon's church. But, a week after debating theology with Moon, Kim joined his church. This was a sure sign from God to Moon's early members. Kim joining the church gave Moon and his members more credibility. His church membership snowballed in numbers.

By 1953, once again, Moon's persecution reached its extreme. The people most perplexed by Moon's church growth were the administrations of Yonsei University's College of Theology and Ewha Woman's University's Graduate School of Theology, who were, in turn, financed by Christian foundations based in the United States. They could not bear the pressure and had to do something to keep their students and faculty from joining Moon's church.

In an effort to counter this trend, they began a campaign of false rumors, such as calling it a "pseudoreligion, "cult" or "brainwashing," which eventually became inseparably identified with Moon's name. After many students were expelled and professors were fired, public opinion began to turn against Moon. False rumors started by the churches in Pyongyang began to surface in

Busan. Unfortunately, the viler the rumor, the more people chose to believe it and repeated it as true until the media got hold of it. On July 4, 1954, the police raided Moon's church and took him and four members to custody. Just like in Pyongyang, ministers and church elders of the established churches and secular authorities wrote letters, demanding his church be closed. In a way, these Christian ministers were like the Pharisees and the Sadducees who gave Jesus so much trouble.

The matter did not end there, however. After an investigation into his past, the authorities charged him with draft evasion and sentenced him to three months in prison and sent him to Seodaemun Prison in Seoul. But, in truth, the charge was unjust. By the time he had escaped the North Korean death camp and headed south, he was already beyond the age of compulsory military service.

Many of the churches that sent him to jail expected his imprisonment to destroy his church and his members would leave. They were wrong. Instead, members couldn't stay away. They visited him every single day. In some cases, they even fought over who would get to see him first. It even amazed the prison guards. Finally, after three months, the court found him not guilty and he was released.

After his release, Moon's church blossomed. With so many people joining the church and membership growing, after seven years, new churches opened in other cities all over South Korea. By 1957, churches were established in 30 Korean cities and towns, and, as the church reached its high stature and recognition, Moon began to evangelize the world.

CHAPTER 32

Judge the Tree by Its Fruit, Not by Its Leaves

First of all, before I launch into the story, I want to remind my readers that what I am about to explain in this chapter is related to signs that were predicted in Matt. 24:3-8 and were prophesied to happen in the Last Days during the Second Coming of Christ. I truly believe this prophecy was fulfilled in the 1960s. As many of us know, the decade of the 1960s was a very fascinating time in our history. There have been hundreds of documentaries and movies made about the 1960s. It was a chaotic period. Kennedy was assassinated. There was a war in Vietnam. Young people rebelled against the status quo and introduced the term, Hippie, to the world. Then, as the Bible predicted, a large number of spiritual gurus from the East came rushing to the United States offering healing and salvation: the Hare Krishnas, Bhagwan Shree Rajneesh, Children of God. In the midst of these gurus came The Rev. Sun Myung Moon. As the Bible says in 1 Thess. 5: 2, "the day of the Lord will come like a thief in the night ..." but the day will come as a surprise.

One interesting thing I noticed was that people couldn't figure the Moonies out. They don't dress in a particular uniform to identify themselves, such as the Hare Krishnas, with their shaved heads and orange clothing, or those who followed Rajneesh, who dressed in orange as well. The Moonies dress and look like ordinary people, and people keep confusing us with Hare Krishnas and the Rajneesh.

With this in mind, I would like to begin.

Most recently, June 10, 2018, to be exact, I watched a documentary on Netflix called "Deprogrammed." The documentary is about the rise of deprogramming and anti-cult movements in the 1970s. Ted Patrick was the featured master deprogrammer. I must add, had Patrick lived during Jesus' time, he would have attempted to deprogram Jesus. The Romans, however, took care of that. He would also have attempted to deprogram the disciples and even St. Francis of Assisi!

After I watched the documentary, I couldn't help but wonder what happened to Patrick and other deprogrammers who were in demand in the 1970s?

If you haven't heard anything mentioned about Patrick in the past 20 years, here's why.

a) His "reverse-brainwashing" technique is violent and unethical (he was jailed and fined numerous times).

b) His technique involved forceful kidnapping and abduction.

c) His claim to have saved and returned children to their families is false. The people he deprogrammed or tried to deprogram were all adults and not teenagers as he said they were.

d) Because of social media, the era of deprogrammers spreading lies was eliminated.

So, let's begin by addressing four major beliefs held by deprogrammers about cults and brainwashing, and, in particular, the Unification movement which was founded by Moon. I have been a proud member for more than 35 years. I joined in 1981.

Because it is difficult to decipher right from wrong, Jesus gave a clue in Matt. 7:16: "You will know them by their fruits."

So, to determine what kind of fruit Moon brought to the world, we need to look at his work. For this, we need to organize his work into a question and answer section to determine the fruit, and whether it is good or bad.

This leads us further to form our list of questions and answers based on the complaints his persecutors had formed against him, which are basically concentrated on four major points.

1) Breaking up families: Taking children away from their loved ones.

2) Brainwashing: His method of teaching and strict disciplinary lifestyle.

3) Riches/profit: He used his followers to get rich.

4) Blasphemy/Heresy: Claiming himself as the Messiah and bringing false teachings.

Complaint No. 1: Breaking Up Families

One complaint against Moon was he was breaking up families.

He was accused of taking children away from their loved families and forcing them into strict training, which prevented them from seeing their parents or coming home.

During Moon's rallies of the late 1970s and early '80s, Christian and Leftist organizations staged counter-rallies to disrupt them. They invited angry parents to demonstrate against him and hoped to disrupt the rallies. But, every attempt failed to turn people away from hearing Moon's message.

The response to complaint No. 1 is quite the opposite.

Moon's whole religious theme revolved around the "true" family. According to his view, the family is the cornerstone of an ideal society. The family is the center of love, and it is in the family that we learn about all types of love. In other words, the family is the School of Love. This is what Moon teaches about family.

Also, in 1990, after visiting his hometown in North Korea and his meeting with Kim Jung-Il, Moon founded a new church project, "Home Church." He told his followers to return to their hometowns and serve and love their parents and their communities. Each family was asked to adopt 360 homes and serve the needs of their communities. But, when we look at today's family in the United States, we find the institution of family and its values have been weakened to such an extent that family breakdown and divorce has reached its highest level.

In the United States, the divorce rate has increased to approximately 54 percent. Troubles in the family can be traced to people's lack of family values, which are embedded in their marriage covenant with God. In addition, there is the free sex, adultery, infidelity, selfishness and greed.

Forty years ago, Moon came to the United States with the mission to restore true family values through the proper order of marriage and brought about the "Marriage Blueprint," which is God-centered and contains true family values. This is what Moon had done.

Members of the Unification Church were not all "kids" when they joined the church. The majority were mature and responsible people. I, personally, am an example of this.

I joined the church movement at the age of 35. Moon came and turned them into responsible, respectful and very successful families recognized by people around the world as examples to be praised.

In divorce, despite mounting problems because of language, racial and cultural differences, families in the Unification Church have the world's lowest divorce rate, with a rate of less than 5 percent, compared with the national rate of the United States: 55 percent.

Moon's interracial and international marriages have played a central role in resolving racial, cultural and religious problems. Couples were matched and blessed, white with black or Asian. In religions, couples were matched and blessed, Christians with Muslims, Jews with Christians and Buddhist and Christian and Muslims with Jews.

The perfect example is my "Matching and Blessing." Moon blessed me with a wonderful wife who has a Christian background and is from Indiana. Our daughter, who is now 22 years old, wanted to be blessed in marriage with a man of Jewish background so she would complete the full circle: Muslim, Christian and Jewish! This is the fruit of Moon. Is there anything better in this world?

Here's another interesting thing. Long before I was matched with my wife, my mother-in-law had hired a deprogrammer who kidnapped her and tried to deprogram her. However, the deprogramming failed, and my wife escaped and returned to her preferred faith.

Looking back today, I see great joy in my mother-in-law's eyes. She is now proud and happy, and that's pretty remarkable! She not only has a smart and beautiful granddaughter who she loves, but she also has a son-in-law who adores her! Even my spiritual mother, Jacinta, the young missionary lady who witnessed to me and brought me to the Unification Church, was kidnapped by deprogrammers. She, too, escaped and returned to her faith and is now a proud mom! So, remembering the 1970s and the leftist media against Moon, one has to ask: Where are those deprogrammers today? And, where are those unhappy parents?

Speaking of Jesus' words about good fruits, these are Moon's fruits! In the years between 1987 to 2000, Moon conducted forgiveness ceremonies and a rededication marriage blessing to more than 450 million couples of all religions and races all over the whole world! Thousands of Unification Church members all around the globe were given the holy wine and signed up people for a marriage rededication blessing.

The first of the larger mass marriage and rededication ceremonies was Nov. 29, 1997, at RFK Stadium in Washington, D.C. There were 3.6 million people there (See the Holy Marriage Blessings: Mass Weddings section of Chapter 33).

Mass marriage and rededication blessing ceremonies grew ever larger after that.

In a blessing in Seoul, South Korea, in 2012, 40,000 couples were married in simultaneous weddings all over the world. Moon presided over these weddings via a satellite link (www.whatsonxiamen.com/news7883.html).

Here in the United States, we went everywhere we could—to parks, churches, streets, state fairs and malls. Wherever a large body of people, gathered we were there, giving the holy wine and blessing marriages.

Complaint No. 2: Brainwashing

This is an accusation against Moon and his church for how new members are taught and trained in a controlled environment. This is silly and borders on stupidity. When people run out of good reasons to prove themselves right, they come up with unintelligent words to prove they're right, such as "brainwashing."

When we examine other religions or denominational methods of teaching and training, we find Moon did nothing different than any other church founder before him. People look and wonder why members of Moon's church separated themselves from their families and friends, dropped out of schools and let their careers die. They call Moon's religion a cult and look at his teaching as brainwashing. Of course, they forget their religion once started as a cult. One needs to look back into Christian history and what people thought of Jesus and his followers 2,000 years ago.

The reason Unification Church members gave up everything is they discovered there is something of greater value than the external pursuits. They found a passion for God, who is alive and active.

It was this passion for the love of God that we find in the stories of early devout disciples of Christ, as well as in the stories that were written about lovers of Christ, such as St. Francis of Assisi and many other devout Christians. They, too, not only left their families and careers but were also tortured and killed for their faith.

Today, Unification Church members occupy high-level successful businesses and jobs. Externally you cannot tell the difference between the so-called normal executive and "the Moonie."

Complaint No. 3: For Riches/Profits

The Rev. Sun Myung Moon was accused of using young people to amass large sums of money, which made him so rich. On Sept.18, 1976, in *The Washington Star*, there was an article "Reverend Moon, a prophet for profit." The article related how Moon, as a religious leader, became so rich because he subjugated young kids and made them sell flowers on the street to accrue money.

In a way, it is true that Moon was rich. But, not because of what they said. It was because God blessed him immeasurably.

But, what incenses me the most is the untruth that Moon kept the money for himself. Moon was doing nothing different than what we might find, for example, in the Catholic Church, or any of the Protestant churches or televangelist outreach networks! They are all rich and their programs cannot function without money!

Speaking of outreach programs and the works that Moon founded in this country, I cannot tell you how much money Moon invested to save this country and lead the United States to her God-given calling. Millions upon millions of dollars were spent yearly on people in humanitarian services, seminars, travels and newspapers, such as *The Washington Times*, which by itself costs more than $40 million a year!

By the way, *The Washington Times* is the only conservative newspaper in Washington D.C.! I am not speaking of things I read somewhere about Moon. I was there. I saw it with my own eyes.

I was fully active on many campaigns that Moon initiated over the years. There were providential, significant events Moon did, in the United States and in other countries in the world, that were ignored by the media.

After suffering an approximately seven-year period of persecution, between 1976 and 1983, sparked by three successful rallies, particularly the Washington Monument rally on Sept. 18, 1976, hard persecution put a heavy toll on the Unification Church. Moon and his church were attacked daily by negative media, deprogrammers and by normal, but misled Christians and others.

The first providential event was the "Video Providence," which occurred between the end of 1982 and the beginning of 1983. Under the direction of Moon, the Unification Church sent and delivered a pack of 12 videotapes all filled with lectures of the Divine Principle, the teachings of Moon, to approximately 100,000 churches. Later, the church issued a pack of three videos to a total of 350,000 churches. Half of all churches in the United States received these lectures!

I was there. I saw it with my own eyes while I was working in Rapid City, South Dakota. For a period of six months, thousands of Unification Church members were actively involved in this awesome providential project. I did this task daily from early morning to late evening seven days a week. I visited churches, met with the ministers and distributed hundreds of videotapes in my assigned area.

Then, the second wave came. This time it was with books. The church delivered a book of Moon's collected speeches titled "God's Warning to the World." I made a second visit to all the churches I previously visited. I mapped churches in such a detailed way that no church was omitted. I listed its denomination, how big it was, what corner of the street it was on and the name of the minister, among other things. These were kept in the church's files for future reference.

Later, there was a third providential mission. This time, it was with CAUSA-USA. Between 1983 to early 1984, more than 15,000 civic and religious leaders attended a three-day seminar. The Unification Church paid for the accommodations at a first-class hotel and the participants' airfare. I was also involved. I actively visited and invited them to the CAUSA program.

Later, from 1984 to early 1986, the providence shifted to ICC conferences (Interdenominational Conference for Clergies), which was held in Korea. For this program, more than 10,000 ministers went to Korea for a 12-day conference. Included were tours to the cities and places where Moon grew up as a teenager and where he met Jesus in a vision at 16 and received his mission. Guests stayed in high-class hotels, all paid by Moon!

I witnessed this myself. I was in Minnesota at the time and had a large coverage area, from St. Paul to Mankato to Rochester. I traveled daily and visited every church to invite ministers to the ICC conference. This is one example of what Moon did with the money.

On Sept.12, 2005, after Moon founded the UPF (Universal Peace Federation), he, his wife, Hak Ja Han, and their children conducted Marriage Rededication and Blessing ceremonies and completed three world speaking tours in the United States and 40 other nations. Afterward, 120 Christian ministers from the United States, as well as 1,200 religious leaders and 12,000 ambassadors for peace from across the globe, traveled simultaneously throughout 190 nations to spread the same peace message that Moon gave on the inaugural day of the UPF. The organization was created to take on the role of the New Abel-UN.

In 2006, Moon sent 120 Christian ministers for a tour around the world for 60 days. They traveled from country to country and preached God's word! There is so much Moon did for God and humanity that the media has kept hidden from people.

To me personally, there is no one on Earth who did as much for God and humanity as Moon, at least, not since Jesus Christ 2,000 years ago. Jesus gave his own life three years after starting his public mission, but Moon gave his entire life in the service of God and humanity. No one knew God's heart and sorrows more than these two most loving people on Earth.

Complaint No. 4: Blasphemy and Heresy

False Teaching

The Rev. Sun Myung Moon was accused of false teaching. When Christians ganged up against him, they called him a blasphemer and an antichrist.

I have seen their anger. I was persecuted many times for my faith and physically pushed out of churches a few times because church ministers knew I was a "Moonie."

One time, a minister came at me, fuming with hate. He shouted, "Get out of my church, get out of my church!" I wanted to reason with him, so I waited until he came closer to talk. But, he wasn't willing. Instead, he started to push me out of the church. I politely resisted and told him, "Stop pushing me out. This church is not your own church. This is Jesus' church! Would Jesus push me out of his church, like you do?" The pastor was stunned. He looked as if he had been struck by lightning He let me go with shock on his face, left me and went away.

In the end, God knows how much Moon tried to wake up the country and the Christians. He did so much that no human being could do in all areas, whether it was by using the money, warning, reaching out or teaching. There is nothing Moon didn't do, so no one can blame him. He tried to reach out to all Christian churches. He spent millions of dollars on videos and books, speaking tours and mass rallies, but only a few listened.

But, Moon understood it was his fate that he must first suffer many things at the hands of others. After all, Jesus prophesied the Lord will suffer many things and be denied by his generation when he comes. And, it would not be at the hands of the atheists or the leftists or other religions, for that matter.

Moon's persecution mostly was under the hand of Christians, themselves! The prepared church believers who would deny him did so just as the prepared chosen people of Israel denied Jesus, 2,000 years ago.

CHAPTER 33

World Evangelism and Ministry in America

Major Organizations Founded by the Reverend Moon

As stepping stones for world evangelism, in 1958, Moon sent missionaries to Japan, and, then, in 1959, he sent missionaries to the United States. In 1965, before coming to the States, Moon had his first world tour. He visited 40 nations. In 1968, Moon founded the (IFVOC) International Federation for Victory Over Communism, which, in the 1980s, developed into what became known as CAUSA. The IFVOC was the first of many organizations and activities founded by Moon to bring about the peaceful downfall of communism. Moon taught that communism should be defeated ideologically through education about the fallacies of Marxism-Leninism. He suggested a counterproposal consisting of universal principles called Godism. Thousands of conferences, global networking, rallies and demonstrations were held in Asia, the United States and Latin America in the 1980s.

In 1971, Moon's ministry in the United States began. God directed Moon to expand his ministry to the world. He saw the goodness of America, which embraces all people, races and religions, and represents the world. He knows that what happens in the States has global repercussions. He expressed his gratitude for the United States' role in liberating his homeland, but he also knew that God expected much more from this land that had been so richly blessed. It was clear to Moon the States had drifted from its original ideas.

In 1972, in response to God's will, Moon launched his first "Day of Hope" public speaking tour in seven cities with the purpose of reviving traditional Judeo-Christian values. By 1972, his church, known then as the Unification Church, was established in all 50 states, and, in the same year, Moon organized the IOWC evangelical witnessing teams that went from state to state in a membership campaign to tell others about the Unification Church.

Just like in Korea, his mission's earlier years in the States snowballed and thousands of people joined his church. Unfortunately, despite the miraculous success he achieved in the United States, he also experienced persecution, with rumors and false accusations beginning all over again. Christian churches, as well as leftist liberals and mainstream media, ganged up on him. Moon didn't have an easy life in the States. He was bitterly rejected and persecuted, called all kinds of names, and, ultimately, he was unjustly imprisoned. As Moon once expressed:

> "Words like heretic and pseudo were placed in front of my name so often that they seemed to become part of my name. Indeed, the phrase Sun Myung Moon came to be synonymous with heresy and pseudo-religion. It's hard to hear my name mentioned without these words" (Moon 2010).

Therefore, speaking about the effect and confusion that false prophets might cause at the Second Coming, Jesus gave a clue for people to help them differentiate between true and false prophets. "You will know them by their fruits" (Matt. 7:16).

Based on Jesus' words, let us now examine the works of Moon for the past 40 years and see if we can determine whether he is a true prophet.

Let us go back to the early years, when Moon first came to the States in the early1970s and to his most popular time, the "Bicentennial God Bless America" rallies in 1976. What did Moon say or do that offended this nation so much that his name would be smeared in the media and he and his church would be made a mockery? What crimes and complaints did Americans have against Moon?

Rallies

From 1974 to 1976, Moon launched campaign rallies in both South Korea and the United States. People flocked to these rallies by the hundreds of thousands. At the height of the Cold War, and during a time of great tension between North and South Korea, Moon held the Yeouido Park Rally in Seoul in June 1975, which drew more than 1.2 million people. Moon spoke out against communism in South Korea and said it is important to establish a world centered on God. In the U.S., he gave a similar message at his numerous rallies. Moon spoke to overflowing crowds of 25,000. The Sept. 18, 1976, Washington Monument rally, as I noted earlier, was the largest crowd of its history. More than 300,000 gathered to hear Moon's speech! Right after the success of the Washington Monument rally, Moon launched a 50-state speaking tour with the same message and gained enormous recognition.

In 1974, Moon urged Americans, through rallies and newspapers ads, to forgive President Richard Nixon during the Watergate Scandal. No one was willing to side with a president who was on the verge of being impeached, but Moon didn't flinch when he received God's directions. He also foresaw the serious consequences of undercutting the U.S. presidency in a world still dominated by the communist threat. His appeal was met with scorn, even though his "forgive, love and unite" message embodied the essence of Christian practice.

Persecution in America Begins

As a result of the rapid growth of his movement in the United States, Moon and the church had to endure a period of persecution similar to what other new religious leaders and movements had faced in the past.

Moon's appeal for a true Christian renewal of America was initially welcomed. However, this receptiveness proved to be hollow when, in 1974, he became an easy target for the now-hostile news media, which were unhappy over his "forgive, love and unite" message.

The fair and objective coverage he had received in the past was now placing Moon and his church in the worst possible light. All sorts of unfounded allegations from Korea were dug up. In this atmosphere of hysteria, the enthusiasm and idealism of his young followers were interpreted as "brainwashing." Moon was portrayed as a hypnotist and an agent of a foreign government. Religious and racial bigotry and persecution, a phenomenon in the U.S. as old as the country itself, reared their ugly faces.

Even though one of the tenets on which the U.S. was founded was religious freedom, regrettably, religious intolerance continues to remain. The Unification Church bore the brunt of America's religious intolerance for three decades. In 1975, Moon launched his worldwide outreach, and, in the midst of persecution, he sent out missionary teams with members from enemy countries—one Japanese, one American and one German—to countries in Asia, Africa, the Middle East, Latin America and Oceania. He managed to bring the total number of nations with Unification Church representatives to 120. His way of resolving prejudice was to have people of different religious, racial and cultural backgrounds work together. He also sought to resolve historic religious and racial conflicts through the interracial and interreligious mass-wedding ceremonies.

In 1975, Moon founded The Unification Theological Seminary (UTS). It is a fully accredited graduate school that offers master's degrees in divinity and religious education. The UTS was founded as an ecumenical seminary and faculty members belong to a broad range of denominations. Rather than concentrating solely on Unification theology, students learn philosophy, psychology, world religions and homiletics, the art of preaching, as well as the histories, theologies and scriptures of Judaism, Christianity, Islam and other world religions. In 1975, international interreligious work begins. Starting with dialogues at the UTS, the New Ecumenical Research Association (NEW ERA), and continuing with other initiatives, such as the Assembly of the World's Religions, Moon worked to promote interreligious discussion, understanding and cooperation to help solve the problems of poverty, war, injustice and breakdown of the family. The 1985 Assembly of the World's Religions in New Jersey was attended by 1,000 distinguished religious leaders and scholars. Moon taught that the world's most difficult problems could be best solved by leaders of various religions working together rather than by purely political and economic initiatives.

I know I mentioned this earlier, but, on Sept. 18, 1976, during America's bicentennial year, Moon spoke to 300,000 people at the Washington Monument Rally on the theme "God's Hope for America." To date, this was the greatest religious rally ever assembled in Washington, D.C. People of all creeds and colors came to hear him speak at the "God Bless America Festival." At this historic rally, Moon called upon the United States to fulfill its blessing as one nation under God and to create "one world under God." He referred to himself as a "doctor" and a "firefighter" from the outside who has come to help and warn the United States of "God-denying" communism and to revive its religious heritage. He proclaimed the Unification Church, with its "absolutely God-centered ideology," had the "power to awaken America, and raise up the model of the ideal nation upon this land."

In 1984, while he was in prison, Moon founded the *Washington Times,* which became the second largest daily newspaper in Washington, D.C. The *Washington Times* was to be instrumental in the peaceful fall of communism, a goal that was achieved in conjunction with the Reagan Administration, and, then, after the Cold War ended, to promote family values and support the role of religion in society.

As I previously stated, Moon organized a major conference of news media leaders and former heads of state in Moscow in 1990, fulfilling a pledge he made in 1976 to organize a "great rally for God in Moscow." Moon and his wife met with then-Soviet President Mikhail Gorbachev and gave the Soviet people a message of hope. After the fall of communism, Moon funded numerous activities that assisted former communist countries as they transitioned to democracies.

In 1991, Moon took a crucial step toward establishing world peace through the peaceful reunification of North and South Korea. Risking his life, he traveled to North Korea in December 1991 and met with President Kim Il-sung, under whose regime he had been tortured and sent to a labor camp. His purpose was to seek ways to bridge the gap between the two countries. The North Korean ruler, who had suppressed religion for 40 years, met and graciously welcomed Moon and his wife. During the same visit, Moon was allowed to return to his hometown and see the house where he was born. He placed flowers on the graves of his parents and was embraced by proud and tearful surviving relatives.

In 1992, Hak Ja Han, Moon's wife and mother of 14, began her own public activities for world peace – she began with a world speaking tour. Her mission was to both lead peacemaking work and promote the central role of women in creating a just and peaceful society. Today, after years of intense international work, Han is recognized as one of the most effective woman leaders in the world (www.reverendsunmyungmoon.org/life_biography.html). She has spoken in such notable venues as Capitol Hill, the United Nations, the Kremlin, the Great Hall in Beijing and congressional buildings in Japan, Korea and Canada. Perhaps no other woman leader has addressed so many large audiences in as many countries as Han (www.reverendsunmyungmoon.org/life_biography.html).

Han took her first world tour in 1993 and visited 44 American cities, 27 Japanese cities, 40 university campuses in Korea and 41 nations. In 2006, accompanied by her children and grandchildren, Han embarked on two tours for peace. She visited a country a day, speaking to enthusiastic audiences in 120 countries in Asia, Europe, Africa, the Middle East, Oceania and Latin America. She met many heads of states, prominent religious leaders and political leaders during the trip.

In 1996, Moon announced the end of the Holy Spirit Association for the Unification of World Christianity. In its place, he founded the FFWPU-Family Federation for World Peace and Unification, which built a network of families from every race, religion and culture who were united in the belief that God's love, happy marriages and successful families are the cornerstones to solving the most fundamental problems of society.

In 1999, Moon proposed the creation of an international council of religious, civic and political leaders to supplement the peacekeeping work of the United Nations. The IIFWP, known as the Universal Peace Federation since 2005, is active in 190 countries. There are 110,000 "Ambassadors for Peace," who work for peace, both in their nations and internationally.

In 2001, after 9/11, Moon organized conferences to address interreligious conflicts. The first, for religious and political leaders from around the world, was held in October 2001 in New York. The second, which was an unprecedented conference for international Muslim leaders, was in December 2001 in Indonesia. It was titled "Islam and the Future World of Peace," and it reflected

Moon's confidence that Islam could potentially be a major partner in the global quest for peace.

In 2003, Moon founded the Middle East Peace Initiative. He was dedicated to addressing the world's most unsolvable challenges, achieving peace in the Middle East and a peaceful reconciliation between North and South Korea. The Middle East Peace Initiative exemplified his approach to peace by calling on leaders of all fields, including government, academia, religion and the arts, to take part in interreligious peace missions to the trouble spots of the world.

Moon didn't stop there, however. In 2005, he founded the Universal Peace Federation (UPF) on six continents. Its mission was to create a global council of religious and other leaders to supplement and support the work of the United Nations. It has a Global Peace Council with distinguished leaders from all continents and maintains a Peace Force to mediate in the world's trouble spots.

Audiences worldwide are inspired that Moon's work is being continued by his wife Hak Ja Han, She began revisiting world religious leaders to network and plan for interreligious peace work.

In 2006, the Cheon Jeong Gung Peace Palace, Museum and Meeting Center opened in Cheongpyeong, Korea. Called the "Vatican of the East," the center sits in the mountains about two hours from Seoul and near the North Korean border (You can read more about Moon's world evangelism in my book, *Jerusalem Appointment with Destiny*). Moon died on Sept. 12, 2012, from complications of from pneumonia at the age of 93. His mission passed on to his wife.

There is much more work Moon did that can fill thousands of pages in a book. To learn more about Moon, please read his book, "As a Peace-Loving Global Citizen," or go to *FamilyFed.org.*

Holy Marriage Blessings: Mass Weddings

The Marriage of the Lamb

One of the greatest miracle work Moon did in our time is the Holy Marriage Blessing. It is by far the most important work ever done in the history of mankind. The Holy Marriage Blessing is also known as the mass-wedding blessing. To understand its significance, one needs to look at prophecies told in the Bible about the Marriage of the Lamb in the Last Days, found in Rev. 19:6-7, and mentioned in Jesus' parable of the 10 virgins in Matt. 22:1-14. If one is looking for miracles, I believe no miracle can surpass Moon's mass weddings. On Nov. 29, 1997, Moon and his wife, known to the Unificationists as the "True Parents," conducted a Holy Marriage Blessing at Washington, D.C.'s Robert F. Kennedy (RFK) Stadium in which 3.6 million couples were married. This was the first major blessing in the United States since 1982 and was an exponential leap beyond the Holy Blessing of 360,000 couples at Seoul's Olympic Stadium in 1995. *The Washington Post* set attendance at 40,000, CNN at 45,000 and the Associated Press at 56,000. Other couples took part in "satellite blessing" at locations across the world. How is that a miracle? In ONE DAY, Moon blessed 3.6 million couples in marriage! This is more like Jesus feeding 5,000 people with five loaves of bread (Matt. 14:13-21). As Jesus said, if "you do not believe in me, believe in the works," (John 10:38). The same can be said of Moon: if you doubt him, believe instead in the works he has done for God. The FFWPU Movement has grown to become a "nation" within nations!

The Bible tells us, at the Second Coming, Jesus Christ is going to be married. Who is the Bride? When does the marriage supper of the Lamb take place? The Book of Revelation contains an intriguing vision in which the Apostle John heard a great multitude say, "Hallelujah! For the Lord our God, the Almighty reigns! Let us rejoice and exult and give Him glory, for the marriage of the Lamb has come, and His Bride has made herself ready" (Rev. 19:6-7).

The passage explains how the Bride will be dressed: "it was granted her to be clothed with fine linen, bright and pure" — for fine linen is the righteous deeds of saints" (Rev. 19:8). This short passage concludes with an instruction to John to "Write this: 'Blessed are those who are invited to the marriage supper of the Lamb" (Rev. 19:9). The key to identifying the Bride is found in her clothing—"fine linen," which I believe represents her purity and sinless status. It was pointed out in Rev. 22:14: "Blessed are those who wash their robes that they might have the right to the tree of life And that they may enter by the city by the gates. "

Not surprising, the marriage supper of the Lamb was also one of the themes on which the Lord Jesus loved to dwell. In many of His parables, He spoke of marriage suppers. For instance, in the parable of the 10 virgins, He told about the preparation for the coming of the bridegroom. In Matt. 22:1-14, He spoke of the parable of the marriage of the king's son. At this festive occasion, the king sent out servants to invite people to come to the blessed event. He ends by saying, "For many are called but few are chosen."

However, the Christian concept of the marriage supper of the Lamb is erroneous. They believe the "church is the Bride of Christ," and after the Rapture and judgment, members of the church will be rewarded for their faithful service (See 1 Cor. 3:10-15 and 2 Cor. 5:10). A marriage will take place. The church, "the bride of Christ," and the Lord Jesus Christ will be officially married in heaven. While the Earth is suffering through the last throes of the tribulation, the church will enjoy a heavenly wedding. And, then, a feast! But, this is not the correct meaning of the marriage of the Lamb.

As we can imagine, The Marriage Supper of the Lamb will be a magnificent occasion. Devout believers through time have wondered about it. It is alluded to in Hebrew prophetic poetry. And, as it is clearly outlined in Revelation Chapter 19, at the Last Days, the elect will be gathered. There, they will be ushered into an experience they have never had. It will be a love feast with their Messiah. This will be a glorious consummation of this age. It is beyond the power of words to describe. This marriage supper of the lamb was none other than the blessing of the Moons in 1960.

The climax of this age will see the saints, Unificationists, come under intense persecution. They will bring the final witness before men and angels on behalf of the Holy Bridegroom and Bride they love. The end-time drama is very much a love story—an epic saga of love and persecution. This particular age is none other than the 20th century "Baby Boomers" of the 1960s!

Surely, this awesome deliverance in the future will be a grand occasion for a party. As in Moon's mass weddings, the Messiah will invite all who have been prepared to partake of the holy marriage blessing and receive the holy wine, which I believe will give them rebirth and resurrection. It will be a grand celebration in which all other victory feasts and toasts cannot compete. As for the Parable of the 10 virgins, let us read it and see what we can we learn from it.

The Parable of the Wedding Banquet

In Matt. 22:1-14, Jesus spoke to a large gathering in parables, saying:

> "The kingdom of heaven may be compared to a king who gave a marriage feast for his son, and sent his servants to call those who were invited to the marriage feast, but they would not come. Again he sent other servants, saying, 'Tell those who are invited, Behold, I have made ready my dinner, my oxen and my fat calves are killed, and everything is ready; Come to the marriage feast.'"
>
> "But they made light of it and went off, one to his farm, another to his business, while the rest seized his servants, treated them shamefully, and killed them. The king was angry, and he sent his troops and destroyed those murderers and burned their city. Then he said to his servants, 'The wedding is ready, but those invited were not worthy. Go therefore to the thoroughfares, and invite to the marriage feast as many as you find.' And those servants went out into the streets and gathered all whom they found, both bad and good; so the wedding hall was filled with guests."
>
> "But when the king came in to look at the guests, he saw there a man who had no wedding garment; and he said to him, 'Friend, how did you get in here without a wedding garment?' And he was speechless. Then the king said to the attendants, 'Bind him hand and foot, and cast him into the outer darkness; there men will weep and gnash their teeth.' For many are called, but few are chosen."

From my understanding of this parable, I believe it is a warning to Christians in the Last Days to not to take God in vain, and worship Him by mouth but not by faith and actions. And, like in the parable of the vineyard, they would be thrown out of God's kingdom, just as the Israelites in Jesus days were destroyed for their lack of faith in Jesus. Having said this, it gives me no greater pleasure than to present you a brief history of the Moon's Blessing Ministry and how I participated in the Marriage Blessing.

Before coming to the United States, the marriage blessing of the Moons took place in Korea on March 16, 1960. This marked the beginning of their mission as the "True Parents" and the beginning of the "Blessing" for the restoration of humankind back into God's lineage. Shortly after the weddings on March 16, 1960, they held the first blessing ceremony for 36 couples in Seoul. The blessing grew from 36 in 1960, to 8,000 in 1982, and to 30,000 in 1992. The one in which I participated took place in Korea on Jan. 12, 1989, and included 1,275 couples. In 1982, the first large-scale blessing of 2,075 couples held was outside of Korea in Madison Square Garden in New York City. The blessing ceremonies have attracted a lot of attention from the press and the public.

For Unificationists, these interracial, interreligious and international mass-marriage ceremonies symbolize the family as the hope for love and peace. The blessing ceremony has become the most famous ritual of the Unification Church. The men and women who receive the blessing are called "Blessed Central Families" and help facilitate Cheon Il Guk (the Kingdom of Heaven.)

In the 1990s, Moon allowed people of other religions to receive the blessing. This liberalization led to a great increase in the number of people being blessed, from 360,000 couples in 1995 to more than 450 million couples, most of whom were already married and not Unification Church members (http://rev-moon.blogspot.com/2012/03/moons-mass-marriages-gift-of-love.html). Ministers of other faiths, including Judaism and Islam, have served as "co-officiators" at blessing ceremonies. Since 2001, couples blessed by Moon have been able to arrange marriages for their own children, without his direct guidance. The last blessing conducted by Moon and his wife before he passed away included 40,000 couples (www.whatsonxiamen.com/news7883.html).

As we have seen, Moon gained fame and notoriety in the 1970s by marrying thousands of followers in mass-wedding ceremonies. As mentioned earlier, there were 40,000 couples at the 2012 mass wedding! The couples often came from different countries and had never met but were matched by Moon in a bid to build an interracial and multicultural religious world. Today, the Unification Church has approximately 1 million members, including 100,000 members in the United States, and has sent missionaries to 194 countries. The church's holdings include *The Washington Times*, the New Yorker Hotel, and a seafood distribution firm that supplies sushi to Japanese restaurants across the United States. It gave the University of Bridgeport $110 million over more than a decade to keep the Connecticut school operating. It acquired a ski resort, a professional football team and other businesses in South Korea. It also operates a foreign-owned luxury hotel in North Korea and jointly operates a fledgling North Korean automaker.

The Holy Marriage Blessing Ceremony is a large-scale wedding or marriage rededication ceremony. It is given to married or engaged couples. Through it, members of the Unification Movement believe the couple is removed from the lineage of sinful humanity and grafted into God's sinless lineage. As a result, the couple's marital relationship—and any children born after the blessing—exists free from the consequences of original sin.

In the Unification Church, marriage is known as a blessing and it consists of three ceremonies. The first is the matching. A person must be a member of the church for at least three or more years and work as a full-time core member before he or she can qualify for matching. Members are often recommended by their local leaders for this ceremony. The second is the Holy Wine ceremony; the third is the blessing (wedding). These two ceremonies were often held during the same three-day period, depending on the size of the mass wedding. For members to receive the blessing, they must have served several years in a "formula course" as full members and offered a seven-day fast. They must also be pure with no premarital sex. The full story on how I was matched and blessed was published in my first book, "Honor Thy God" in 2010. However, I would like to share a profound spiritual experience I had during the Holy Wine Ceremony. It is as follows:

My Marriage Blessing

During the Holy Wine Ceremony at my mass wedding in Korea (there were 1,275 couples), all the candidates stood in pairs facing each other in meditative prayer and observing the ceremony. The Rev. and Mrs. Moon offered a prayer. The holy wine had been prepared and put in cups on trays that were placed on the long altar, which was on the stage. Offstage, 30 elder representative couples were assigned to distribute the wine. Each couple had a row of approximately 120 couples, which stretched from the stage to the end of the room. My wife and I were about 20 couples toward the back. The True Parents were dressed in white gowns that were decorated with gold embroidery and had crowns on their heads. They handed trays to the representative couples, who were also dressed in white gowns and wore white gloves.

As the distribution of the holy wine began, I began to meditate, and pray: "Heavenly Father, please allow the holy wine to enter into every cell of my body, into every cell of my blood, and into every cell of my soul." Suddenly, I transcended into a higher state of consciousness and had a powerful vision:

The Vision: Ocean of Blood

> *As the Rev. and Mrs. Moon began to pass out the holy wine trays, I saw thick blood pouring out of the True Father (Father Moon) and dripping down to the stage. The platform was covered with blood almost 2 inches high, and the blood started to cascade off the stage toward us as we stood in silent meditation. As the blood flowed toward us, it began to get thinner and flow even faster. With a sudden rush, it felt like we were being washed away by a huge tidal wave, and the room turned into an ocean of blood!*

Astonished by what I had just envisioned, I opened my eyes. The couple who was passing the holy wine was right next to us. I was amazed. The vision was still fresh in my mind when I received the holy wine with my wife!

This vision confirmed Moon's teachings about the importance of rebirth and changing of blood lineage. In the Unification Church, this can only be done through the blessing of the marriage ceremony and the partaking of the holy wine. Members of other faiths are also invited to participate. All they need to do is to have faith in God and keep the four points of the pledge: (1) Husband and wife should not commit adultery; (2) They should never divorce; (3) Parents must teach their children abstinence before marriage; and (4) The family should support world peace.

Speaking of the "seed" God sows in our life's path, remember the story I mentioned earlier about my wedding day in England and how my ancestors went berserk in disapproval? Well! This is what that experience was about. As if they knew, my ancestors went into a frenzied panic because they didn't want me to miss out on this holy marriage blessing. It is this blessing of marriage that they want me to have, not just a regular and normal marriage. It also wasn't about me marrying someone of a different religion, which would destroy everything about Islam. I believe this is the reason my ancestors retaliated against me when I got married in England in such an overwhelming way.

CHAPTER 34

Other Spiritual Experiences

The following are personal experiences, dreams and visions I experienced during my first workshop with the Unification movement, which solidified my faith.

In addition to the few dreams you have read in previous chapters, I will leave you with a few more dreams and spiritual experiences that made a difference in my life. These dreams and spiritual experiences were confirmation and support of Moon's teachings and in support of me being part of the Unification movement, which came during difficult years of Moon persecution. I would like to start with the vision I had right at the end of the workshop with the Unification movement on October 1981. I titled it "Conversion Experience-I prayed and God answered my prayer."

Conversion Experience

I prayed and God answered my prayer.

Then came the most profound moment in my history! On the last day of the workshop, I was asked whether I wanted to accept the teaching of Reverend Sun Myung Moon and, would I like to join the movement? I was a little hesitant in the beginning, and I didn't quite know what to do. I needed a little help or a nudge, and so came Jacinta. After John and I talked for a while and stood outside the house waiting for my decision, Jacinta came and said, "Ali, we are not here to push, nor to force you to join our movement; you are old enough to make your decision. There is nothing hidden about our movement. You spent almost forty days with us learning about our teaching; we have done all we could to help you, and if this is not enough," as she pointed to the forest and said, "Go there and pray and ask God for help to tell you what to do." She physically, but gently, pushed me toward the forest. I mildly retaliated and made a cheap comment saying, "Oh, yes,

God is going to answer me and tell me what to do...just like that... If God can do that with me, why couldn't he end the suffering of mankind?" I knew deep inside that I was crossing the line with God. Anyway, Jacinta insisted and said she was not going back inside the house until I spoke with God and she stood there as I walked hesitantly toward the deep wooded hills.

I walked for approximately half a mile until I found a deep ravine nestled between two hills. I walked around and found what I thought was a good spot. When I felt I was ready, I stood straight facing the ravine and began looking for words to say to God. I closed my eyes, and muttering like a little boy I said, "Heavenly Father, I am sorry to call you Father. My religion (Islam) forbids me to call you Father. But I would love to be your son. I would love to call you Father, but I am not worthy. I love this group. I learned so much about you in their teaching, but there is so much controversy about them."

Suddenly, from the sky, a message came down to me as fast as the speed of light. The words were written on my forehead and spoken simultaneously, and the words said, "Son! Why are you so troubled? If you are sincerely doing it for me, wouldn't I be with you? Wouldn't I save you even if you are in the most dangerous group?"

The message was so powerful and so clear that I immediately fell on my knees, bowed down to the ground, prayed, cried, and talked to God like he was the real True Father. There were no words to describe that precious moment. I cried and cried for hours. Approximately ten minutes after I received the conversion experience, while I was still in the meditative spirit, I looked up to the sky. I received a very revealing vision. It is as follows:

> *Lo and behold, the whole sky turned into a huge round building like a football stadium with gates on both ends. People were rushing into it, but there were people who didn't want to go in, but other people were dragging them in. Others wanted to go in, but people were holding them back, forcefully, not allowing them to enter.*

After I received this crystal-clear vision, I couldn't leave the place. It began to get a little dark, and I could hear my friend John calling me a few times, but I didn't answer him.

Finally, I felt it was time to go back. With puffy and red eyes, I walked in the house and asked for the papers (membership application form). I wanted to sign, and I demanded that I fill out the application form to join the movement and sign it right away! People were so surprised and curious to know what had happened! They sensed something special had happened to me. They gathered around me and comforted me as I was crying again while I was telling them my story. At the end of the workshop, everybody went back to their centers in different cities of the region, and I was assigned to go to the regional headquarters in Atlanta, Georgia where my spiritual mother, Jacinta, and Mr. Howard Self, the regional director of Southeast CARP lived. And I began my spiritual leadership training there.

The human mind is the temple of God.

"Do you not know that you are God's temple and that God's Spirit dwells in you?" (1 Cor. 3:16).

Our mind is God's temple. When I first heard this verse, I was spellbound by this concept. I had never heard of such a concept before. After hearing about it, I experienced déjà vu.

I recalled a time from my childhood. It happened about 35 years before. It was about noon, and I was sleeping. My parents left me at the house to work on the farm. For some unknown reason, about an hour later, I awoke, and the room was dark. There were no windows, and all I could see was a beam of light piercing through a hole in the door about an inch. This beam had rainbow-colored rays and dust floating through it. It got my full attention. I got up and went to investigate. After examining it, I looked through the hole to see where the light and dust were coming from and was almost blinded by the Sun! I knew then that the beam of light was from the Sun, but I couldn't understand what the rays of color or dust particles were. As I continued to examine the beam of light, I wondered if God, who is in the sky, in the Seventh Heaven, could see me through this hole. It was amazing. This was my "déjà vu" moment. God chose to answer my question approximately30 years later! It was from a lecture called "Divine Principle (Principle of the Creation Chapter) I learned for the first time that humans were created to be the images and temples of God, and God's spirit dwells in our hearts and minds as we grow to perfection. As Jesus said, "You, therefore, must be perfect, as your heavenly Father is perfect" (Matt. 5:48). I found this to be quite profound. As I noted earlier, the interesting part about this workshop is I was not only there to hear lectures, I was also a participant. God, or the Spiritual World, was engaging with me and reminding me of things I had experienced in the past and connecting them with things addressed in the lectures. More on this subject in coming sections.

Moscow Dream

In late 1983 or early 1984, I had a dream foretelling a dramatic event on a world scale that would happen in Moscow, U.S.S.R., and would change history! The dream was about a rally held at an airport in Moscow. Despite intervention from the government, hundreds of thousands of people jammed the airport with media from all over the world, waiting for the arrival of an important leader who was coming with a message of hope and change! The man they were waiting for was the Rev. Sun Myung Moon! As my wife once told me, "dreams don't lie." See this dream below and observe how crystal clear it was, confirming facts about future events with the World Media Conference. It was clear the dream revealed the imminent end of Communism, which was brought about by Moon! The following is the dream:

> *Moscow Dream. I dreamed I was standing while watching a rally held at the Moscow airport. People were waiting at the airport arrival gate for a very significant figure who was to bring them freedom, prosperity and peace. There were government agents in uniforms beating people over their heads and shoulders with big batons. The agents were trying to stop the rally and disperse the people from gathering to meet this important man. The people were strongly pushed forward to the arrival door. There were many television cameras paused at all angles. Newspaper journalists, photographers and television reporters from all over the world gathered at the door with great anticipation. Suddenly, the man people*

were waiting for, the Rev. Sun Myung Moon, walked through the door. News reporters, photographers and TV cameras rushed forward to Father Moon. Television cameras zoomed in on him, and cameras flooded the place with flashlights. An American TV reporter was going wild in joyful disbelief. He was reporting the news, screaming loudly and saying, "My God, he did it! My God, he did it!"—of Father's arrival in the Soviet Union. While this was going on, the people were still pressing forward to see Father Moon. Government agents, in fear of being caught by TV cameras, stopped hitting people on their heads and shoulders while still trying to stop people from coming forward. The people were so compressed together, there was no room for the agents to hit hard, so they finally gave up. The pictures were so real! Cameras recorded close pictures of Father Moon walking in fast with a huge crowd of press and dignitaries. Following the dramatic entrance, Father Moon and I were alone on the other side of the airport inside the Soviet Union. Suddenly, Father Moon became double! As he was walking in, he kept on switching from one person to another and then back to his real self. This other person, which Father Moon kept on switching into, was shorter, smaller, different in appearance, and had a shiny bald head. The end.

Fast forward to the actual event I saw in the dream. I found that not only had the dream come true but, most importantly, what it had foreshadowed. It is amazing that seven years after I had this dream, Moon attended the 11th World Media Conference in Moscow in 1990! In real life, Moon, a staunch anti-communist, had visited Moscow with the World Media Association, which was sponsored by The Washington Times Foundation, an organization he founded. More than 3,000 diplomats, journalists, TV reporters and 50 former heads of state attended the conference. It appears I was put in place to witness the physical birth of my dream.

God works in mysterious ways! My wife and I were selected from the UTS (Unification Theological Seminary) staff to be part of the World Media staff in Moscow. From thousands of Unification Church leaders and more than 40 UTS professors and employees, my wife and I were among the very few selected! Could this be a coincidence? Upon hearing the news of going to Moscow, the "Moscow Dream" suddenly began to replay in my mind, just like a videotape. I was so astonished to receive a powerful prophetic dream of such magnitude. Father Moon's dramatic arrival in Moscow was so strong in the dream.

The scenes in the dream were so crystal clear I was compelled to write a letter to Dr. David S.C. Kim, founding president of the Unification Theological Seminary (UTS), to tell him about my dream. However, the fascinating part of the dream was after Moon began to transmogrify. I began to analyze my dream, reflected and wondered who Moon was turning into? Suddenly, it dawned on me. It was Dr. Song Han Lee, head of V.O.C teaching (Victory Over Communism)! The dream was very revealing, not only because of Moon's transmogrifications but, also, most importantly, how the dream symbolized Dr. Lee. He symbolized Father Moon's thoughts about the V.O.C. In other words, Father Moon walked into the Soviet Union "On the Wings of his Victory Over Communism!"

Interesting! In the United States, most conservatives and Evangelical Christians credited President Ronald Reagan for the downfall of communism because of his charismatic leadership. Speaking of charisma, Moon boldly marched into Moscow in 1975, the same year the Soviet Union declared him as its No. 1 enemy! His V.O.C ideology speaks for itself. Hundreds of thousands of religious and civic leaders were taught V.O.C. ideology through CAUSA-USA in all 50 states in the early 1980s. Moon supported Reagan wholeheartedly, and Unification Church members were fully engaged in supporting Reagan's election. Therefore, Moon's V.O.C ideology was one of the prime forces behind the downfall of communism!

Even Nostradamus predicted he'd come "delivering a great people from subjugation" (Hogue, 1987). In his book, "Nostradamus: The Complete Prophecies," John Hogue was referring to Moon and not Reagan! It is really fascinating! The Moscow dream revealed the events of the 11th World Media Conference in detail:

1. The period in which the 11th World Media Conference took place (1990s Gorbachev era) was a period of great change in

the former Soviet Union. The Russian people were demanding a change from the communist system. This is depicted in the dream by people's rallying at the airport to welcome their great new leader (Moon) despite government intervention.

2. The dream depicted the conference as being coverage by the world, with television cameras posted at all angles. This again foreshadowed the events of the 11th World Media Conference sponsored by Moon!

3. The dream clearly emphasized the importance of Moon's World Media Conference in Moscow and his victory in the breaking down of the communist system! This was depicted as Moon's transmogrification into Dr. Sun Han Lee.

It is remarkable how clear the dream was, and how seven years later, God proved it to me just as He had in all my dreams!

Dreams are not wishful illusions. They are real and destined to come true! Therefore, we need to pay attention to them. It is through them that God reveals His secrets and calls on His people! A few days before the conference, during the world media's staff meeting on job assignments, I was surprisingly selected to take care of the needs of the VIPs—most were former heads of state. This included meeting them at the airport to assigning them to their hotel rooms and all hospitality-related items to their transportation to various sites, such as the Kremlin and the Bolshoi Theatre. Fascinating! God made sure I witnessed my dream unfolding in real life the day I went to the Moscow airport to meet the Rev. Moon and his family (Mahjoub, 2015).

Rhadia's Dream

The following dream I believe, is a confirmation and encouragement of me being in Moon's Unification movement. It is a dream my sister, Rhadia, had that revealed my brother Mohammed's support of me being in the movement.

In late 1984, my brother, Mohammed, was killed in a car crash in Italy. In 1985, my family back in Tunisia was still mourning his death. To comfort them, I sent a nine-page letter to my family offering them spiritual guidance and healing from Moon's teaching on life and death. He taught that death is one of God's creations and is just as important as life. We, humans, are made to pass through three stages of life: first in water, in our mothers' wombs; second in the air, when we are born; and third in the spiritual world, when we die and return in the spirit to God. I also asked them to watch for my brother, who may appear to them in dreams and reveal to them the spiritual meaning of his death. Surprisingly, about a month after I sent the letter, I received a long letter from my sister, Rhadia, who had experienced a dream.

Rhadia's Dream

In her dream, Rhadia, our younger sister, Mabrouka, and our younger brother, Habib, were playing behind the house, when, suddenly, Mohammed appeared to them, laughing, joking, and full of life. He said to them, "Let us sing a song for our brother, Ali. Let us make him happy." He asked Rhadia to sing something. As she was singing, Mohammed was singing with her. Then, our mother came to them. Suddenly, Mohammed got a little nervous and uneasy. Rhadia looked at Mohammed and asked, "What happened, my brother? Why are you so nervous? Have you forgotten? This is your mother who you loved so much."

As our mother got closer, Mohammed began to tremble, got up and began to back away as if he were going to run away. Rhadia held him by the hand and insisted he wait and greet our mother. However, as our mother got closer, Mohammed fell to the ground as if he had fainted or dropped dead. Then, as Rhadia let go, he woke up and was upset at Rhadia for forcing him to stay. He then ran and Rhadia ran after him.

The picture changed, and the scene was repeated with my father! Again, Rhadia tried to force Mohammed to meet with him. He fell to the ground again, as if he were dead, but when she let him go, Mohammed came alive again. She tried a second time. Again, he got so angry at her, he ran away. Before she could get to him, he looked up at the sky and saw the "moon." He lifted up his hands, gave a loud shout of "Father," and shot up into the sky. He disappeared into the moon!

What could be more obvious than this sign?! It is interesting that, in this dream, Mohammed clearly expressed his acceptance of the "True Parents" and his support for me being in the Unification Church.

Khaled's Spiritual Experience

Another story that was just as frightening as the one that occurred when I was in Saudi Arabia is a story that my brother, Khaled, told me on my last visit to Tunisia in 2001. I was there to attend my mother's funeral. Khaled had this experience the same year Mohammed died but had kept it secret until I visited. Khaled's story is not a dream, but a paranormal experience he never forgot. The following is his story.

Back in 1982, approximately six months after I joined the Unification Church, I sent my family a long letter informing them of my new life commitment and about my joining the Unification movement. In the same envelope, I sent them pictures of the Rev. and Mrs. Moon, one picture for each one of them, and told them to keep the picture next to their beds. I explained to them the importance of the True Parents and that they should pay their respects to them. In return, the True Parents would bless and protect them. And, this is how Khaled's story started.

> *One day, while he was away in the capital city staying at a hotel in a famous village called Sidi Bou-said, Khaled went out with friends and had a few drinks. Then, he returned to his hotel room. Later that night, as he lay on his bed, something prompted him to look at some of the pictures in his wallet. One of the ones he looked at was the picture of the Rev. and Mrs. Moon. He looked at it for a moment and, then, began to talk to the picture as if he were talking to the Moons face to face. He addressed his disappointment and resentment against them for taking his brother (me) from them and leaving them in financial shame.*
>
> *After he poured out his heart, he spat at the photo, tore it into pieces, threw it into the garbage can, and returned to his bed. A few minutes later, as he began to relax, an unusual and very frightening thing happened. A spirit in the form of a*

person came and struck him across his cheeks as if to teach him a lesson! He got up, trembling with fear. The smacks felt very real, but he could not see anything! There was no physical presence.

After thinking about the strange experience for a while, he doubted it was real. He went back to bed but was attacked again. This time, he received stronger smacks. He jumped out of his bed, realizing he possibly made a big mistake with Moon and he might actually be a good prophet. He then went to the garbage can, picked out all the pieces of the photograph, put them together, and began to pray, asking Moon to forgive him. That night, he did not sleep until the sun rose! Since that experience, Khaled has been very cautious, and never said a bad thing about Moon nor tried to dissuade me from following him!

Many people wonder why members of the Unification Church have so much love and loyalty to Moon. They only think of it as "brainwashing." But, they forget the earlier believers of any religion, whether it was Islam or Christianity, had the same love and loyalty to their religion's founders, Mohammed and Jesus. Personally, my love for Moon grew ever stronger because he had awakened my spiritual senses and made me discover the loving God who was lying dormant in me. God's love can be experienced personally and is very intoxicating. This was a love I had never experienced or known before. In the "Water of Life Dream," I had expressed how deep my love and loyalty was for Moon. Although I named the dream, "Water of Life," it wasn't literally water. It was a supernatural element, a sort of "supernatural drink of life." Personally, I understood it to be the holy wine that is offered during the Marriage Blessing in the Unification movement.

CHAPTER 35

Conclusion

In conclusion, I have done all I could to reveal everything I have learned from my spiritual journey. There is nothing of great importance left untold. I have systematically written this book, starting with my birth, and traced how God has worked in my life, by revealing great things through dreams and visions to me. He raised me from a humble Muslim farming family in Tunisia, had me living intermittently in 20 countries, and, finally, settling in the United States. God taught me and, eventually, led me to the Rev. Sun Myung Moon and the Unification Church in the most phenomenal way.

I talked about the problems faced by the three Abrahamic religions, one by one, and what I learned from Moon's teaching regarding Jesus' true story, the Second Coming of Christ and the true meanings of the Last Days. I have given a brief history of the life of Moon, from his childhood up to his death. I have also included predictions and prophecies from some of the world's most influential Western and Asian prophets.

Since 9/11, there have been books, movies and documentaries focusing on the Last Days. Many prophecies predicted the end of time would be 2012! One of the most powerfully written book on 9/11 is *The Harbinger: The Ancient Mystery That Holds the Secret of America's Future"* by Jonathan Cahn (2012), where a 3000-year-old mystery, hidden in an ancient biblical verse from the Book of Isaiah, precisely predicts recent American events, particularly 9/11 and the 2008 stock market collapse to the exact days!

Moon gave a two-way prediction, depending on which direction world leaders would choose. (1) A hopeful bright future full of great blessings depends heavily on the unity of Judaism, Christianity and Islam. These Abrahamic religions must unite and work together for peace. (2) A Third World War! Without a doubt, it would have been a nuclear war. What would have been the result? Just thinking about it makes the body tremble. It would have meant not only the demise of the Soviet Union, but also the downfall of world civilization, and/or the end of humanity (Pak 2002).

Regarding the problem of Islamic radicals today, I had hoped this problem could best be resolved with negotiations between the Muslim states and Muslim-on-Muslim negotiators. Unfortunately, Arab nations couldn't do it because of fear of putting themselves and their countries in the line of fire. The moderate Arab states need to come out of hiding, put their faith on the line, and speak the truth to their citizens. As I predicted in *Honor Thy God*:

> "Muslim States who have been enjoying freedom and peace in their country will soon find themselves in the same situation as in Afghanistan, Pakistan and in other stronghold religious extremist nations, such as, Iraq, Egypt, Sudan, Yemen and Syria. They, then, find themselves pinned under the merciless dictatorship of these blind self-righteous and self-appointed Islamic radical groups" (Mahjoub 2010).

Not surprisingly, this prediction has already happened and is still going on. The fact the Arab Spring, which began in 2011, is spreading like wildfire from Tunisia, to Egypt, Libya, Oman, Morocco, Algeria, Nigeria, Sudan and Syria is a perfect example of that prediction. With the recent rise of new militant groups, ISIS in Syria and Iraq and ISIL in Iraq, the Arab states need to be extremely careful about extremist movements that are growing quickly all over Africa and the Middle-East like a wild weed!

As for Arab-Israeli conflict, acceptance, respect, love and peace are the only remedies for peace. What I learned from the scriptures, including the Qur'an, is the essence of God is love, compassion and mercy. When people die and face their creator, they will not be judged based on their religion, but, rather, by how they lived their lives.

Based on what I learned from Moon's teaching, the real and true competition between the religions should be a competition of "True Love" for God and humanity.

The God that Moon taught about is not an abstract supernatural being living somewhere in the sky. He is a being that feels like a human. After all, the Bible tells us we were created in His image. He wanted to be understood, loved and appreciated. Like humans, He loves joyful relationships, good tasty food, sports, the arts, clothes, fancy cars and space shuttles. He also feels sad and experiences pain when he sees his beloved children killing each other in His name. He feels lonely when he has no one with which to share his heart. He feels hurt and sorrow when bad things happened to his children, and He cries and weeps in sadness and joy. He experiences all these things through us.

The Bible says, in 1 Cor. 3:16: "Do you not know that you are God's temple and that God's Spirit dwells in you?" This is what is missing in the God portrayed in the teachings of Judaism, Christianity and Islam. Two thousand years ago, God sent Jesus to the chosen people to teach them this truth, but they weren't ready.

We are living in stirring times, on all levels. The world needs a place where it can go to meet the living God, a place where God alone rules. Unfortunately, established religions pushed God aside and took matters into their own hands. Biblical history tells us God's providence of restoration moves from one religion, organization, people or nation to another when it cannot keep God at the center.

I believe God sent the Rev. Sun Myung Moon to be a vehicle for God's will for this time. His teachings in the Divine Principle were a guide that anyone who longs for God's love could encounter the living God and know His truth. His teachings answered my key questions: What is God trying to achieve and how is He working to solve this seemingly unending conflict between the three religions? Meeting Moon confirmed he was indeed a man of God and his religious movement is the place where God alone rules.

I am not suggesting everyone should leave his or her religion and blindly join Moon's religious movement. I am asking that one at least try to study the Divine Principle, and meditate, pray and find the truth for himself or herself. Moon's desire was you believe in him and receive his anointing blessing in the "Blessing of Marriage" or marriage rededication and become a Blessed Family, free from satanic attachment. In John 5:39, Jesus said to his opponents, the Pharisees, "You search the scriptures, because you think that in them you have eternal life; and it is they that bear witness to me." In this verse, Jesus was speaking of Deut. 18:15, when

Moses told his people: "The Lord your God will raise up for you a prophet like me from among you, from your brethren—him you shall heed." So, again, I will pose this same anecdote to the three faiths, Christians in particular, and ask them to review these Bible verses and consider Moon's teachings.

Finally, I want to apologize if I have offended anyone. I meant no harm, but only wished to express truths about which I was led to speak. I love all religions and revere all saints, prophets and sages. And, I love all people, races and colors. I am of the Unification faith. I embrace Jews, Christians and Muslims and people of other faiths and races. When people ask me what religion I follow, I would tell them "I am a Unificationist. I am all three. I am a Jew. I am a Christian and I am a Muslim, all put together." This is what Moon taught me to believe and do!

God Bless you all!

Bibliography

Aslan, Reza. Zealot: The Life and Times of Jesus of Nazareth. New York: Random House. 2013.

Bae, Aram. "Korean Independence Outbreak, 1919 – [192?]." The Burke Library Archives of Columbia University. Union Theological Seminary. October 2007.

Baker, Mike. "Billy Graham's Wife Ruth Dies at 87." *The Washington Post*. June 14, 2007. Accessed April 19, 2018. http://www.washingtonpost.com/wp-dyn/content/article/2007/06/14/AR2007061401568.html.

Bhutto, Benazir. *Reconciliation: Islam, Democracy and the West.* New York: HarperCollins Publishers. 2008.

"Biography of Rev. Sun Myung Moon." Universal Peace Federation. Accessed April 25, 2018. http://www.reverendsunmyungmoon.org/life_biography.html

Breakwell, Tom. "Saudi Arabia Beheaded 59 People So Far This Year – But Hardly Anyone is Talking About It." Published October 17, 2014. https://news.vice.com/article/saudi-arabia-beheaded-59-people-so-far-this-year-but-hardly-anyone-is-talking-about-it.

Breen, Michael. *Sun Myung Moon: The Early Years 1920-53*. New York: HSA-UWC. 1997.

Buckingham, Wendy Lee. *Free Will, No Choice.* Bloomington, IN: Xlibris Corporation. 2010.

Bullard, Roger, A. and Joseph A. Gibbons, translators. "The Second Treatise of the Great Seth." The Gnostic Society Library. Accessed July 1, 2018. http://gnosis.org/naghamm/2seth.html.

Cahn, Jonathan. *The Harbinger: The Ancient Mystery that Holds the Secret of America's Future.* Lake Mary, FL: Frontline Charisma Media/Charisma House Book Group. 2012.

Choudary, Anjem. "People know the consequences: Opposing view." *USA Today*. January 8., 2015. Accessed March 22,

2018. https://www.usatoday.com/story/opinion/2015/01/07/islam-allah-muslims-shariah-anjem-choudary-editorials-debates/21417461/.

ChristianHome (2017, June 16). *Second Coming of Christ.* Retrieved from www.facebook.com/christianhome11/videos/1189057204542134/.

Deffinbaugh, Robert L. "John the Baptist and Jesus Matthew 3: 1-17." Bible.org. Published 22, 2004. https://bible.org/seriespage/john-baptist-and-jesus-matthew-31-17/.

Eberly, Clark. *I Am In This Place: Testimonies About Jesus and Sun Myung Moon.* Washington, D.C.: American Clergy Leadership Conference. 2009.

Evans, Mike. *The Return.* New York: Thomas Nelson. 1996.

"Exposition of the Divine Principle." Unification.net. http://www.unification.net/dp96/dp96-2-1.html. Accessed April 13, 2018.

Feather, Robert. *The Secret Initiation of Jesus at Qumran: The Essene Mysteries of John the Baptist.* Rochester, VT: Bear & Company. 2005.

Ford, Arthur. *Unknown, But Known: My Adventure into the Meditative Dimension.* New York: Harper & Row. 1968.

Gibbs, Mark. *The Virgin and the Priest: The Lost Secrets of the Messianic Code.* Port Jefferson, NY: The Vineyard Press Ltd. 2008.

Gibbs, Nancy and Michael Duffy. "Billy Graham, Pastor in Chief." *Time.* Aug. 20, 2007. http://time.com/5168522/billy-graham-pastor-in-chief/.

Graham, Billy. *Just As I Am: The Autobiography of Billy Graham.* New York: HarpersCollins. 2007.

Graham-Harrison, Emma. "Drawing the prophet: Islam's hidden history of Muhammed images." *The Guardian.* January 10, 2015. Accessed March 22, 2018. https://www.theguardian.com/world/2015/jan/10/drawing-prophet-islam-muhammad-images.

Halberstam, Yitta, and Judith Leventhal. *Small Miracles of the Holocaust: Extraordinary Coincidences of Faith, Hope, and Survival.* Guilford, CT: Lyons Press. 2008.

—*Small Miracles of Love and Friendship: Remarkable Coincidences of Warmth and Devotion.* Holbrook, MA: Adams Media Corporation. 1997.

Hall, Manly P. *The Secret Destiny of America: The Occult Significance of the United States.* Milton Keynes, England: Lightning Source UK, Ltd. 2011.

Hoge, John. *Nostradamus and the Millennium.* New York: Doubleday. 1987.

—*Nostradamus: The Complete Prophesies.* Rockport, MA: Element Books, Ltd. 1997.

"How long did it take Noah to build the ark?" Gotquestions.org. Accessed June 6, 2018. www.gotquestions.org/Noahs-ark-questions.html.

Inglis, Brian, and Ruth West. *The Unknown Guest.* London: Coronet Books. 1989

Jobs, Steve. (2005, June). *Stay Hungry, Stay Foolish.* Speech presented at the Stanford University Commencement, Stanford, CA.

Josephus, Flavius. *The War of the Jews: The History of the Destruction of Jerusalem.* Scotts Valley, CA: IAP. 2009.

Kadi, Wadad, and Aram A. Shahin. "Caliph, caliphate." In *The Princeton Encyclopedia of Islamic Political Thought.* Princeton, NJ: Princeton University Press. 2013.

Kennedy, John F. *Public Papers of the Presidents of the United States: John F. Kennedy, 1961: Containing the Public Messages, Speeches, and Statements of the President, January 1 to November 22, 1963.* Washington, D.C.: U.S. Government Printing Office. January 1, 1964.

Le Elef, Ner. "World Jewish Population," Judaism online. Accessed March 22, 2018. https://www.simpletoremember.com/vitals/world-jewish-population.htm.

McCarthy, Kevin. *The Master Plan: God's Hope to Heal Humanity.* Dale City, VA: New Family and Church Foundation. 2003.

Mahjoub, Ali. (2015). Jerusalem Appointment with Destiny. (n.p.): Author.

—*Honor Thy God*. Indianapolis, IN: IBJ Book Publishing. 2010.

"Mashiach: The Messiah." Judaism101. Accessed April 19, 2018. www.jewfaq.org/mashiach.htm.

Moon's Mass Marriages: The Gift of Love [blog]. http://rev-moon.blogspot.com/2012/03/moons-mass-marriages-gift-of-love.html

"Moon's Unification Church's biggest mass wedding in South Korea." What's on Xiamen. Published October 15, 2009. www.whatsonxiamen.com/news7883.html.

Moon, Sun Myung. *As a Peace-Loving Global Citizen.* Washington, D.C.: The Washington Times Foundation. 2010.

—*Divine Principle.* New York: HAS-UWC Publications. 1977.

—"God's Will and the World, The Change of Blood Lineage: The Real Experience of Salvation by the Messiah," Unification Church, Accessed March 13, 2018. www.unification.net/gww/gww-04.html.

Noory, George and William J. Byrnes. *Worker in the Light: Unlock Your Five Senses and Liberate Your Limitless Potential.* New York: Tom Doherty Associates LLC. 2006.

"Number of Christian Denominations." Numberof.net. Published March 5, 2010. http://infomory.com/numbers/number-of-christian-denominations/.

O'Connell, Mark, Raje Airey, and Richard Craze. *The Ultimate Illustrated Guide to Dreams, Signs and Symbols: Identification and Analysis of the Visual Vocabulary and Secret Language That Shapes Our World and Dictates Our Reactions to the World.* London: Anness Publishing, Ltd. 2012.

O'Reilly, Bill and Martin Dugard. Killing Jesus. New York: Henry Holt & Company, LLC. 2013.

Pak, Bo Hi. *Messiah – My Testimony to Rev. Sun Myung Moon Volume II*. Lanham, MA: University Press of America. 2002.

Price, John. *The End of America*. Cambridge, OH: Christian House Publishing, Inc. 2013.

Prince of Peace. 2012, April 15. Billy Graham: Second Coming of Christ [Video File]. Retrieved from https://www.youtube.com/watch?v=SFZXJmAljl4&feature=share.

Quebedeaux, Richard. Lifestyle: Conversations with Members of Unification Church. Erick Rodriguez, 1982 Google books. Archived *from the original on October 12, 2017—via* Google Books.

Rushnell, Squire. *When God Winks at You: How God Speaks Directly to You Through the Power of Coincidence*. Nashville, TN: Thomas Nelson, Inc. 2006.

Six Megathemes Emerge from Barna Group Research in 2010. Barna Group. Accessed June 6, 2018. www.barna.com/research/six-megathemes-emerge-from-barna-group-research-in-2010/?

Strand, Paul. "Vice President Pence Blasts ABC's 'The View': Christianity Is NOT a Mental Illness." CBNnews.com. Feb. 14, 2018. Accessed Feb. 20, 2018. www1.cbn.com/cbnnews/politics/2018/february/vice-president-pence-reacts-to-abcs-attack-on-his-faith-christianity-is-not-mental-illness?cpid=:ID:-24305-:DT:-2018-02-14-14:19:47-:US:-JR1-:CN:-CP1-:PO:-GC1-:ME:-SU1-:SO:-FB1-:SP:-NW1-:PF:-TX1-.

Sung, Mo Koo. "Who Is He?" tparents.org. Published August 1998. ww.tparents.org/Moon-Books/Cta-ik/Cta-ik-6-2.htm.

Walavat, Nadeem. "Dow Jones Stock Market 777 Point 7% Crash." The Market Oracle. Published September 29, 2008. www.marketoracle.co.uk/Article6528.html.

Zacharias, Ravi. Ravi Zacharias International Ministries. 2012, April 2. How do you know that Christianity is the one true worldview? [Video File]. Retrieved from https://www.youtube.com/watch?v=nWY-6xBA0Pk.

About The Author

ALI B. M. MAHJOUB was raised in a Bedouin Muslim family in Tunisia, North Africa. At seventeen, he became a farm laborer for three years before obtaining a job in a government-run hotel chain. Currently living in Fishers, Indiana, he is married and has one daughter.

After being sent to Brussels, Belgium, for management training, he worked as a maître d' at London's prestigious Green Park Hotel and Hyde Park Hotel. His career took him to Iran in 1976, and then to Saudi Arabia, while his passion for travel took him to more than twenty countries in Europe, the Middle East, and Asia.

In 1981 God delivered him to the United States and to Reverend Sun Myung Moon's Unification Church. He eventually studied at the Culinary Institute of America in New York, and in 1991, he went to Indiana to become the food and beverage director at the Canterbury Hotel. And since 1995 Ali was hired by Sakura Seafood, Inc. as the manager of Ocean World restaurant till present.

Mr. Mahjoub has published two previous books, *Honor Thy God* and *Jerusalem Appointment with Destiny*. If you have a question or would like to contact the author please send an email to mahjoubworld@yahoo.com.

Made in the USA
Lexington, KY
28 September 2018